Hip Hop on Film

HIP HOP

ON FILM

Performance
Culture,
Urban Space,
and Genre
Transformation
in the 1980s

Kimberley Monteyne

University Press of Mississippi / Jackson

www.upress.state.ms.us

Chapter 2 is a revised and expanded version of the essay "The Sound of the South Bronx: Youth Culture, Genre, and Performance in Charlie Ahearn's Wild Style," originally published in Youth Culture in Global Cinema, edited by Timothy Shary and Alexandra Seibel (University of Texas Press, 2007). Used by permission.

The University Press of Mississippi is a member of the Association of American University Presses.

Copyright © 2013 by University Press of Mississippi
All rights reserved
Manufactured in the United States of America

First printing 2013
∞

Library of Congress Cataloging-in-Publication Data

Monteyne, Kimberly.
　Hip hop on film : performance culture, urban space, and genre transformation in the 1980s / Kimberly Monteyne.
　　　pages cm
　Includes bibliographical references and index.
　ISBN 978-1-61703-922-5 (hardback) — ISBN 978-1-61703-923-2 (ebook)　1. Hip-hop in motion pictures.　2. Motion pictures—United States.　I. Title.
　PN1995.9.H46M66 2013
　791.43'611—dc23   2013015244

British Library Cataloging-in-Publication Data available

To Robert Sklar

Contents

Acknowledgments ix

Introduction 3

1 The Case for the Hip Hop Musical 39

2 The Sound of the South Bronx 85
Wild Style Reinvents the Urban Musical

3 Hip Hoppers and Valley Girls 124
The Economic and Racial Structuring of Youth Cinema in the 1980s

4 *Flashdance* 164
Breaking, Ballet, and the Representation of Race and Gender

Conclusion 209

Notes 213

Bibliography 259

Index 269

Acknowledgments

I have many people and institutions to thank for the completion of this project. The scholars that I worked with at New York University's Cinema Studies Department have been instrumental in my own development as a film historian and in shaping the initial research that would eventually lead to the writing of this book. Antonia Lant taught me a great deal about historiography and navigating the archives, and it was through her that I first became interested in musical film. Robert Stam always offered unique critical perspectives that imbued my later work with a breadth and vitality not present in the project's initial stages. Richard Allen met my writing with demanding questions and insightful criticism as I worked to define the historical scope and methodology of this project. Ed Guerrero offered many helpful suggestions and criticisms. In particular, Robert Sklar, who has unfortunately passed away, met my research with challenging questions and meticulous attention to issues of style and historiography. He was extremely generous with his time and always encouraging in the face of difficulties and setbacks. I miss his thoughtful criticism of my work, his profound knowledge of American film, and, especially, his kindness.

This book would not have been possible without funding from The Social Sciences and Humanities Research Council of Canada, who supported my work at NYU. The Cinema Studies Department at NYU also awarded me a grant as I completed the final stages of research on the project. I have been fortunate to live in New York City, a metropolis of outstanding research institutions. In particular, my work was greatly enhanced by access to archives at the Schomburg Center for Research in Black Culture in Harlem and the New York Public Library for the Performing Arts at Lincoln Center. The new online *Afro-American* archive has enriched the project by facilitating access to the publication dating back to the teens. I also made use of film archives at the Library of Congress in Washington, D.C., and the American Film Institute's online collection of silent film company production summaries. The George Amberg Memorial Film Study Center in the Cinema Studies Department of NYU generously allowed me to view films pertaining to this project.

Gathering images for the book has been more demanding than I had initially anticipated, and the visual material has been amassed from a variety of sources, including the Library of Congress, the *Afro-American*, the *New York Daily News*, and the *Chicago Defender*. I would especially like to thank filmmaker and artist Charlie Ahearn for his assistance with the project. Firstly, I am grateful that he made the film *Wild Style*, which inspired the initial project, and secondly, I am indebted to him for providing all of the visual documentation of his film that appears in these pages. Joe Neumaier, film critic for the *New York Daily News* (and my neighbor), also deserves a special thank you for tracking down the photograph of Jimmy Tate that appears in Chapter 4.

Leila Salisbury, my editor at the University Press of Mississippi, has been supportive and enthusiastic about the project from the beginning, and I am grateful to her for selecting such thoughtful and knowledgeable readers for the manuscript. I would also like to thank Valerie Jones at the press for her assistance with visual material, historian Krin Gabbard for his astute and valuable criticism, my copyeditor Peter Tonguette, and film scholar Timothy Shary for his advice, close reading of the manuscript, and interest in my early scholarship on *Wild Style*.

My parents have been supportive of my academic career since my undergraduate days. I would not have been able to follow this path without their kindness and generosity. Many thanks also go to my good friend Holly Wood, who took care of my daughter when I didn't have the ability to simultaneously write and keep up with an active toddler. My husband, Joseph, who shares my interest in hip hop movies and music, deserves a warm thanks. He has been patient and kind during this process and also offered many fruitful suggestions and criticisms of my work. I must also thank my beautiful daughter Cleo, who taught me to value playtime as much as work time.

Hip Hop on Film

Introduction

It is conventional wisdom that hip hop culture has become the mainstream—a multi-billion dollar industry that caters to the urban underclass as well as the wealthy suburban teen. Americans love success stories and no other cultural phenomenon is quite as demonstrative of the acquisition of material wealth as the rap video industry with its ever-present images of gold jewelry, luxury cars, bottles of Cristal champagne, and multi-million dollar pads. In fact, in the fall of 2008, high-end auction house Simon de Pury hosted "Hip-Hop's Crown Jewels," where one could purchase "bling" from the personal collections of Missy Elliot, LL Cool J, and the late Tupac Shakur. The auction included a microphone-shaped pendant worn by LL Cool J, Biz Markie's pendant designed to look like a cassette tape, and a twelve-pound diamond encrusted necklace consigned by Lil Jon, which reads "Crunk Ain't Dead."[1] There can be no mistake: hip hop as a representational trope encompassing graffiti, breakdance, DJing, rap, and most recently, poetry has come full circle, and the irony of a twelve-pound diamond necklace proclaiming the viability of crunk, a subgenre of hip hop music, cannot be ignored. Once invisible to both the mainstream and academia, and then an object of study for folklorists in the early 1980s, hip hop has now become a symbol of media driven capitalist excess even as "old-school" performers like Grand Wizzard Theodore and Grandmaster Caz perform at the National Folk Festival in Richmond, Virginia.[2]

Hip hop has also "made it" in the world of academia where we find books, conferences, and entire courses devoted to its study. While Simon de Pury auctioned off Missy Elliot's black diamond and gold turntable ring, the English Department at North Carolina A&T University offered a course entitled "The History, Literary Connections, and Social Relevance of Hip hop." Cornell University's Music Department has conducted a graduate research course designed to utilize the institution's collection of hip hop print and ephemera; Georgetown University has structured an entire course around the subject of rapper and entrepreneur Jay-Z entitled "Sociology of Hip-Hop: Urban Theodicy of Jay-Z" for their 2011 fall semester; and students around the globe are reading *That's the Joint: The Hip Hop Studies Reader*.[3]

Rap artists, because of their constant visibility in the popular music industry, are generally given the most attention in mainstream media, and likewise, academia has focused most intensely on elements of hip hop music. Hip hop cinema and films that feature a hip hop soundtrack have also received a moderate amount of study in scholarly circles, yet nearly all of this attention has been directed towards the urban centered so-called "New Black Realism" of the late 1980s and early 1990s, associated with the work of Spike Lee, the Hughes brothers, and John Singleton.

The very first hip hop film musicals made in the early 1980s—the subject of this book—have generally been considered poorly made works, sandwiched in between two notable, and for the most part highly regarded, periods of African American cinema: the Blaxploitation films of the 1970s and the aforementioned "New Black Realism." At best, this corpus of hip hop centered films, which includes *Wild Style* (1983), *Beat Street* (1984), *Body Rock* (1984), *Delivery Boys* (1984), *Breakin'* (1984), *Breakin' 2: Electric Boogaloo* (1984), *Rappin'* (1985), *Krush Groove* (1985), and Disney's made-for-television *Breakin' Through* (1984), has been regarded as a disposable and unremarkable cinematic effort, and at worst, an embarrassment to the later genesis of "real" films about the "hood." For instance, Gary Dauphin argues that most hip hop musicals of the early to mid-1980s were simply awful. He writes,

> Unlike the wholly indie-minded *Wild Style*, the crop of B-monikered breakdancing films that appeared in 1984 and 1985—*Beat Street*, *Breakin'*, *Breakin' 2: Electric Boogaloo*, and *Body Rock*—were products of LaLa Land interest and production techniques, industry attempts to shake what was then a still-growing money tree before the fad died or contracted back to its local roots. With that kind of pedigree it's no surprise that three out of the four pictures mentioned above quite simply stank.[4]

Paula Massood's impressive study of "black city cinema" only spends two pages on these musicals, which she describes as "hip-hop influenced films" that "bear the early traces of the urban look, sound, and themes that Spike Lee developed in his films and the hood films of the 1990s would further refine" and Murray Foreman's extensive and otherwise very comprehensive account of space and place in hip hop culture only devotes three pages to the films.[5] Nelson George indicts all hip hop-oriented cinema and observes that "the most consistently disappointing cultural offshoots of hip hop have been the movies made about it. Feature films or documentaries, by and large, have been technically crude, clueless about the culture, juvenile, or unfocussed missed opportunities."[6] In speaking specifically about *Krush Groove* David Toop writes, "In the years to come, like the rock and roll features of the '50s, the only reason for watching will be the brief musical performances—in this case by LL Cool J, Run-D.M.C. and the Beastie Boys."[7] On the whole, the initial instances of hip hop on film have either been excoriated or ignored in journalistic accounts as well as in academic writing.[8]

The tendency to omit these films from hip hop film history is undoubtedly related to the heterogeneous and rather unruly nature of these early productions. They do not fit easily into the kinds of categories that tend to structure film histories of hip hop-oriented cinema, including those organized around the experiences of black directors, the trope of the African American gangster figure, and the delineation of exclusively black urban neighborhoods.[9] In fact, black and white directors were involved in the production of early hip hop cinema, the communities depicted in the films cut across racial and ethnic divides, and any traces of "gangsterism" were generally relegated to the narrative periphery. I intend to show that the significance of these films, and especially their wide-reaching explorations of the contemporary urban environment, racial inequity, and the perpetually transformative nature of the inner city, is enabled by their protean subject matter, varied production histories, multiethnic focus, as well as, surprisingly, their adherence to the generic tropes and iconography of the musical film.[10]

Early documents of hip hop culture that utilize the musical format are divided here into two categories. What I call the true hip hop musical features recognizable urban locations, sympathetic portraits of inner city communities, and politicized communal performance strategies, while the surface hip hop musical designates films that move away from social exposition and location shooting in order to emphasize dynamic breakdance choreography, outlandish costuming, and the aesthetic rather than political aspects of hip hop culture. These terms will be further unpacked in the following chapter. This book will also discuss films that use breakdance sequences within narratives that are not broadly concerned with hip hop culture or even specifically with breakdance. *Flashdance* (1983) and

Fast Forward (1985), for instance, belong in this latter group and are not technically hip hop musicals. They do not have hip hop soundtracks, they focus on other settings besides black and Latino neighborhoods, and most importantly, breaking is not the predominant form of dance within these films. However, I have included them in this discussion because they use aspects of hip hop culture in ways that help to illuminate the racial politics of music and dance in Hollywood film within the context of the 1980s.

When hip hop musicals appear, however briefly, in accounts of 1980s cinema culture, historians have neglected to address how these films employ the tropes of the musical genre in innovative and transformative ways.[11] As already indicated, criticism has tended to focus on the quality of their soundtracks and the street credibility of their performers. Notably, all of these films follow rather prescribed generic film musical structures and patterns through a sustained focus on communal harmony, romantic unions, and performance success—familiar aspects of the genre traditionally associated with conservative American values. However, I argue that these conventions have been taken up and transformed by the hip hop musical in order to present an unusually positive view of inner city life during this decade. This book explores such unique and innovative elements of the hip hop musical while also revealing the connections between cinematic musical performance, the recording of city space, and the social and political climate in which these films materialized.

Furthermore, no attention has been given to the ways in which these films provide a set of visual and aural signifiers though which one can trace the mainstream media's adoption and transformation of black and Latino cultural products. This process, whereby entertainment produced by communities of color is repackaged and sold to a wide audience as youth entertainment through the mass media, also shaped the most significant and enduring postwar musical phenomenon when Alan Freed first renamed rhythm and blues rock 'n' roll.[12] In truth, a similar process has also characterized much earlier forms of American popular entertainment. During the nineteenth century, for example, Irish entertainers appropriated African American performance traditions in the staging of minstrel shows for white audiences. White American musical film actors also imitated the style of black dancers, and dubbed African American voices remain notoriously uncredited in Hollywood classical cinema.[13] Whether this process involves the actual "theft" of black cultural forms by white entertainers or refashioning performers of color into acceptable forms for the consumption of broad audiences, this cultural meeting point speaks to particular historical inequities within the entertainment industry itself and to the limits of the representational modes and performance spaces that define a particular era.

It is not a stretch to argue that the concept of "American freedom" promised in the Declaration of Independence of 1776, and the literal making of the United States of America as a sovereign entity in the years that followed, have been premised upon the appropriation of Indian land and the expropriation of black labor. These twin atrocities guaranteed white freedom through the oppression of other racial groups by placing limitations upon the latter's rights to geographical expansion and spatial ownership. The discourses of social hierarchy enabled in cultural and artistic spaces produced through the "making" of the nation, not surprisingly, mimicked the racialized political conditions of "American freedom." As a distinctly American strain of commodified leisure and entertainment culture developed out of the class formations and social reorganization engendered by the rapid processes of industrialization in the nineteenth century, variously sketched "borrowings" from communities of color by mainstream interests (albeit often marked by particular class affinities) relied upon an alternately imitative and derisive relationship with racial "Otherness." These cultural formations and their vast legacy have been intimately and inextricably wedded to myriad social and political forces working to profoundly shape the American experience, particularly in relation to interracial social engagement, class formation, economic as well as labor struggles, and the perceived tensions between rural and urban identity.

This introduction is not meant to serve as an exhaustive study of the historical relation between popular entertainment, mediated culture, race and ethnicity, and the spatialization of political as well as social struggles. Rather, my purpose here is to bring together some illuminating examples of this nexus in order to show how the hip hop musical is a unique and fascinating phenomenon within a much larger historical current. For instance, a series of broadsheets produced between 1819 and 1832 mocked black public music and dance celebrations commemorating America's official prohibition of the Atlantic slave trade in 1808. These prints, including *Grand Bobalition, or "Great Annibersary Fussible"* (1821) and *Grand Celebrashun ob de Bobalition ob African Slabery!!!* (1825), burlesqued African American popular urban revelries and processions through both visual caricatures of black bodies and the use of an intentionally derisive dialect ascribed to black figures.[14] The prints gestured to the tradition of

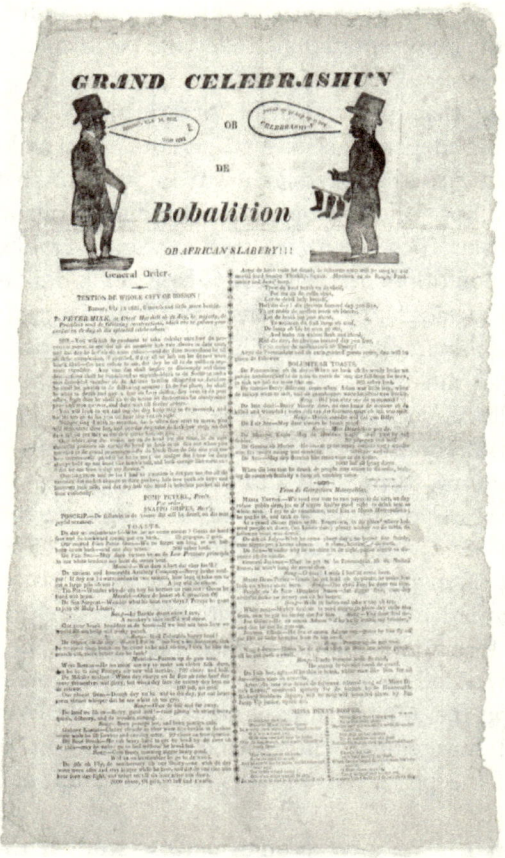

Fig. 0.1. *Grand Celebrashun ob de bobalition ob African slabery !!!* (1825). Broadside Collection, portfolio 53, no. 28 c-Rare Book Collection, Library of Congress, Washington, D.C.

the broadside ballad and featured crudely rendered images of black bodies and occasionally white rioters, achieved through an anachronistic woodblock technique.[15] These bodies occupied the top of the sheet with columns of text underneath. The prints not only imagined the corporeal elements and speech acts of African American identity but some, such as *Grand Celebrashun* (fig. 0.1), also usurped black social rituals as the text mockingly describes a program of festivities, songs, and toasts to be undertaken during the revelries. Such sheets appropriated black bodies for white viewing pleasure, and also expropriated black cultural forms, transforming them into ritualized mockery.

The violence of this gesture became fully realized when actual black communal festivities that claimed access to white urban spaces, such as

"Election days" and Pinkster, were subject to frequent attacks by white mobs (often made up in blackface) even as white urbanites continued to participate in such events.[16] That the prints deliberately referenced an outmoded representational form in the broadsheet ballad, a format associated with spontaneous public performance, ritualized actions, and oration rather than private silent reading practices, further underscores the link between representational hostility and the provocation of actual mob violence. Such a vicious reaction to black public performance in celebration of abolition is further explained by the fact that rural black folk music, derived from slavery, made clever use of simple lyrics in order to deride white slavers or even communicate acts of revolt.[17] Moreover, the history of black dance during slavery was also linked to slave rebellion and insurrections.[18]

As the desire to punish black public celebrations materialized in printed form, the theatrical stage offered yet another cultural arena in which to negotiate such anxieties. Racial and ethnic-based satire was a staple of mid-century theatrical productions as African Americans, both rural and urban, were burlesqued in working-class minstrelsy productions in Northern city centers such as New York City's Bowery theater district.[19] The minstrel show offered white spectators a purportedly faithful rendition of black culture through music, dance, stump speeches, and comedic routines. Stock characters such as the Northern "Coon"—a dandy who "put on airs" and was often in search of white women to seduce—and the Southern plantation "darkey"—a sentimental and dimwitted slave character—allowed Northern audiences to experience an "imaginary resolution to intractable social conflicts" that racialized all spaces of social interaction.[20] Such shows, and the unease that they provoked, could not be separated from anxieties over maintaining the differences between Southern rural traditions that depended upon established racial hierarchies and an emerging Northern urban culture, which promised more fluid spaces of racial interaction and fluctuating ethnic identity.[21] The transformation of blackface minstrelsy—the first and most popular form of indigenous American nineteenth century theater—from *entr'acte* spaces and marginal venues to a codified and highly structured form of lower-class urban theater in the 1840s was, as Eric Lott points out, directly related to contestations over the fate of white workers in the North. Their desire for class stability and economic autonomy alternately united them with the cause of abolitionism and drove them to burlesque and to repudiate "blackness" as a protection against emasculation and downward class movement initiated by the forces of industrial capitalism.[22]

Fig. 0.2. *The Great Fear of the Period That Uncle Sam May Be Swallowed by Foreigners: The Problem Solved* (1860–69). Prints and Photographs Division, Library of Congress, Washington, D.C.

The particularly class conscious theatrical circuit and volatile social milieu of minstrelsy also gave rise to low-comedy figures of the stage such as Mose and Liz—working class types associated with Irish descent, who could slip in and out of mock black dialect.[23] As a social group similarly stigmatized, Irish immigrants were often portrayed as analogous to enslaved black Americans in numerous caricatures of the nineteenth century. Printed material proved remarkably effective in suggesting ethnic and racial affinities, and it could also indicate with astonishing economy the relationship between performance traditions and geographical spaces. Lithographs such as *The Great Fear of the Period That Uncle Sam May Be Swallowed by Foreigners: The Problem Solved* (1860–69 San Francisco: White & Bauer) (fig. 0.2) equated Irish immigrants with free blacks and slaves by appropriating representational tropes such as the devouring mouth of blackface minstrelsy to represent Irish and Asian immigrants. As these "Othered" ethnicities and races overwhelm Uncle Sam in the print, consuming him and then each other, a vast railway network spreads out over the landscape to signify the conditions of urbanization and industrialization that led to such an apparently precarious situation.

Minstrel shows frequently evoked the transgressive topography of black bodies—especially black female bodies—as porous, monstrous, and consuming, while emphasizing their "perverse" orality in song verses, skits, and make-up.[24] Further, evidence suggests that Irish dance steps and the performance traditions of African slaves were already entwined through cultural exchanges that occurred on British plantations in the West Indies during the seventeenth century.[25] As these groups entered the United States in the following centuries, the American cultural imagination was keen to exploit such affinities as a way of denying newly arrived immigrants the social status and access to jobs that established European ethnic groups possessed. Evoking the "black minstrel mouth" as racially fluid, *The Great Fear of the Period* drew upon an established representational ethos of racial and ethnic doubling that effectively conflated the movements of black dancers and Irish "jiggers" so that the word "jig," which was "originally used to describe an Irish folk dance," came to denote black dance generally, and could even refer to a black person.[26]

The race-conscious discourse of the stage flowed outward into newly enabled forms of mass culture at the close of the nineteenth century through stereograph images, postcards, and other popular forms of printed material. Freed slaves had been promised entry into citizenship and the pleasures of an urban-centered industrialized free market economy after the Civil War (even as poll taxes and literacy requirements for voting rights continued to erode black political empowerment) but conventional spaces of representation usually worked to confine African Americans to impoverished rural scenarios and occasional urban buffoonery. Such representations persisted in using the established motifs of Southern black caricature—predilections for watermelon and chicken—in demeaning ways. Numerous stereoview images from companies such as Underwood & Underwood, a plethora of "coon songs" with visually sophisticated sheet music covers published by Jos W. Stern Company, among others, and postcards from the turn of the century all depicted African Americans flanked by watermelons and chicken and positioned them near rustic shacks and fields or within a squalid interior setting. Occasionally, the urban "zip coon" figure emerged while brandishing a razor on a handful of sheet music covers. When "respectable" urban vaudeville shows arose from the rowdy performance traditions of working class theater and the tawdry dens of concert saloons—where drink, prostitutes, and live entertainment were purported to mix freely—this new form of popular amusement coalesced, more or less, into an established mode of performance that attempted to tame and then unify the motley audiences of late nineteenth century American cities.[27] In this conciliatory mixing and blending of cultural and racial accents, blackface traditions continued to flourish when African Americans such as Bert Williams and George Walker entered the vaudeville circuit in blackface, gaining prestige and fame as they negotiated the constraints of blackface theatrical codes. Southern "darkey" themes remained an inescapable aspect of conventional expectations in the newly respectable variety format and the watermelon itself found its way onto the vaudeville stage with electrified glitz and sex appeal in a 1903 Brooklyn based act entitled "McMahon's Water-melon Girls," which included an enormous replica of the fruit illuminated with electric lights and dancing girls in watermelon costume.[28] This conjunction and profusion of imagery and live performance across disparate cultural forms undoubtedly whet the cinematic appetite for the deluge of watermelon and chicken eating films that would prove to be popular for the first ten years of cinema, even as pre-cinematic sites of mass culture continued to churn out all of the familiar tropes of the stereotype well into the twentieth century.

Once the cinema emerged as an exceptional site of representation, it on the one hand transformed racial stereotypes and ethnic identities, while on the other upheld preestablished codes of depicting race and ethnic markers in American culture. For instance, the Irish domestic worker, a common figure of caricature on the later nineteenth century stage, was revived on the screen only to be increasingly and viciously objectified and victimized through the cinematic apparatus in films such as *How Bridget Served the Salad Undressed* (1898), from American Mutoscope and Biograph Company, and the *The Finish of Bridget McKeen* (1901), an Edison Company production. Her screen persona mimicked conventional Victorian theatrical codes of the Irish domestic—incompetent, dimwitted, unattractive, and often dirty. At the same time, the technology of moving pictures could realistically render her body torn asunder by fire and the darkness of the theater increasingly facilitated the objectification and sexualization of her body.[29] Early silent cinema defined and mobilized "blackness" in a variety of ways: supposedly objective recordings of domestic activities such as washing children that were rooted in anthropological photography, short dance routines, and vaudeville performances of popular entertainers, or narrative comedies that directly appropriated earlier nineteenth century minstrelsy characterizations. The watermelon and chicken subject, as well as the figure of the Southern "darkey," were popular early film subjects and remained an integral part of black representation in later silent cinema and even persisted well into the classical Hollywood era.[30]

Chicken and watermelon themed productions were particularly plentiful at the turn of the century with many titles recycled within and between film companies. American Mutoscope and Biograph Company's *A Watermelon Feast* emerged in 1886; Lubin released *Watermelon Contest* in the following year; the Edison Company's *Watermelon Contest* (1900) was released in June; and later films from Lubin followed with *Who Said Watermelon* (1902) and *Watermelon Eating Contest* (1903).[31] Edison's *The Watermelon Patch* (1905), a neglected *tour de force* of racialized anxiety directed by Edwin S. Porter, is a relatively late entry within the general category of early "theft films." The "chicken subject" proved nearly as popular with American Mutoscope and Biograph Company releasing *Who Said Chicken?* in July 1900, while Lubin's *Who Said Chicken?* followed in July of the subsequent year. Lubin released *The Chicken Thief* in 1902 and a different version of the same title in 1903, while American Biograph and Mutoscope Company offered yet another film of the same title in 1904. This list encompasses static, one-shot images of black Americans engaged in eating but also extends to include longer and more complex "theft films" such as *A Nigger in the Woodpile* (1904), a film about black thieves (whites in blackface) pilfering firewood. As technological advances in filmmaking provided an increasingly complex system that could be exploited to elaborate on the narrative assumptions of early African American eating films, filmmakers could now explain the origins of the food being consumed by blacks, construct elaborate chase sequences, and concoct violent scenarios to punish black thieves.

Early single-shot watermelon and chicken films usually located black Americans in rural settings with little narrative exposition. They offered viewers a spectacle of alternately grotesque and childlike consumption for the purpose of emphasizing the perceived instinctual and voracious nature of African Americans. The glee with which Lubin's summary of *Who Said Chicken?* emphasizes the bodily proportions of its black subject is particularly telling.

> All coons like chicken. This fellow is no exception to the rule and to see the expression on his face when somebody mentioned the toothsome bird to

him proves the fact conclusively. The subject is that of a darkey of immense proportions talking to the audience. The head occupies the entire screen. Incidentally, the subject was that of a southern darkey, said to be 98 years of age. He has about three teeth left and they look like old fashioned tombstones. A perfect picture of facial expression.[32]

The subject emerges as an immense specter of Southern slavery—he is after all, reputed to be born in 1803, long before slavery was officially banned following the Civil War, and even prior to the American cessation of the international slave trade in 1808. As his consuming and overwhelming visage fills the frame according to the summary, the film firmly locates black identity within the antebellum South, and black subjectivity within physical rather than intellectual qualities.

Filmmakers repeatedly returned to popular one-shot eating contests, but these corporeal spectacles of consumption were produced alongside more complex narratives of theft and punishment. When American Mutoscope and Biograph Company released a film with the title *Who Said Chicken?* a year before Lubin's, it took place in an urban setting; the primary emphasis of this production was on the theft rather than consumption of goods. The American Mutoscope and Biograph Company summary alerted exhibitors to the urban setting of the film in the first sentence. It simply read: "A street scene," and it went on to describe a scenario in which a "colored chicken thief" outwits a policeman, with the help of an Irish maid.[33] This film is unusual in that its black thief escapes punishment by white authority—he thus appears to have control over the urban environment—yet it is typical in that it makes an association between black and Irish subjectivity as disruptive elements within the social order.

More often than not, black thieves pursued by white farmers and policemen are dealt violent and horrific punishments within the theft narrative. Bear traps (*The Chicken Thief*, 1904), exploding dynamite (*Nigger in the Woodpile*, 1904), and the horror of being burned alive (*The Watermelon Patch*, 1905) are all meted out as justifiable and comic results for the thievery of food and other necessities by African Americans. Such films were made more than a quarter century after blacks were granted suffrage and I suggest here that they are in many ways preoccupied with the relationship between African American citizenship and industrial capitalism. If such productions are connected to Southern arguments suggesting that thievery was pervasive among the freed slave population because blacks were no longer provided for by white masters, and had also slipped out from under the disciplining gaze of slavery, they also spoke to contemporary anxieties about the ability of African Americans to perform wage labor and navigate a commodity marketplace.[34] As black men competed with each other in acts of cinematic gluttony in the typical watermelon and chicken picture, they were simultaneously displaced from Northern industrial life through both the films' rural setting and the staging of black masculine competitive energy as bodily, inane, and animalistic. This is in contrast to the measured, constrained, and repetitive nature of urban wage labor that had been cultivated by Republican political forces and ideology in nineteenth century Northern cities. Blacks were frequently playing themselves in these films rather than having their images usurped by whites in blackface, but the pictures invariably mocked black citizenship and diminished the role of productive African American labor within industrial capitalism.

Early silent film catered to the racialized economics nurtured by slavery and the volatile processes of Southern reconstruction in the wake of the Civil War. Yet, it also worked to negotiate new anxieties stemming from the growth of urban black communities and the rise of an African American middle-class that threatened to encroach on hitherto white residential city blocks around the turn of the twentieth century.[35] As the cinema established itself as a major commercial force by the mid-teens, African Americans struggled to gain a foothold in better paying industries and worked to create black owned business networks in urban centers.[36] Silent film, as noted above, negotiated these anxieties by circumscribing black Americans within a cinematic fantasy of the Antebellum South in a barrage of chicken and watermelon eating productions. The Northern dandy of minstrelsy occasionally emerged as a haplessly inept negotiator of urban territory—for instance, in later "race movies" produced by the Chicago-based, white-owned Ebony Film Corporation. The company's *Two Knights of Vaudeville* (1915) was a cinematic meditation on the unruly nature of African American audiences in metropolitan entertainment venues, while *Spying the Spy* (1918) mocked black patriotism in an urban context even as thousands of African American soldiers participated in the Great War.

In light of such productions, African American critics continually assessed the ways in which filmmakers refused to acknowledge the advancements of blacks since the end of slavery. This implied, of course, not only educational and monetary gains, but also a distinct move from rural to urban settings for many black families. The migration of African

Americans to urban centers at the beginning of the twentieth century has been thoroughly studied by contemporary historians, and this phenomenon became an important aspect of self-definition for the black community during the teens and twenties. For example, in 1921 a reporter for the *Chicago Defender* noted that

> during the last ten years there has unquestioningly been an amazingly large migration. In 1910 there were, already 1,049,000 out of a total population of 9,787,000 living in the North and West, and in twelve Northern cities there has been an increase of 200,000 Colored people since 1910, most of them unquestionably coming from the South . . . in the North he can get better educational advantages for his children, at least theoretical equality as a worker, fairer trials, and greater security from mob violence.[37]

The article also asserts that "the migration northward was a protest" and that its reverberations will force a change in attitude towards black citizens by the white population. It was registered as a transformative and politicized demographic shift that would prove "the old Northern attitude toward the Colored population no longer . . . adequate for a group rapidly increasing in numbers, intelligence, and self-respect."[38] The move northward was clearly equated with a rising tide of collective self-respect within the African American community that had the power to both transform white prejudice and facilitate the social, political, and educational gains of blacks.

Significantly, the black community was seeking to consciously transform itself. African American writers and intellectuals seized upon and attempted to direct a great and unprecedented explosion of artistic, theatrical, musical, and literary talent largely centered around the Harlem neighborhood of New York City. This movement, the Harlem Renaissance, and the discourse of the New Negro—a term that had been utilized and consistently refashioned by the African American community in the preceding decades—produced a body of artistic output and political thought that was directly tied to a particular sense of new black urban identity, as well as to the exploration of racial identity in a sociological and psychological context throughout the 1920s and into the 1930s.[39] Writers, artists, and intellectuals such as Zora Neale Hurston, Langston Hughes, Claude McKay, Marcus Garvey, W. E. B. Du Bois, and Jacob Lawrence, transformed white conceptions of black culture as they articulated a complex and multifaceted sense of contemporary African American identity that explored the historical conditions of black identity rooted in slavery and looked forward to alternative social and political formations such as Pan-Africanism and Socialism.

Musicians and actors, including Bill Robinson, Louis Armstrong, Josephine Baker, and Paul Robeson, were also central to this movement. Yet the status of actors, dancers, and musicians was complicated by class-inflected tensions between key players of the Harlem Renaissance and an increasing disdain for "low" entertainment in tandem with a fervent embrace of black "folk" culture. In truth, Harlem Renaissance intellectuals never embraced the "race film" industry.[40] The proliferation of the African American press at this time, however, gave voice to black critics who were acutely aware that the representation of music and dance performance, and the role of the black entertainer in general, were unmistakably related to political and social mobility. For instance, perspicacious black critics such as Lester Walton emphatically decried the persistence of Southern plantation "dialect" ascribed to black actors in film intertitles. Walton alarmingly noted in 1918 that this practice was becoming more evident in the pictures while at the same time black Americans were increasingly divorced from the social and geographical milieu of the South.[41] Stressing the incompatibility of such "dialect" with the reality of contemporary lived black experience, he noted that "to be able to speak Negro dialect is as much of an accomplishment for the average colored American as it is to know Spanish or French."[42] An anonymous article from the *Afro-American* lamented in 1923 that *How Come*, a current play showing at the Gayety, a white theater, insulted the black race through its use of an iconography steeped in stereotypical Southern minstrelsy. The author writes that

> the resentment we have in mind is first concerned with the plot. In casting about for a framework for the show, it is to be regretted that the librettists could find nothing more commendable than the chicken subject, which with its ally watermelon, have served the white comedian, humorists and others for a half century or more in burlesquing the Negro.[43]

Although language is not specifically mentioned in the above article, a burlesque production centered on "chicken and watermelon" would have undoubtedly employed "dialect" in its characterization of African American subjects. Adding to the complexity of discussions centering on "dialect" in white-produced narratives, the African American literary community debated the use of "dialect" in works produced by black writers.[44] It is important to note that while Walton and other black critics routinely criticized the limitations of black subjectivity within theatrical and cinematic avenues, the African American performer was simultaneously constructed in the black press as a formidable icon of political progress. As Hollywood film continued to relegate blacks to peripheral roles during the transition to sound, and the triumph of the musical genre in the early 1930s offered very limited opportunities for performers of color, the African American press seized upon the body of the black entertainer as a privileged site for tracking the social and political progress of black Americans. Far from only offering a pleasing spectacle of docility to white audiences, black entertainers often played unique roles in representing collective values and "race progress" in the African American community. During the 1920s, for instance, the black press became acutely aware of the ways in which musicians and dancers acted as emissaries for the African American community both in the United States and overseas. A regular column that ran in the *New York Amsterdam News* during the 1920s, "News of Our Entertainers in Europe," boasted that the newspaper was the "Only Publication of Its Kind That Offers This Feature to the Thousands of Its Readers in This Country." Undercutting this claim, the *Chicago Defender* consistently ran articles that meticulously charted the reception of black entertainers in the United States and Europe during this decade. These columns also reported the mistreatment of black entertainers, including large-scale protests against prominent African American performers such as Josephine Baker as well as individual incidents involving relatively unknown chorus girls in smaller shows. For example, Ivan H. Browning reported in 1928 that

> it is rumored that Jack Bucannan the English actor and producer who is producing Topey and Eva with the well-known American Duncan sisters wanted eight or ten red hot American dancing girls to do a couple of feature numbers in the show, but the idea was turned down flat by the Duncan girls who did not fancy that at all and did not want the Colored girls in the show at all, and now it has been decided to have white girls make up brown in order to carry out the idea.[45]

An anonymous article from the following year reports that foreign jazz musicians, including black Americans—"Our jazz boys who have been and are making a fine living in Paris"—will be losing their jobs overseas when a recent law limiting the employment of non-native-born entertainers is enforced.[46]

At the same time, these pages are filled with stories that privilege the connection between race progress and the entertainment industry, and announce with pride the various advancements made by blacks in the field of entertainment. In 1922, an advertisement appeared for a musical show entitled "A Night with the Negro," which proclaimed itself "an inspiring exposition of the advancement of our people."[47] In 1923, the *Defender* reported that Ethel Waters was the "first of the Race" to perform a "real 'radio' stunt," while an ad below this article boasted that Black Swan records, an African American-owned-and-operated business, offers the first opera record ever by a "colored singer."[48] The *Defender* also printed prominent theater critic Mark Hellinger's remarkable account of Bill Robinson's performance in *Blackbirds of 1928*, following the show's interruption by a group of agitators. These agitators, described as white, male, and "fairly well ginned" were, according to Hellinger, "members of some southern society in New York City for a reunion" who "applauded in the wrong place and did their best to break up a show."[49] The insults were further intensified when "one chap rose from his seat unsteadily and waved a $10 bill at the chorus" and apparently shouted, "Get hot here, Colored gals. This is for the first one that meets me after the show. Don't kill yourselves in the rush. Ha, ha, ha."[50] I quote at length from the rest of the article because it demonstrates so strongly the ways in which the African American press articulated Robinson as both a "star" and an engaged member of the black community who could use his privileged position in unique ways to counter the negative experience of white racism and invert established racial hierarchies. This article gives voice to Robinson as a politicized figure as it transcribes the sounds of his "taps" and intersperses them with his eloquent castigation of white interlopers during the stage performance. Hellinger writes:

> Robinson stepped to the footlights. "Keep playing boys," he said softly. The music went on. Bill Robinson danced. Slowly. Tap. Tap. Tap. Tap. And as he danced he spoke. "What you men have done tonight," he murmured, "is a disgrace to your race. You down there. You. And you. And you." Tap. Tap. Tap. Tap. "If I stepped down the street," he continued, "entered the New Amsterdam theatre and waved a bill before a chorus girl, I'd be mobbed. If I did a thing like that I'd deserve whatever punishment I received." Tap. Tap.

Tap. "For 30 long years I've been dancing and trying to entertain everyone to the best of my ability. The thing that happened here tonight has never been done before. I consider you—and you—and you the lowest men I have ever played before." The audience went wild. For five solid minutes they applauded. One by one the "gentlemen" reached for their hats and disappeared into the night. Good boy Bill.[51]

This account deftly weaves the story of Robinson's triumph over white animosity and racially inflected sexual threats towards the chorines into a corporeal "recording" of the dancer's routine. Hellinger notes that "no one did anything" until Robinson ascended the stage and tapped out his measured and intelligent assessment of the situation, which galvanized the crowd into action and drove the hecklers—who apparently numbered in the dozens—from the theater. The art of tapping and the body itself becomes inscribed within the story as a profound tool of resistance, and vestiges of this corporeal politicization will be explored through the performances of breakers and rappers in the later hip hop musical. As extraordinary as Hellinger's account might appear, tap dance always incorporated a verbal dimension that facilitated boasting, jeering, and general bravado.[52] What Robinson did was to deftly deploy this aspect of tap in order to defend his community from a group of Southern "good ole boys," and it is a significant testament to the politicization of the dancer's body for the African American community. Further, when the *Baltimore Afro-American* reviewed *Bert Williams, Son of Laughter*, a posthumous literary tribute to the vaudeville sensation, Broadway player, recording artist, and arguably most successful black entertainer of the early twentieth century, they quoted Booker T. Washington, a highly influential African American political leader. Washington said of Williams: "He is a greater man than I am. He has done more for the race than I have ever done. Why? Because he has made people laugh. He laughed his way into the hearts of men and into the hearts of the greatest men of every race in the whole world."[53] In fact, as late as 1934, John Frederick Matheus, who penned plays and wrote for the black press, noted that it was performers such as Josephine Baker, Florence Mills, Adelaide Hall, Jules Bledsoe, and Ethel Waters who fought "the caricature that masquerades as Negro personality" and who on their tours abroad "have waged and are waging war for its suppression."[54] There are of course numerous weekly performance reviews and listings in the entertainment sections of African American newspapers at this time, but it is really these pages that constructed the black entertainer as the figure *par excellence* who would directly influence general attitudes about the black community in the United States and throughout Europe, and who would become the primary figure around which social change could actually be experienced and recorded. Performers of color continued to bear this burden many decades later as dance groups like the Kid Fresh Break Dance Crew, Rock Steady Crew, and New York City Breakers entered into arrangements with institutional dance promoters and corporate entities who promised to bring their talent to mainstream American consumers and overseas audiences in the early 1980s.

During the 1940s, unfortunately, it became clear that such a correlation between the elevated status of some black musicians and dancers and the plight of the ordinary black American was not immediately at hand, as the United States prepared its citizens (and transformed its manufacturing process) for entry into the Second World War. The reorganization of industrial production only exposed the degree to which African American entertainers had not been able to fully transform the attitudes and laws that oppressed black citizens in quotidian life. Indeed, racial tensions increased regarding the demand for black civil rights, beginning with A. Philip Randolph's call for a march on Washington in 1941 to protest the exclusion of African Americans in the wartime defense industries. Randolph's pressure eventually resulted in an executive order that banned racial discrimination in defense manufacture, and the years that immediately followed were met with deadly race riots in Detroit and New York City.[55] Increased industrial production in preparation for the war effort, however, coincided not only with cases of de facto racial exclusion in the work place, but also organized labor's continuing indifference to blacks who did gain a foothold in some industries. This created a volatile situation. For instance, the infamous Ford strike of 1941, which erupted before President Roosevelt issued the executive order to ban racial discrimination in defense manufacture, escalated into violence as the automobile company encouraged African Americans to cross primarily white picket lines while the CIO (Congress of Industrial Organizations) charged that the employer was hiring black boxers to help physically defeat striking workers.[56] The *Afro-American*'s coverage of the Ford strike ran with a photograph depicting violent black workers brandishing iron pipes on the picket lines. Further, Randolph's scathing editorial piece, which decried FDR's indifference to black workers, graced the front page of the same

Fig. 0.3. Newspaper illustration depicting African Americans demanding jobs in the defense industries, Apr. 12, 1941. Courtesy of the *Afro-American*.

issue, and featured a drawing of angry black Americans taking to the streets with placards announcing "WE WANT OUR SHARE OF JOBS" and "DEFENSE JOBS FOR ALL."[57] (fig. 0.3)

As the collective frustrations of an understandably incensed African American population emerged to occupy public spaces in industrial strikes and promised to materialize en masse in the nation's capital, Hollywood representations of blacks, with few exceptions, remained largely depoliticized and constricted to rigid codes of musical or comedy performance, and a handful of roles as maids and household domestics. Hollywood black-cast folk musicals, including *Hearts in Dixie* (1929), *Green Pastures* (1936), and *Cabin in the Sky* (1943), showcased tremendous African American musical talent but repeatedly placed the black community within a timeless rural setting or antebellum past. This had the effect of depoliticizing black performance by removing it from the present and cleaving the African American entertainer from the contemporary stage of political action, the urban milieu—a move that would not be undone in any meaningful way until the rise of Blaxploitation and early hip hop film.

Another representational space briefly opened up between 1940 and 1947 with the introduction of the "Soundie," a three-minute musical film exhibited in a jukebox-like machine.[58] They featured established and burgeoning white artists, as well as black jazz musicians, comedians, and dancers, including Duke Ellington, Bill Bojangles Robinson, and Dorothy Dandridge. The "Soundie" frequently placed its performers within non-realistic fantasy spectacles or rigidly defined stage parameters. Yet when the medium shouldered the burden of wartime propaganda, it was also used to transmit a unified and supposedly realistic portrait of the American people. As this depiction of hardworking yet happy citizens demonstrating labor skills, intellectual acumen, and even beauty emerged on film, black Americans, and indeed most traces of ethnic difference, were banished from the screen. Particularly telling is the racial exclusion in patriotic "Soundies" such as *Defend America* (1941) and *America I Love You* (1942), which imagined the United States as a uniformly white nation of farmers, lawyers, financiers, preachers, bakers, munitions workers, and lovesick girls. Furthermore, wartime newsreels habitually repressed the contributions of black soldiers and cut their images from documentary footage before the films were screened.[59] Randolph may have been given the full force of the law in his bid to end discrimination in defense manufacture, and black soldiers were a vital part of America's victory in the war, but the American cultural imagination continued to produce spaces of startling racial exclusion.

The circumscription of black performers within fantasy settings and rigid prosceniums in the "Soundie" also coincided with the use of African American musical talent in Hollywood features as musical interludes in otherwise non-musical films that usually took place in an urban setting. Donald Bogle elaborates on this Hollywood practice, noting that "because musical numbers were not integrated into the script, the scenes featuring the blacks could be cut from the films without spoiling them should local (or Southern) theater owners feel their audiences would object to seeing a Negro."[60] This practice reveals how easily economic concerns within the film industry could be aligned with discriminatory desires and passed off as good business sense.[61] For the most part, Hollywood musicals of the 1940s, especially those made by Fox, such as *Down Argentine Way* (1940), *Orchestra Wives* (1942), and *The Pirate* (1948), also followed this pattern.[62] They almost exclusively featured all-white dramatic performers, romances, and social situations, yet introduced black entertainers in dinner club performances and other proscenium settings. When the musical adopted wartime concerns as subject matter in productions such as *Star Spangled Rhythm* (1943) and *Carolina Blues* (1944), patterns of racial exclusion remained in place with black actors barred from the narrative setting while appearing in musical numbers.

"Soundies" were viewed in a public entertainment context but, unlike the site of feature-length cinema practice, they were screened in bars, hotels, or taverns with a potentially fluctuating audience. Just as the status of these machines was rather indeterminate, their use by patrons was also somewhat imprecise. As the reels contained a certain number of films which changed weekly, the viewer could not control what program they would see next and therefore a certain element of randomness characterized the spectatorship of these films in a hitherto unprecedented way.[63] However, if "these eight-song preassembled reels adhered to a loose formula, which included a variety of set genres" there was one element of performance that appeared to be more rigidly controlled through reel placement—the racial identity of the entertainer—and it became customary to place an African American performer in the last position of the reel.[64] This practice echoes the racial organization of vaudeville, which typically included only one African American act per show.[65] Amy Herzog notes that "shorts by African American artists were listed in a separate 'Negro' section," implying that "racial divisions might have affected the distribution of these Soundies, although little data regarding actual distribution patterns has survived."[66] This is more than likely the case, given the fact that this practice so closely mimicked contemporary Hollywood racism cleverly masquerading as "business" savvy, and the organization of earlier pre-cinematic forms of variety entertainment. In addition, just as black performers were bracketed from the narrative of mainstream cinematic productions (in their restriction to proscenium performances)—and Southern exhibitors could simply remove all traces of black performances in feature-length films if desired—the "Soundies" were also organized to precisely control the dissemination of African American entertainers through their variety format, which was, after all, not as "random" as a cursory viewing might suggest. Political and economic tensions threatened to bring the African American community into hitherto predominantly white public spaces, and indeed into fully desegregated civil life in the years to come, yet mainstream American entertainment continued to find ways to delimit and even "cut" black Americans from its cultural imaginary.

The immediate postwar era ushered in a significant social and spatial shift—the flight of white American families to suburban enclaves and the further expansion of communities of color within urban centers—which would come to form the dominant frame of reference for depicting social rituals and familial organization in teen cinema beginning in the 1980s, including hip hop musicals. White families benefited from unprecedented expansion in financial freedom, rates of home ownership, and leisure time. Such improvements were largely facilitated through governmental initiatives to ease returning GIs entry into civilian life immediately following the Second World War. Not surprisingly, black soldiers and their families, while making some progress in educational opportunities and housing standards, were habitually denied access to these programs, which gave white families of blue collar status access to middle-class educational opportunities and financial security.[67] Even if an African American family did qualify for mortgage assistance through the home loans program administered by the Veterans Administration, many of the newly planned prefabricated suburban idylls, such as the ubiquitous Levittowns developed by Levitt and Sons, found ways to prohibit black families from moving in, further constricting them to urban ghettos and rural poverty.[68] Indeed, the exclusionary nature of the postwar suburban dream was enacted on multiple fronts.

Despite such a pronounced and rapidly expanding racialized geographical fissure however, the emergence of rock 'n' roll and the increasing consumer power of American youth threatened to destabilize this growing divide in the following decade. The intensified struggle for African American civil rights, sparked by the reversal of *Plessy v. Ferguson* in 1954 and the racial integration of public schools, also coincided with tremendous public anxiety over the potential for both racially motivated violence and interracial socializing at rock 'n' roll venues, particularly when the roster included white musicians and black performers.[69] As conventional teen music culture embraced black musicians, live rock 'n' roll gigs, radio shows, fan culture, teen films, and record sales became part of a larger discourse about interracial "mixing," the dissolution of sexual mores, the integration of urban and suburban performance traditions, as well as the apparent gap between parental values and youth culture.

Most dramatically, teenagers could not only hear their favorite rock 'n' roll performers on the radio and attend the odd live show, but they could also witness the extraordinary talent of The Platters, Chuck Berry, Little Richard, and Frankie Lymon and the Teenagers in a steady run of teen rock flicks—the first popular cinema directed exclusively at a youth audience. Black musicians remained firmly within the proscenium and outside the narratives of young love, irresponsible spending habits, and an inexplicable (to the parents' generation, at least) need to dance in such films as *Rock Around the Clock* (1956), *Don't Knock the Rock* (1956), and *Rock Rock Rock!* (1956), but the newly created intimate settings for white suburban teens' engagement with black entertainers in these films suggests an increasingly erotically charged and porous threshold between audience and performer.

When Little Richard performs at a teen dance in *Don't Knock the Rock*, his piano is set on the dance floor as he shakes and shouts just a few feet from his young fans. During the performer's second song of the set, "Tutti Frutti," the film awkwardly gestures towards the possibility of interracial socializing as the winners of the Harvest Moon Contest (presumably a dance competition) are announced. The all-white rural teen audience, with their frenzied footwork, dizzying lifts, and wildly swaying blond top knots, return to their seats as a lone African American couple emerges to celebrate their victory with a dance while the white teens look on in admiration. In this film, black and white dancers and musicians were sharing the same intimate entertainment spaces, although, admittedly, teens were not dancing together at the same time. Nonetheless, this certainly nudged at, and was undoubtedly meant to unsettle, the most sensitive anxieties that rock 'n' roll evoked for conservative pro-segregationists like Asa Carter, executive secretary of the North Alabama Citizens Council, who just months prior to the release of the film, fretted about not only interracial mixing but went so far as to call for juke box operators to "ban 'rock and roll' music and records with colored performers."[70]

During the final performance in *Rock Rock Rock!*, which takes place at a white high school prom, Lymon and his band, made up of young African American and Puerto Rican New Yorkers, sway on the stage to their hit song "I'm Not a Juvenile Delinquent." In this moment, the intimacy of the setting suggests that Lymon, or perhaps one of his older bandmates, could have surely descended the stage to dance side by side with any high school girl of his choosing. This possibility is particularly heightened by a reaction shot from a female prom-goer who gazes lovingly at the charismatic performers during their number.[71] Prior to this spectacular musical denouement, Tuesday Weld and a teen friend moon over the sentimental pleas of black vocal group The Moonglows' hit "I Knew From the Start" in the privacy of the living room while watching music impresario Alan Freed's *Rock 'n' Roll Jubilee of Stars* on the tube. It is unclear, however, whether their emotional reaction is initiated by the appearance of the suave crooners on the television and their image as teen heartthrobs or merely the sentiment of their highly romantic and suggestive lyrics—or perhaps both. Furthermore, in *Rock, Rock, Rock!*, Lymon's group boldly appears at the high school prom hosted by Alan Freed with the letter "T" on the front of their sweaters and the word "teenager" emblazoned across

Fig. 0.4. Frankie Lymon and the Teenagers performing in the film *Rock Rock Rock!* (1956). Courtesy of Photofest.

their backs, calling for entry into the emergent youth-oriented consumer culture of the postwar era. (fig. 0.4)

While there were obviously black people between thirteen and eighteen years old in the United States at this time, the word "teenager" was largely synonymous with middle-class white suburban identity during the 1950s, if one looks to popular magazines, film representations, and literature.[72] Indeed, the panic over juvenile delinquency in the early twentieth century and the birth of the modern, youth-oriented culture industry (which, according to most accounts of teen culture, more or less crystallized conceptions of the American postwar teenager) primarily imagined, evoked, and addressed the white family unit.

This last point is especially revealing, since it has largely gone unremarked that the black press used the word "teen-ager" at least as early as the 1940s.[73] Black-oriented beauty product companies like Dr. Palmer's targeted teenagers in their advertising beginning at mid-century, as they attempted to entice them to both control teen acne and lighten their skin.[74] In 1954 Lester Granger, the director of the National Urban League and black civic leader, painted the African American teenager as a dangerous buffoon when he addressed the annual convention of North Carolina Teacher's Association. According to the *Washington Afro-American*, he suggested that blacks were demonstrating that they were "not ready" for racial integration because of "the clownish behavior and hep cat ways" of "teen-agers" and the "high incidence of delinquency."[75] Granger may have connected delinquency with music ("hep cat ways" is a reference to an appreciation of and involvement in jazz music) in black teen culture yet Lymon cleverly insisted through his songs and musical persona that he and his group were without a doubt teenagers, but certainly not juvenile delinquents. The band even appears in similar letter sweaters on album covers and promotional photographs. I have already mentioned The Teen-agers' hit "I'm Not a Juvenile Delinquent," but it is worth looking more closely at its lyrics since it is hard to imagine a more emphatic declaration of this sentiment. After several lines imploring that they are not juvenile delinquents, with the word "no" preceding the statement numerous times, the song continues with:

> Do the thing that's right
> And you'll do nothing wrong
> Life will be so nice, you'll be in paradise
> I know, because I'm not a juvenile delinquent

Certainly black youth were less apt to be summoned in the pages and electronically mediated imagery of mainstream postwar advertising culture, given that white adolescents were more numerous and had more disposable income, but appeals to a black teenager did exist, at least within the pages of African American–oriented media. And these appeals were remarkably extended through the format of the postwar teen rock film as its threshold spaces—marked by a variety of novel proscenium settings (television studio audience, at-home television viewership, prom stage)—flirted with the possibility of representing interracial socializing and even desire on screen.

I dwell at length here on the rock 'n' roll teen film because it is one of the only instances where performers of color appear regularly in a cycle of youth-oriented American cinema. Although the political and transformative results of such an inclusive practice may be debated, it shows the extent to which popular culture and the intersection of racial politics and American youth had the potential to signify meaningful and significant challenges to prescribed racial boundaries. Even though white Americans were motivated to move to the suburbs and create racially homogenous social and geographical boundaries, these new intimate spaces and their attendant technology—Levittown living rooms with televisions and radios, and spacious bedrooms equipped with turntables—as well as the desires of an increasingly autonomous and powerful teen culture that was enthralled by African American music, could potentially hasten the forces of social integration. Black bands may not have played regularly at predominantly white high schools immediately following the integration of the public education system, but Alan Freed's racially integrated performances certainly gestured towards the pleasures of that possibility.

When African American funk bands infiltrated the music scene two decades later in the midst of the Black Power Movement, geographical concerns literally moved to the center stage of both black musical performance and lived experience. While organizations like the Black Panther Party armed themselves in an effort to protect their neighborhoods from the racially motivated violence of the Los Angeles Police Department and other hegemonic entities of power, bands such as Parliament and its sister act Funkadelic (both led by George Clinton) created a lexicon of black imagery that inverted conventional attitudes of derision towards working-class communities of color.[76] Parliament recorded and celebrated the growth of African American urban communities in their 1975 release "Chocolate City" and also created an outer space mythology of black history in which the origin of black people was not only *not* American—it was literally out of this world. If mainstream America had a problem fitting black citizens comfortably within its geographical contours there was another option. Parliament's ingenious response was to stage an outlandish extravaganza during their live shows, which included a shimmering spacecraft descending from a cloud of smoke to deliver black mythical figures and entertainers in the guise of alien beings such as Dr. Funkenstein and Star Child (both alter egos of Clinton). That funk music became the soundtrack for Blaxploitation cinema during the 1970s is no accident. If this emergent African American-centered form of popular cinema produced a new and sometimes harrowing vision of Afrocentric urban geography, funk was a musical form that could occupy multiple politicized spaces. These ranged from Curtis Mayfield's socially engaged vision of ghetto life in songs such as "Freddie's Dead," from the soundtrack of *Superfly* (1972), to Funkadelic's fifth studio album, *Cosmic Slop* (1973), which addressed the issue of prostitution on at least two tracks, and Parliament's insistence on Dr. Funkenstein's fantastical and otherworldy origin. Together, Blaxploitation cinema and its funk soundtrack formed a new aesthetic of imaginative black American geography that was constantly being reinvented. When Parliament took to the stage in the 1970s, their futuristic, yet ghetto-centric grooves were felt by black and white audiences alike; black funk artists charted on both popular and R & B *Billboard* music charts; African Americans owned successful record companies (even as white music executives continued to exploit many entertainers of color); and African American directors of Blaxploitation cinema were able to produce successful films that directly spoke to the black community (even as some black political groups—such as the NAACP—condemned them).

This heterogeneous historical preamble is admittedly abbreviated and far from complete, and I have not explored related topics such as the representation of American Indians in early anthropological dance films, which served to displace anxieties about colonial atrocities and the appropriation of Indian land. Rather, I have chosen to focus primarily on delineations of African American identity and agency. This is due to the fact that the relationships between American entertainment culture, race, and social struggle have been most significantly dramatized within black American history, especially as it relates to defining community and conceptions of rural, suburban, and urban spaces. With this caveat in mind, the preceding historical discussion establishes several key points about American performance traditions. Firstly, entertainment culture in the United States has, at numerous historical junctures, facilitated negotiations between social mobility, urban and rural identity, and perceptions of racial and ethnic identity. Secondly, although the most significant and enduring social "Other" in mainstream American culture—the African American community—has frequently been maligned and grossly misrepresented through theatrical performance and the circulation of music and dance traditions by the mass media, black entertainers have also served as exemplary figures of political agency, from Bill Robinson's percussive admonishments of white theater hecklers to George Clinton's mapping of extraterrestrial black geography. Thirdly, I emphasize that my historical examples indicate instances where mainstream representational spaces expropriate the performance traditions of culturally and racially "Other" bodies—for instance, in nineteenth century print culture. Yet I also gesture towards examples in which historically disempowered groups seize the avenues of mass media and/or entertainment forms for progressive ends, such as the formidable entity of the black press in the early decade of the twentieth century. I am cautious, however, to eschew a reductive binary historical framework whereby cultural production concerning race, geographical space, social mobility, and class is viewed as either wholly positive or negative in its effects. As my discussion of hip hop cinema in the following chapters will show, mainstream film, and even outright exploitation hip hop fare made by people outside of the hip hop community, could incorporate radical political and social plot elements and themes, while the contemporary African American press, on occasion, castigated the burgeoning facets of hip hop culture and its practitioners.

The hip hop musical film of the 1980s featured entertainers from different ethnic populations and enabled a performance tradition that negotiated race, cultural difference, and economics within recognizable geographical parameters on screen. Urban locations central to the films that I discuss, such as Pittsburgh's Hill District, The South Bronx, and East Los Angeles, have hosted successive waves of European and Latino immigrants as well as migrating African American communities. These regions (and other similar inner city neighborhoods) have become symbols of population instability, cultural transformation, and economic impoverishment—an "Othered" space of ethnic and architectural flux frequently targeted for redevelopment initiatives and the erroneous miscalculations of social scientists. Such neighborhoods have also come to represent important literary and artistic centers of black culture throughout the twentieth century, and more recently, regions like East Harlem have emerged as the core of Latino social and political life in the United States. Indeed, while African Americans have historically fashioned significant elements of music and dance traditions in the United States, a growing Spanish-speaking population has recently transformed conceptions of social categories and identities as well as contributed to American popular music and dance styles, including hip hop.[77]

Many aspects of hip hop culture and the geographical regions where it first thrived in the United States are multiracial and ethnically diverse—Puerto Ricans were at the forefront of breakdancing talent in the early 1980s and there were many white graffiti writers such as New York City's Zephyr "bombing" the trains when Ed Koch waged his war against the "graffiti disease"—yet both the mainstream media and the black press often presented it, or at least individual facets of hip hop, as a uniquely African American enterprise. Significantly, the hip hop musical functioned as a highly adaptable and malleable space of racial and ethnic consolidation. I present cases where hip hop, and the hip hop musical film in particular, evoked a pan-ethnic performance culture that served as a panacea for social conflict. I also present moments where it alternately signified black cultural uniqueness and urban identity. The point is that these films capture a historically important nexus in which American social life is negotiated through performative gestures that reformulate the urban milieu within ethnic and racial markers. These films also show that gender, class negotiations, and differing forms of economic relations play a significant role in the mobilization and politicization of such performance cultures.

While the racial inequities of nineteenth century America were written into law, the plight of many different ethnic populations in the United States at the closing decades of the twentieth century were far less easily defined in terms of access to communal empowerment, jobs, education, and space. The hip hop musical repeatedly imagines fluctuating coordinates of power through the relation between an artist (or group of artists) and his community. Some films, such as *Wild Style*, envision a pan-ethnic street crew where place of residence takes precedence over racial identity. Overwhelmingly, however, the hip hop musical calls forth a struggle between street culture and the commodification of performance. The "threat" to cultural authenticity takes on many guises, including the recording industry, the world of professional theater, and the art gallery. A persistent dualism raised within these films is the negotiation between "selling out" by achieving personal success and the individual's role in bettering their community.

In fact, a battle between the "authentic" and the commercially contrived makes its imprint upon all aspects of the hip hop musical film. This issue is so important because it dramatizes the economic and social inequities that defined racial categories and their contingent geographic boundaries in the 1980s. The films do not directly tell us that their young characters have no opportunity to attend college; it is implied simply by their geographical location and economic status. As the main characters of these hip hop musicals straddle a precarious position in relation to mainstream cultural institutions and the entertainment industry, their situation is symptomatic of the subjection that many inner city communities actually faced when confronted with larger entities of power, such as civil government, real estate development, and federal programs and agencies during the Reagan years.

The social groups depicted in several hip hop films were deeply affected by federal cuts to social service programs, gentrification, and rising rates of dereliction. In 1981, the year that Ronald Reagan ascended to office, nearly half of all black children and 36 percent of Hispanic children in the

U.S. lived below the poverty line, while the poverty rate for whites was just over 15 percent, and all children, regardless of race, was 20 percent.[78] Madeline Kimmich notes that "federal outlays for twenty-five programs affecting children—social services, health, nutrition, education, employment, and income support—decreased by 11 percent between fiscal years 1981 and 1984, after adjusting for inflation."[79] In 1982 John E. Jacob, president of the National Urban League, summarized the contents of the NUL's "annual assessment of the status of blacks" for 1981.[80] He noted:

> Never in that time (since the report was first issued in 1976) has the state of black America been more vulnerable. Never in that time have black economic rights been under such powerful attack. Never in that time have so many black people been alienated from their government.[81]

Moreover, a variety of housing programs that had been initiated in the 1970s to alleviate the problem of unfit housing stock and dereliction in urban communities of color were either reduced or terminated under the Reagan administration, further straining the cohesion of the family unit in urban communities of color.[82] The structure of the Hollywood musical film, with its emphasis on community, family, and the home, neatly crystallized the increasingly vexed engagement with, and outright obliteration of, official channels of governance experienced by inner city populations in the 1980s. This project explores such crucial issues and examines hip hop's actual spatial movement from inner city neighborhoods to various mainstream venues (such as large ballet productions), while also analyzing the ways in which hip hop culture took root in more conventional representational spaces, moving from the independent art film (*Wild Style*) to mainstream cinema (*Flashdance*) and parody (*Delivery Boys*).

The book grew out of a paper I wrote for a graduate course on the musical film as a doctoral student at New York University. Viewing Charlie Ahearn's *Wild Style* piqued my interest in historical and theoretical writings on musical film and led to an exploration of the roots of hip hop in New York City. As I watched *Wild Style, Beat Street, Krush Groove, Breakin' Through, Rappin', Delivery Boys, Body Rock,* and the *Breakin'* films, I realized that such early incarnations of hip hop cinema had as much, if not more, to say about the plight of inner city youth, hip hop as a social practice, and the instability of urban spaces than the subsequent films of "New Black Realism" which emerged just a few years later. This book thus provides an interdisciplinary investigation into the emergence of hip hop musical cinema that places these films in a variety of relevant contexts, including urban history, dance culture, and youth studies. It emphasizes the contradictions and complexities of these films, while stressing their importance to the social history of the 1980s, particularly in relation to urban culture. Some productions—for instance, those that present a singular historical achievement or unique narrative strategy, such as *Wild Style* and *Flashdance*—are discussed more fully than others as the book proceeds. Such a method of analysis reveals that the hip hop-oriented musical, and the use of hip hop in musical films more generally, constitutes a profoundly important development within this genre because it pushed the boundaries of musical cinema to include the images and sounds of an emergent inner city youth culture, while also frequently acknowledging contemporary social and economic inequities.

In Chapter 1, I make the case that these early hip hop-oriented films are indeed musicals through a close examination of their structural and thematic elements. The book also provides a revisionist history of the postclassical musical that makes room for early hip hop-oriented cinema, and significantly alters theories about the trajectory of the generic development of the musical. In doing this, my account challenges several of the assumptions made by scholars of this era. For example, this book troubles the notion that musical film from the 1980s was either conservative in its thematic concerns and narrative structure, or a deconstructionist exercise, which called into question the values of the so-called classical-era "music man"—a character who historically embodies both successful romantic partnering (he gets the girl) and triumphant musical/dance performance (he becomes a star). These arguments by scholars suggest a binary schism within the genre, and are largely based on an analysis of the trio of successful conventional youth-oriented musicals that defined the teen musical in the 1980s—*Flashdance* (1983), *Footloose* (1984), and *Dirty Dancing* (1987)—as well as earlier films like *Saturday Night Fever* (1977), *All That Jazz* (1979) and *Pennies From Heaven* (1981), which curtailed the expressive power and romantic grasp of the conventional "music man."

I attempt to do something different here. Firstly, discussions of postclassical, youth-oriented musical film have largely overlooked the racial diversification of the teen musical at this moment. In fact, I argue that hip hop culture made its biggest entrance into mainstream media through the narrative format of the musical film. Nearly all hip hop musicals embrace several features of the classical film musical: the formation of a romantic couple, the desire for communal harmony and order, as well as a final show. While these features are generally put to conservative ends in the classical era, when they form the structural base of the hip hop musical they instead allow for innovative and often radical social and political transformations. This is achieved through their documentation of contemporary urban landscapes, use of non-professional actors, centrality of communities of color, and, in the case of *Wild Style* especially, innovative cinematic language.

Secondly, I argue against the assertion that postclassical "music men" of the 1980s are no longer invested with the ability to make claims upon space through the act of performance. The appropriation of space and subsequent narrative manipulation through dance was a hallmark of classical-era "music men" such as Fred Astaire and Gene Kelly, whose routines in *Top Hat* (1935) and *An American in Paris* (1951), respectively, emphasize their mastery and in some cases even ownership over public spaces. While previous scholars have argued that the postclassical "music man" can no longer orchestrate or signify ownership of space through performance in films such as *All That Jazz* and *Pennies From Heaven* or that his ability to do so is present but highly limited in its impact (*Footloose*, *Dirty Dancing*), hip hop musicals repeatedly show us "music men" who are able to appropriate city spaces (and in some cases enact important social change) through the various performative outlets of hip hop culture. This is a crucial development in the larger context of the history of musical film because classical-era Hollywood musicals have habitually denied African American performers and other people of color the transcendent abilities of the "music man."

As I move onto a close study of Charlie Ahearn's groundbreaking independent hip hop film *Wild Style* in Chapter 2, I provide an even more in-depth examination of the relationship between hip hop culture and the musical genre. This film redefines notions of home and community as it transforms traditional generic parameters in order to document the resourceful and creative South Bronx community in the early 1980s. Additionally, the chapter addresses *Wild Style*'s reflexive strategies, location shooting, and use of animation, all of which are derived directly from hip hop artistic strategies.

Chapter 3 puts the hip hop musical in dialogue with other youth-oriented cinema of the same era in order to reveal how early hip hop film presented a challenge to the dominant values of white-centered suburban teen cinema of the same decade. The former evokes hip hop culture as a social and economic system that celebrates difference, innovation, and creativity. This is in sharp distinction to the emphasis on conformity and consumption found in 1980s mainstream youth cinema, such as in the films of John Hughes. Culture is made, not just consumed, in the hip hop–oriented youth musical. In the end, this chapter argues that teen film from this era was acutely concerned with the perceived racialized geographic contours of American life that associated white America with suburbia, and people of color with the city. The teeming, racially homogenous malls of *Fast Times at Ridgemont High* (1982), *Valley Girl* (1983), and *Weird Science* (1985) are spaces of semi-private community ritual in which teenagers shop as well as socialize. However, they also function as symbols of racial exclusion that screen out both poverty and ethnic diversity. The hip hop musical, by contrast, defines community ritual as inclusive, spontaneous, and public through its staging of music and dance numbers in a variety of civic venues and spaces within the urban environment.

Latent social tensions regarding the transgression of boundaries between urban neighborhoods and suburban communities came to the surface in teen film, not just in representational form, but in cinema spectatorship as well. My research uncovered instances of violence and public unrest that broke out during screenings of *Krush Groove*, and demonstrates that youth audiences responded to the content of teen films in ways that dramatized the apparent dichotomy between the racialized geographical spaces of this cinema. The rise of the multiplex theater frequently allowed for encounters between groups of teens from different racial backgrounds and communities, yet the implications of this aspect of multiplex spectatorship have not, to my knowledge, been fully examined. By shedding some light on this history, I hope that I have opened up a fruitful avenue of exploration for future research. Racial diversity was banished from the mainstream 1980s teen film by setting the narrative action in supposedly all-white communities but the hip hop musical focused on underprivileged urban communities of color rather than white middle-class teens. By examining these two distinct but related cycles of films together, I provide a more nuanced account of youth-oriented cinema from this historical period than has been previously drawn.

The last part of the book focuses on the evocation of breakdance—an inner-city dance practice originating in the 1970s that was an integral part of hip hop culture—in both film and print. It offers a history of the dynamic relation between ballet and breakdance, drawing on popular magazines, academic and professional journals, newspapers, and film of the 1980s. A vigorously contested gender dynamic allowed breakdancing to express significant aspects of cultural identity in a broad array of media and performance traditions that included an unusually heterogeneous audience and devoted legion of practitioners. Here I establish that, contrary to popular opinion, breakdancing in the early 1980s was practiced by women and girls. Furthermore, the female breaker was able to use the dance form in a critical manner that negated the marginalization of women in certain avenues of hip hop culture.

As the art of breakdance came to national attention in the early 1980s, it was continually redefined by a negotiation between "authentic" street culture and the protean arms of institutional power—the ballet academy, advertising, and dance magazines—that tried to grasp for control over its meaning and place within American life. This chapter reveals that institutional forces initially brought the two dance forms together through both community outreach programs and theatrical shows. When street trained breakers were courted by the world of professional ballet and jazz dance, the relationship was presented as a way to invigorate and even "remasculinize" the rigid performance codes of ballet. Paradoxically, it was also envisioned as a mechanism of control used to "tame" an apparently wild and uncultivated mode of expression. This unusual aspect of 1980s dance culture found its way into the first wave of hip hop films including *Breakin'*, *Breakin' 2: Electric Boogaloo*, and *Breakin' Through*, while also influencing, and even to a degree, structuring the enormously successful mainstream film *Flashdance*.

The short breakdance sequence in this 1983 blockbuster is generally considered to be the earliest inclusion of this aspect of hip hop culture in mainstream cinema. And, although it is usually dismissed as a curious footnote in the history of American film, the use of breaking in *Flashdance* can actually be read as a complex instance of ambivalent desire underpinned by the musical genre's historical negotiation of race, gender, erotic energy, and performance on screen. Previous accounts have ignored race as a significant factor in this film, and instead focused on *Flashdance*'s delineation of female subjectivity. Upon close examination of the cinematic text, however, it becomes apparent that the definition of gender and sexual identity in the film were inseparable from issues of race, class, and performance. My reading demonstrates that the transformation of the female heroine from working-class stripper to upper-class dancer is actually predicated on her relationship to black and Latino youth culture. Further, it establishes that *Flashdance* works towards the expulsion and repression of all racially "Other" aspects from the main narrative, while at the same time these repressed elements, however marginalized within the narrative, return as surplus visual cues. *Flashdance* is usually understood to be a transparent window into the regressive gender politics of the 1980s, but I argue that much more complex operations are at work in this film, revealing that gender cannot be cleaved from an understanding of the categories of both race and class.

This book fills a gap in hip hop scholarship in that it examines hip hop culture on film and its relationship to classical film genres and institutional dance traditions. Moreover, this connective understanding of early hip hop cinema reverses the claim that, with few exceptions, the hip hop musical was uniformly apolitical and unworthy of serious narrative analysis. Rather than simply expressing the angst of inner city youth or merely providing a backdrop for partying, hip hop culture, I argue, is actually the catalyst for social change in many of these films. It presents a blueprint for communal cohesion by including everyone and by literally taking place everywhere—any stoop, street corner or basketball court will do.

1

The Case for the Hip Hop Musical

Between 1983 and 1985 no fewer than nine hip hop-oriented musical films were released in the United States, including *Wild Style, Beat Street, Body Rock, Breakin', Breakin' 2, Breakin' Through, Rappin', Krush Groove,* and *Delivery Boys*. Although they have been all but forgotten in most historical discussions concerning the development of the musical genre, many aspects of these films are, in fact, overwhelmingly consistent with the thematic contours and narrative structures of the classical-era musical, a form that emerged in the late 1920s. The American musical film genre includes "star" vehicles like *The Jazz Singer* (1927), which established an enduring backstage narrative, all-black cast folk musicals, such as *Hearts in Dixie*, and *Top Hat* and *Swing Time* (1936), eloquent romantic comedies in which heterosexual union is central to both the film's plot and musical numbers. Hip hop musicals emerged in the aftermath of significant challenges to the genre that have been loosely gathered by historians under the banner of the postclassical musical. These films renewed some classical-era generic elements, while directly challenging others as they navigated contemporary urban settings, social anxieties, and political struggle through the conventional iconography of Hollywood musical cinema. This chapter has four main concerns: to demonstrate the diverse ideological, thematic, and stylistic aspects of the hip hop musical; to show how the hip hop musical directly engaged with aspects of the classical musical film genre; to reveal the extent to which the racialized history of urban transformation impinged upon the representation of community and social action in the film narratives; and to reconstruct a history of the postclassical musical that includes a space for this initial hip hop-oriented cinema.

All hip hop musicals deal with themes of urban space, race, youth culture, and performance, but I do not want to suggest that this is an ideologically coherent group of films. Hip hop musical cinema offers diverse criticisms and celebrations of American social values, while adopting myriad positions regarding approaches to communal activism and the individual's path towards success through music and dance performance.[1] Not only were these films significantly varied in terms of the degree to which hip hop functions as a progressive and political performance strategy, but their production histories ranged from independent art cinema to exploitation fare. The entire corpus of the hip hop musical thus represents an array of ideological positions, and within particular texts themselves we find multiple social and political attitudes. These films might be understood to "reflect" the social and political currents of their historical moment, yet they do so in ways that are contradictory, ambiguous, and potentially even liberating for various members of historically oppressed groups within the United States, such as women and people of color. What is so apparent in examining the entire corpus of hip hop cinema is, in fact, the *differences* between films in terms of their social and political elements (or lack thereof), filming techniques, and actual presentation of hip hop culture through the cinematic lens.

Crucially, these films also rely on the various facets of hip hop culture to structure the cinematic text in different ways. For the purpose of this discussion, I have organized the corpus into two categories: the true hip hop musical and the surface hip hop musical. The first category—the true hip hop musical—which includes *Wild Style*, *Beat Street*, *Rappin'*, and *Krush Groove*, utilizes the interrelated set of cultural and social practices within hip hop as the organizing principle of the film. They also feature identifiable inner city locales, offer sympathetic portraits of the community inhabitants, and all but *Krush Groove* make a point of revealing the poverty of ghetto life. These films also show how the collective neighborhood body comes together in unconventional ways through the various facets of hip hop culture, while stressing the democratic nature of this process whereby everyone participates in music and dance performance.

Films such as *Wild Style*, *Beat Street*, and *Krush Groove* were the product of filmmakers and producers who were personally invested in the lives of urban communities of color. For instance, *Wild Style*'s director, Charlie Ahearn, was a constant presence in the South Bronx community for years before the film was finally released. *Wild Style* chronicles the romance of two Latino South Bronx graffiti writers—Rose, who works with a crew that paints legal murals, and Raymond (Zoro), an "outlaw" writer who works alone "bombing" train cars at night. As Ahearn gathered material for this romantic and creative docudrama of the South Bronx community, he painted graffiti with its stars, went to clubs in the neighborhood, and enlisted local residents to appear in the film and work on its soundtrack and artistic production.[2] Moreover, as Ahearn sought to capture the emergence of hip hop culture in New York City on film, he became part of its artistic process and transformation. After the director photographed graffiti writers at work, club events, as well as other local happenings, he produced a series of slide shows that were projected at local venues, while MCs rapped over the unfolding narrative. Ahearn recalls this experience at a party space named The Ecstasy Garage:

> I would bring two sheets and hang them on the wall behind the DJ and project slides that I was snapping in the yards and the clubs. I would edit them like a storyboard, adding some shots taken the week before at the Ecstasy. It was like projecting a rough version of the movie. Busy Bee would be on the mic. He'd see himself up huge on the screen and would get the crowd to yell, "Hey Busy Bee, ho!" One night Phase2, who was an originator of early subway art and was designing the most beautiful party flyers, brought some slides from the early '70s of his incredible train pieces and of him posing in front of some of his bubble-style paintings. I popped them into the carousel and they became part "of the movie."[3]

Hip hop is a collaborative form that privileges the integration of different artistic mediums, and Ahearn's documentary imagery became part of an energetic, multimedia cultural performance that reinforced the collaborative, direct, and improvisational nature of hip hop culture.

Beat Street, a semi-independently produced film directed by Stan Lathan, features the exploits of two fictional South Bronx brothers, Kenny (Guy Davis) and Lee (Robert Taylor), who are heavily enmeshed within the hip hop culture of their community. The older brother, Kenny, embarks on a romantic affair with a wealthy Manhattan girl named Tracy (Rae Dawn Chong), while Lee, played by real-life breakdance prodigy Taylor, boogies his way into police custody. Lathan's film also explored the subculture of graffiti writers, and even romanticized this practice through its depiction of Ramon (Jon Chardiet), a fictional Puerto Rican writer. Ramon, who dreams of tagging a pristine subway car, ultimately dies while attempting to apprehend Spit (Bill Anagnos), a rival writer who has been destroying his work throughout the film. *Beat Street*'s producer, Harry Belafonte, was not as directly involved in hip hop culture as Ahearn, but he was a committed civil rights activist and vocal critic of the Reagan administration.[4]

Belafonte also grew up in Harlem and dedicated his film to the people of the South Bronx.⁵ He undoubtedly had a political vision of hip hop as a revolutionary tool, and much has been made of his subsequent influence on Cuba's burgeoning rap culture at the turn of the millennium.⁶

Krush Groove was directed by notable African American filmmaker Michael Schultz. He had previously made two important films about the black urban experience in the 1970s—*Cooley High* (1975) and the funk musical *Car Wash* (1976)—while also maintaining a steady presence in television directing. This hip hop musical was a fictionalized account of the life of record producer Russell Simmons (renamed Russell Walker in the film and played by Blair Underwood), his relationship with Run-D.M.C., Kurtis Blow, and other luminaries in the world of rap music, and the Def Jam record label. In the midst of money troubles, musical rivalries, disagreements, and familial strife a competition emerges between Walker and his brother Run (of Run-D.M.C.) for the affections of club performer Shelia E. The film was co-produced by Simmons, and as such he had some input into the narrative and casting. *Krush Groove* was released by Warner Bros. and made a respectable $11 million at the U.S. box office. While Schultz has worked on a wide variety of subjects, his output reveals a consistent interest in evoking a sympathetic and complex account of the African American experience, which is undoubtedly evident in this film.

Rappin', directed by Joel Silberg, was an entry in the Cannon Group's cycle of hip hop-oriented exploitation extravaganzas. It featured John Rappinhood (Mario Van Peebles)—an ex-con who returns to his inner city Pittsburgh community to protect it from nefarious real estate developers and rival thugs. While saving the Hill District from peril, Rappinhood also jump-starts his musical career and wins the affections of his longtime love interest Dixie (Tasia Valenza).

The second category of hip hop musical films—the surface hip hop musical—includes the two other films belonging to Cannon's hip hop run, *Breakin'* and *Breakin' 2*, as well as *Delivery Boys*, *Body Rock*, and *Breakin' Through*. These films make references to select aspects of hip hop culture and feature breakdancers or practitioners of "street dance" as central characters. What sets them apart from the true hip hop musical is the way in which the emphasis shifts from exposing the social conditions of inner city life to highlighting choreographed numbers and brightly costumed performers. These films relinquish (or at least reduce) the centrality of graffiti as a clandestine practice, rapping as a communal exercise, and the art of DJing in favor of utilizing the energy and visual interest to be found in breakdancing. The surface hip hop musical also evokes a far less specific image of the inner city ghetto, almost never featuring explicit images of recognizable urban locales.

Breakin' and *Breakin' 2*, along with *Rappin'*, were produced in a furious bid to exploit the news media's intense interest in hip hop culture. *Breakin'*, released in May 1984, was the first and most financially successful mainstream breakdance-oriented feature film. The sequel followed with moderate success just a few months later. Historically, Thomas Doherty notes that the term exploitation was utilized by the motion picture industry at mid-century to refer to films that aimed to exploit a particular audience (usually teenagers), had a second-rate budget, and included "controversial, bizarre, or timely subject matter amenable to wild promotion."[7] Cannon has closely followed the model of early exploitation cinema and the company has profited from turning out cheaply made films structured around a variety of fads appealing to a youth demographic.[8]

Breakin' was directed by Joel Silberg, while Sam Firstenberg made *Breakin' 2*. In the first film, professionally trained upper-middle-class jazz dancer Kelly (Lucinda Dickey) teams up with "street dancers" Ozone (Adolfo "Shabba Doo" Quinones) and Turbo (Michael "Boogaloo Shrimp" Chambers) to bring urban dance forms within the purview of institutional performance. The trio battles the resistant forces of academic dance culture as well as other "street dance" crews on their journey towards performance success. *Breakin' 2* reworked subject matter from its predecessor, such as interracial and cross class desire. However, it also explored broadly defined themes of urban gentrification and communal empowerment as the group organizes a fundraiser in order to prevent the destruction of Miracles, a neighborhood dance center. Even though breakdancing is referenced in the title of the *Breakin'* series, it is always described as street dance within the films while rapping, graffiti writing, and DJing are either completely obliterated or relegated to peripheral roles. The breaker moves to center stage in these two productions, but the dancer's tie to hip hop culture more generally is severed as a result of the films' refusal to name either breakdancing or hip hop within the narrative. This dislocation between the practice of breakdancing and the other performance traditions of hip hop are characteristic of the surface hip hop musical.

Evidently, spectators found the initial glimpses of an emergent black and Latino folk culture exciting and pleasurable given that a film with relatively low production values such as *Breakin'* became the eighteenth highest grossing film of the year.[9] It returned over $38 million at the box office, edging out such productions as *The Terminator* and Clint Eastwood's *City Heat*.[10] That *Breakin'* cracked the top twenty might astonish viewers today, but as Robert Sklar has noted, historically (between the 1930s and the 1970s) the yearly top earning pictures also tended to be films which garnered industry awards and praise, whereas during the 1980s there was no longer a correlation between the highest earners and perceptions and distinctions of "quality" within the film world itself.[11] Many hip hop musicals made a tidy profit but none repeated the financial success of Hollywood's first attempt at exploiting the nation's increasing interest in hip hop culture.

Body Rock was a New World Pictures release that featured soap opera star Lorenzo Lamas, who had recently emerged as a "heartthrob" on the primetime hit series *Falcon Crest*. In the film, Lamas portrays Chilly D, a poor unemployed New York youth who is part of a hip hop crew. His crew dances at the underground nightclub Rhythm Nation until Chilly is lured into the decadent world of wealthy patrons who install him as the MC at a swank new dance club. Chilly leaves his friends and would-be girlfriend from the old neighborhood. Next, he is divested of his newfound fame and fortune after rebuking the affections of his male patron. The posh club steals the name Body Rock and attempts to assemble a new group of performers under the same moniker. Angry at this turn of events, Chilly and his old gang get even by crashing the unveiling of the new Body Rock and taking over the show. Following its debut at Cannes, *Body Rock* was poorly received; it netted two Razzie nominations (for worst original song and worst actor), performed dismally at the box office, and director Marcelo Epstein was never to helm another feature film.

The made-for-Disney Channel film *Breakin' Through* cleverly avoided any references to specific social problems while still loosely conforming to the structure of the hip hop musical. Like *Breakin'* and several other films I discuss, *Breakin' Through* staged an artistic "showdown" between the "legitimate" theatrical world and street dance. The film brings two performance spaces—the stage and the street—together through the genre conventions of the Hollywood musical. However, this generic twist does not contain any critical edge but rather defuses all of the radical possibilities inherent within hip hop musical cinema. With the exception of the opening sequence, the film alternates between two settings. In the first instance, we witness street dancers in tightly framed shots that reveal little of the surrounding urban environment. The rest of the film takes place in the rehearsal space of a theatrical dance company as they prepare for the opening of a new musical show. When a choreographer attempts to bring the breakdancers into the space of the theater, friction develops between the street crew, headed by an Italian youth named Ripsaw, and the rest of the professionally trained dancers in the production. A happy finale is achieved when the choreographer utilizes these tensions and appropriates them for the subject matter and formal arrangement of the final show. Thus, the class conflict inherent in the acrimonious relation between different dance traditions in the film is neutralized with the final scene. The film completely aestheticizes the "real" inequity and conflict that is at the heart of the true hip hop musical—the tension produced by the meeting of two different performance spaces or traditions, which signify two different socioeconomic populations. It also attempted to avoid the association between hip hop and the empowerment of black and Latino youth by casting a black actor, Broadway veteran Ben Vereen, to represent institutional dance. *Breakin' Through* further separated hip hop culture from any specific community or racial group by featuring an ethnically mixed street dance crew and locating practitioners of hip hop culture in an insulated space, which had no connection to any larger community or actual urban environment.

Delivery Boys is perhaps the most unique hip hop musical explored in this book. Not only was it a cheaply made exploitation film targeted towards a juvenile audience, it also transformed the subgenre into a complete farce. Promotional material for the film emphasized its blatant aspirations towards juvenile sex comedy status rather than its relationship to hip hop culture. Images on posters and VHS covers for *Delivery Boys* (fig. 1.1) featured not breakdancing or graffiti, but an interior bedroom scene suggestive of sex (red bra hanging casually over the bed frame) and partying (room in general disarray, open pizza box from the night before)—advertising strategies that had proved successful in promoting earlier teen sex films like *Animal House* (1978), *Losin' It* (1983), and *Meatballs II* (1984).

The film features a multiethnic (Jewish, Italian, and Puerto Rican) hip hop crew named the Delivery Boys, most of whom also deliver pizza for Ben's, a local restaurant. The plot of the film focuses on their desire to perform in the Brooklyn Bridge Break Dance Contest, which promises a prize of ten thousand dollars to the winning crew. However, the Devil Dogs, a rival dance team, attempt to prevent the Delivery Boy's entry into the competition through a series of absurd scenarios, in which the hapless breakers are lured into "dangerous" situations on their pizza delivery

Fig. 1.1. *Delivery Boys* (1984) poster.

route. For instance, delivery boy Max (Josh Marcano) is sent to an uptown apartment for a delivery only to be seduced by Elizabeth (Kelly Nichols), an older girl who then keeps him in her room by installing a vicious guard dog outside her door. In order to avoid detection by the girl's father, Max dons a wig and dress and attempts to sneak out of the apartment. He successfully escapes and performs at the breakdance contest while still in drag. In the end, all of the Delivery Boys arrive at the competition only to have the dance showdown turn into a literal battle. There is no progressive, political, or even remotely critical aspect to this film; it relies on bathroom humor and absurd scenarios to keep the narrative afloat. The film's director, Ken Handler, also suffered the same fate as the director of *Body Rock* with this film effectively ending his career.

From this point on, I will use either the terms "true hip hop musical" and "surface hip hop musical" to refer to this group of films. Additionally, the more general "hip hop musical" will be used to denote instances when both the true and the surface hip hop musical are referenced. These terms do not imply value judgments on the quality of the films but rather suggest important differences within the range of musicals that adopted various aspects of hip hop culture during the 1980s. While it can be generally stated that the true hip hop musical is overtly political in its content because it insists on the visibility of urban conditions—poverty, dilapidated housing, and crime—there are some instances in which particular features of the surface hip hop musical also contain potentially radical social critiques in their narrative structure. However, the reduction of location shooting in the surface hip hop musical tends to diminish its radical possibilities because social conditions are rarely connected to images of actual, recognizable urban neighborhoods. The use of location shooting and the "documentary impulse" in the true hip hop musical will be more fully elaborated in relation to *Wild Style* in the following chapter.

The divisions used here are meant to organize material for the reader and to reveal similarities and differences within the films. These categories prove useful in many instances, but the corpus of films discussed in this book is also viewed as a multifaceted, ambiguous, and often contradictory set of material. I adopt such a structure so as to avoid organizing these productions in terms of a linear progression, with *Wild Style* as the first genuine representation of hip hop culture in a feature film, followed by other hip hop musicals that increasingly exploit an authentic cultural form, eventually resulting in films conceived by corporate interests for the sole purpose of exploiting the youth market's interest in African American and Latino urban music and dance. This is something I want to resist, since it does not help to accurately explain the historical circumstances that facilitated the diffusion of an emergent urban ethos from the margins to the center of cultural representation. For instance, writing in 1984, Gene Siskel noted that

> after the success of *Flashdance*, corporate Hollywood began filling its dance card in earnest. *Breakin'*, made cheaply and quickly by the exploitation-oriented Cannon Film Group to beat the competition, opened three weeks ago and already has grossed $22 million, making it hugely profitable. A sequel with the same cast, called *Electric Boogaloo*, is due to be released in record time—September. *Beat Street*, from Orion Pictures, opens June 8, and is

getting a media buildup that suggests it may even outgross *Breakin'* . . . Breakdancing movies are cheap to make. They don't need stars; you can't see an actor's face anyway when he's spinning on his head. Breakdancing movies simply need a strong, self-realization storyline, easy-to-relate-to characters, and fabulous dancing. Much more expensive than the movie is the obligatory TV ad campaign.[12]

Siskel accurately remarks that some breakdancing films were the product of youth market-oriented film companies looking to exploit a seemingly new dance craze. Later in the article, Siskel makes reference to issues of racial inclusiveness within these films, although he never addresses the ways in which breakdance, and hip hop in general, function as fluid vectors of cultural interaction. He does notice, though, that *Beat Street*, unlike *Breakin'*, does not contain a white character in a central role, and remarks that "it will be interesting to see if that hurts *Beat Street* at the box office. By comparison, *Breakin'* was packaged more as a commercial vehicle, because its central character is a young white waitress who learns to breakdance from a black and a Puerto Rican youth in sunny Southern California."[13] But there is no attempt to explain how this white character intervenes in, or is incorporated into, the world of black and Latino performance on screen, or how race figures into the history and structure of American musical cinema in general—issues that will be fully explored in what follows.

Genre Theory and the Hip Hop Musical

The hip hop films with which this book is concerned satisfy the most basic film industry definition of the musical genre articulated by Rick Altman in his important work *The American Film Musical*: "a film with music, that is, with music that emanates from what I will call the diegesis, the fictional world created by the film (as opposed to Hollywood's typical background music, which instead comes from nowhere)."[14] They also correspond to, or are in dialogue with, several musical subgenres, such as the fairy tale musical, the show musical, and the folk musical. Altman has also argued that classical-era Hollywood musical films frequently relied upon conservative elements, such as communal harmony and heterosexual pairing, to form the main strands of narrative progression.

For example, the parallelism between triumphant heterosexual courtship and success in the entertainment world is a hallmark of the Hollywood show musical.[15] From Depression-era Busby Berkeley extravaganzas, such as *Gold Diggers of 1933* (1933) and *Dames* (1934), to the elaborate unmasking of cinematic production in *Singin' in the Rain* (1952), the show musical is constructed around both the creation of a romantic couple and a successful final performance.[16] Class differences, meddling families, and chance mishaps may stall or frustrate the pair's successful coupling until the concluding moments of the film but eventually the couple's tensions are resolved and the viewer's desire for romantic fulfillment is satisfied through a final victorious show or performance in which the male and female leads are ultimately revealed as an amorous pair.

The hip hop musical, though, exploits the conservative plot structures and narrative elements of classical film in order to comment upon contemporary urban conditions, often with very radical and subversive results. It nearly always features a potential heterosexual pairing and the amorous trajectory of this couple becomes completely entangled with the world of music, dance, and performance as the film progresses.[17] Incarnations of the film musical featuring aspects of hip hop culture usually equate this generic romantic musical ending with the potential to bring different city spaces or performance environments together. In some examples, very specific urban imagery is evoked through the consistent use of location shooting. For instance, in *Wild Style* the concluding performance involves the staging of a rap concert featuring uptown (the Bronx) talent in a downtown space (the Lower East Side) in the spirit of both communal celebration and exposure of local talent.

In *Beat Street*, the two would-be lovers come from different socioeconomic classes, symbolized by their place of residence, the South Bronx—a poor inner city neighborhood characterized by dereliction and crime, and the wealthiest regions of upper Manhattan bordering Central Park. After the death of his friend Ramon, Kenny organizes a party to celebrate the fallen graffiti artist's life. The event is Kenny's big chance at stardom as a DJ, and his decision to create a "hip hop wake" is initially viewed by his friends as a potentially disastrous career move. This final performance extravaganza presided over by Kenny is a triumph which both connects him to his South Bronx community and cements his ability to maneuver outside of it in the entertainment world. In fact, the final images of the film reveal Kenny on stage performing with the wife of the deceased Ramon on one side and his love interest/music producer on the other. He straddles the forces of communal integration (represented by Ramon's wife) and the ability to transcend the limitations of inner city life through a romantic link to Tracey, his wealthy upper Manhattan girlfriend. The final performance sequence magically erases any contradictions regarding the ability to succeed outside of the neighborhood, as well as underscores the importance of using music and dance to nurture the community. In this film, the link between romantic partnering and success in the entertainment world is even more emphatically stated because Kenny's love interest is a powerful figure in the "legitimate" music world. In *Breakin'*, *Breakin' 2*, and *Breakin' Through*, the two potential lovers come from different ethnic and racial backgrounds. The *Breakin'* series also emphasizes the vastly different socioeconomic realms occupied by the two leads. Further, *Breakin'*, *Breakin' 2*, *Beat Street*, and *Breakin' Through*, like so many successful Hollywood fairy tale musicals, including *Love Me Tonight* (1932) and *Top Hat*, use romantic pairing to symbolize the blending and merging of opposites. Unlike these earlier precedents, however, the hip hop musical's romantic pairings always signify contemporary socioeconomic inequities and tensions.

The final show or performance number in *Rappin'* also works to bridge the relationship between local performance traditions and success beyond the community. This number brings these themes together as Rappinhood dances through the streets while rapping with the entire community and his girl, Dixie, at his side. In the concluding moments of this film, a white music producer, Dixie's boss, suddenly appears with contract in hand. Previously, the producer's repeated attempts to get the rapper to sign a recording deal were rebuffed by Rappinhood, but during this final attempt the producer is met with a smile and a willing future star. Rappinhood signs on the dotted line, assuring his success in the commercial rap industry after having just single-handedly saved his community from destruction. The film makes a point of emphasizing his signature on the contract, and thus his guarantee of commercial success, by cutting to a close-up as he pens his name in very large black letters across the document. Interestingly, this close-up recalls what has been left out of the hip hop scene in this film, the act of graffiti writing. *Rappin'* downplayed the importance of graffiti writing and reduced the multiple and interconnected performance aspects of hip hop culture, instead focusing on Rappinhood's rise towards stardom. The hip hop practitioner's signature is penned on a corporate document instead of a neighborhood wall but the film reassures us that Rappinhood will not leave his community behind, though, as they contribute to the final number in this scene by singing along with the star.

According to Altman, the final production number within the show musical assumes the quality of a commodity whether or not it follows the usual pattern of the backstage musical, which almost always culminates in a polished and professional theatrical show produced for a paying audience.[18] He notes that "the show musical is a white-collar genre, consistently showing only upper echelon production personnel and performers, while masking the blue-collar work of production."[19] While this may be true for many musicals of the classical era, by the 1980s the genre had undergone significant changes, and several hip hop musicals remarkably end with a show or final number that is emphatically not a commodity, or at least not one that conforms to middle-class expectations of entertainment. The final shows of both *Beat Street* and *Breakin' 2*, for instance, are fundraisers. As noted above, the concluding number in *Rappin'* takes place in the street as the entire community performs together to symbolize their triumph over the forces of corporate greed and gentrification. *Krush Groove* envisions the final show as an impromptu rap number performed by the Fat Boys, Run-D.M.C., Shelia E., and Kurtis Blow at the legendary South Bronx club Disco Fever, while the final rap concert of Charlie Ahearn's independent art film *Wild Style* is a free event produced for the community, by the community.

Music and dance performance circulates in the realm of the everyday in nearly all hip hop musicals. Thus, the final show of the hip hop musical in several instances works against the production of a middle-class commodity, instead functioning to undo the thrust of the traditional show musical that "perpetuates a romantic mythology whereby creativity is vested in the hands of the few."[20] Nonetheless, in other examples—those that work toward reconciling the spaces of the street and the academy within dance performance such as *Breakin' Through* and *Breakin'*—we witness a concluding number that comes closer to Altman's articulation of the final show musical performance as middle-class commodity. They both include highly choreographed finales that take place in large theatrical venues intended for paying audiences.

The traditional parameters of the show musical are opened up far beyond the conventional theatrical proscenium in these hip hop-centered films. When the musical's traditional resolution—a juxtaposition of successful public performance with the romantic union of the two leads—is used to conclude the hip hop musical, it frequently transgresses the historically conservative features associated with the classical-era show musical. This is achieved through the former's emphasis on emergent and inchoate urban youth performance, as well as its broad and inclusive racial spectrum. A hip hop–oriented finale that is explicitly concerned with illuminating contemporary urban relations replaces the classical musical's emphasis on familial and communal harmony within white middle-class America, and the mechanics of producing bourgeois entertainment.

The hip hop musical also centers on communal performance, spontaneous song and dance, and the talents of the untrained amateur, all facets of the traditional American folk musical. This may seem an obvious point, but even though the various practices of hip hop within these films have been described by academics as folk culture, a direct relation to the folk musical has been left unexamined—a surprising oversight considering several important early Hollywood musicals featuring a predominantly African American cast are, in fact, folk musicals. The hip hop musical resists the semantic demands of the folk musical as a setting that stages the recollection of the American past as an idealized state (early black-cast musicals did not necessarily take place in the Old South; nevertheless, they usually reflected the stereotypes about black rural communities that were perpetuated in this era) but emphatically retains the folk musical's emphasis on collective interaction through performance.

A less obvious but still relevant relationship exists between the hip hop musical *Wild Style* and the fairy tale musical. Emerging from a European stage tradition, the fairy tale musical is based on the Viennese operetta, a form that privileges sexual intrigue as its central theme.[21] The plots of early Hollywood musicals influenced by the Viennese tradition often took up the theme of class transcendence, which was frequently facilitated through an elaborate play of mistaken identity that allowed "the characters on stage to play out their hidden desires."[22] This is specifically relevant to two of the productions discussed in this book, *Wild Style*, as mentioned above, and *Flashdance*, films that will be examined in depth in Chapters 2 and 4, respectively. In these musicals, the employment of a secret identity in relation to the musical plot is radically reoriented in ways that foreground a link between race, class, gender, and performance culture in the urban milieu. For instance, the revelation of a secret identity in *Wild Style* is staged to dramatize the difficulty of balancing personal success with communal and familial obligations, while the device is used in *Flashdance* to call attention to audience expectations regarding gender, race, and class within a working-class environ.

I am not the first to argue for a subversive element present within the musical genre. Matthew Tinkcom has recently challenged a primary focus on narrative progression in Hollywood musical film, suggesting that, in the case of musicals made by the Metro-Goldwyn-Mayer Freed

Unit, potentially subversive elements were introduced into the films via the *mise-en-scène*. An emphasis on artifice, costume, and pure spectacle, rather than plot and dialogue, he proposes, undermined the apparently conservative and heteronormative features of *Yolanda and the Thief* (1945) and *The Pirate*. His reading calls attention to the number of homosexual men who labored in the Freed Unit, working together to create the unique style of visual excess associated with MGM musical films of this period. The look of these mainstream films was highly influential, yet their visual codes have now been reclaimed by academics as "camp," a queer subcultural aesthetic.[23] On the one hand, the classical musical genre insists upon heteronormativity and conservative notions of community and family, and on the other, its structure allows for highly transgressive sexual "play" within the text. Apparent dualities within musical film in this instance highlight the contested nature of the genre, and while subversive elements are arguably present in a number of classical musical films they are usually brought within the purview of rigid sexual codes. Such dissident elements in the hip hop musical are undoubtedly enabled by a *mise en scène* that frequently gestures toward contemporary urban transformations and social struggle as well as a cinematic practice that engages deliberate "play" with established generic conventions.

The majority of hip hop musicals combine elements from all three categories of the Hollywood musical genre. Aspects of the fairy tale musical, such as class boundaries and conflicting value systems, are nearly always resolved at the end of the hip hop musical through a feature of the show musical, a final stage production that equates performance success with romantic paring. Thus, a structural aspect of the show musical allows for the "merging of cultural values once defined as mutually exclusive," a thematic feature of the fairy tale musical.[24] Whereas Altman predominantly defines the American musical as a form that privileges distinct subgeneric categories, the postclassical hip hop musical insists on blending and recombining elements of all three types of musical film. It is tempting, therefore, to discuss the mixture, recombination, and transformation of classical-era musical elements in the hip hop musical in terms of postmodernism. The postmodern is recognized as a historical shift emerging in the 1960s (dates vary somewhat across disciplines) in which cultural products are no longer defined by their particular singular qualities. Rather, they are concerned with plurality and the conjunction of different styles, eras, and methods following a crisis of faith in a culture's predominant master narratives (e.g., high modernism in both art and architecture, the classical Hollywood film, etc.). Many accounts of postmodernism argue that this era and its cultural products are marked by a distinct depoliticization as historical elements are integrated into new forms.[25] The hip hop musical, in truth, reveals a contrary operation at work. As elements of the classical Hollywood musical are resurrected in these films, they allow for a uniquely politicized viewpoint of contemporary urban life to emerge. This reversal is only possible because the films materialize at a singular moment in which the urban environment is in flux. The specific cinematic imagery found in these musicals (photography of inner city decay and its accompanying urban youth, the emergent practice of graffiti art, etc.) and the new generic iconography it introduced (the diffusion of violence into dance, the creation of multiracial dance and artistic spaces, and the absence of a traditional nuclear family) symbolized a national economic crisis that was rapidly changing the contours of American urban centers as inner city problems grew in tandem with suburban sprawl.

Topographies of Urban Ruin

When the hip hop musical emerged during the early 1980s, the inner city ghetto in general, and the South Bronx in particular, were emblems of domestic ruin and dysfunctional urban governance.[26] Haunting images of the region's perishing housing stock were revealed to the nation on the front page of the *New York Times*, following President Carter's initial visit to the South Bronx in 1977.[27] As the president surveyed the wasted urban vista of Charlotte Street—one of the most dilapidated segments of the borough—he grimly stated to the secretary of the federal Department of Housing and Urban Development, "See which areas can still be salvaged."[28] The great towers of rubble and debris rising up from the street in both *Wild Style* and *Beat Street* several years later reminded spectators that poverty, a preponderance of damaged housing, and myriad social problems threatening the stability of the family structure were still affecting South Bronx residents and diverse urban ghettos to a far greater degree than other types of communities.

President Carter's highly publicized visit to Charlotte Street was undoubtedly an attempt to assuage the government's perceived neglect of African American communities and social problems. Less than two months before Carter's visit, Vernon E. Jordan, Jr., a reporter for the *Washington Post*, had called on the president to visit black New York neighborhoods as a sign of commitment to African American urban citizens.²⁹ In a lengthy criticism of the Carter administration's first six months in the White House, Jordan writes,

> It is not enough simply to pursue aggregate policies that increase the number of jobs or homes, for example, without targeting those policies to ensure that Blacks and other disadvantaged minorities get their fair share of those jobs and homes. Alongside such basic policy steps, the President and his administration could make those symbolic gestures that are vital ingredients of national leadership. In his actions and rhetoric, the President can demonstrate his concern for America's poor and her minorities. The symbolic acts of his first days in office signaled to the nation the new administration's openness and its more populist style. So, too, can the President send signals to the urban poor. One such signal, costing no more than the fuel for Air Force One, would be to visit deprived urban neighborhoods. A President who went to Clinton, Mass., and Yazoo City, Miss., should also walk the mean streets of the South Bronx or Brooklyn's Bushwick section to assure people of his concern and of his determination to help them change their lives.³⁰

The South Bronx's legacy as a symbol of national bureaucratic neglect and insensitivity to urban communities of color continued for the next two decades. Indeed, presidential hopeful Ronald Reagan also visited Charlotte Street in 1980 in an attempt to show that Carter did not fulfill his initial promise of salvaging and restructuring the area.³¹ Jesse Jackson, too, visited the area in 1984 during his bid for Democratic presidential nominee to again stress the continued governmental neglect of the region.³²

Visualizing these particular urban spaces within the hip hop musical could have been construed as a risky undertaking by the film's financial backers. The mainstream news media routinely and excessively showcased the black and Latino spaces of the South Bronx and Pittsburgh's Hill District as nothing but violent crime and drug-riddled neighborhoods worthy of demolition rather than rehabilitation. For instance, an article from the *Washington Post* declared of the South Bronx in 1979 that

> if you add up that area's problems—the many blocks of vacant lots and vandalized buildings; the high percentages of people on welfare and out of work; the drugs, the crime, the flight of jobs and hope—it's hard to see how

any project that can be paid for can make much of a dent. To put it another way, the urban strategy that is currently popular, shoring up existing neighborhoods, won't work where there is no real neighborhood left to save.[33]

Lee Lescaze, writing for the *Washington Post* in the same year, refers to the South Bronx as "a moonscape of block after block leveled by arson and virtually uncontrolled crime."[34] The wrath of rampant arson and subsequent depopulation in the South Bronx prompted Ronald Reagan to famously compare the neighborhood in 1980 to the devastation caused by the Blitz during World War II.[35]

Interestingly, the most prominent national symbol of urban squalor and despair in the 1980's had previously signified prosperity and hope for white immigrant New Yorkers in the early twentieth century. The South Bronx had been a destination for aspiring Jewish New Yorkers looking to escape the slum tenement neighborhoods of Manhattan during the 1920s and '30s.[36] Yet, even while ethnic whites were moving into the Bronx in search of a better life, plans were already afoot for the area's degeneration. Plans to construct a roadway system that would connect Manhattan to the outer boroughs were initiated by the New York Regional Plan Association in 1929.[37] The fruition of these efforts, resulting in the construction of modern highways such as the Cross-Bronx Expressway designed by Robert Moses, would eventually cut through the heart of neighborhoods like the South Bronx, leaving a wake of rubble, displaced tenants, and destroyed communities.[38] Marshall Berman's poetic description of this massive project, recounted from the very center of the construction belt, emphasizes the birth of a newly formed landscape rising up out of the ground with a terrifying grandeur:

> For ten years, through the late 1950s and early 1960s, the center of the Bronx was pounded and blasted and smashed. My friends and I would stand on the parapet of the Grand Concourse, where 174th Street had been, and survey the work's progress—the immense steam shovels and bulldozers and timber and steel beams, the hundreds of workers in their variously colored hard hats, the giant cranes reaching far above the Bronx's tallest roofs, the dynamite blasts and tremors, the wild, jagged crags of rock newly torn, the vistas of devastation stretching for miles to the east and west as far as the eye could see—and marvel to see our ordinary nice neighborhood transformed into sublime, spectacular ruins.[39]

White residents fled the South Bronx in tandem with the erection of the Expressway at mid-century, and as their numbers significantly dwindled over the years, black and Latino families began to move into the area.[40] These new residents inherited a mutilated urban landscape left in the wake of the highway's construction.

As the images of *Wild Style* and *Beat Street* reveal, by the early 1980s a great deal of New York City's low income housing structures were dilapidated, abandoned, or simply no longer appropriate spaces for domestic dwellings. This problem had in fact surfaced in the late 1960s and the city responded by concluding that rent control laws were to blame since they prevented landlords from raising rents sufficiently to continue adequate maintenance regimens.[41] Following from this, the municipal government amended rent control laws and in 1970 initiated the Maximum Base Rent system, which guaranteed mandatory yearly increases.[42] As a result of these drastic changes to New York municipal law, a large-scale grassroots tenant movement gained momentum throughout the city. The movement was somewhat fractured and ad-hoc, incorporating groups from different income levels and ethnic affiliations, including black and Latino neighborhoods. Over the years, participants and community activists rehabilitated abandoned structures, initiated rent strikes, and fought rent decontrol.[43]

When Jimmy Carter visited the Bronx in 1977, he was exposed to the shocking images of inner city decay but he also witnessed the results of a Sweat Equity rehabilitation project.[44] This type of urban program allowed tenants to perform the physical labor of regenerating a building in exchange for a unit within the apartment complex. The visibility of ruined residential streets following the *New York Times'* coverage of Carter's visit sparked a renewal in funding to different neighborhood organizations working to combat urban decay.[45] The city invested large amounts of capital in neighborhood regeneration projects such as the DAMP (Division of Alternative Management Program) initiative within the municipal housing agency, and overall made a concerted effort to help tenants organize cooperative housing ownership systems.[46]

Unfortunately, the flourishing urban renewal efforts of the late '70s lost most of their funding in the early '80s when the Reagan administration redirected the capital reserved for these projects.[47] As a result, the New York City Sweat Equity program ended in 1980, and there was a severe reduction in the availability of monetary aid for neighborhood regeneration projects throughout the city. When government sponsored rehabilitation programs were reduced or terminated, tenants were forced to either return to grassroots avenues of activism that circumvented state and city channels or compete with each other for shrinking funding opportunities offered by municipal agencies.

The hip hop musical emphasizes the public spaces of communal exchange and civic activism within the South Bronx and other historically black neighborhoods, including the front stoop and the residential street. This practice draws upon a long tradition of African American literature and film that uses the city as "a metaphor for African American experience."[48] Paula Massood, among others, remarks that "the hood" has represented both a dystopic and utopic trope in African American film and literary production, functioning as a signifier that allows hitherto invisible spaces of urban life to reveal themselves.[49] The city, with its racially demarcated boundaries, is evoked in the work of early black twentieth century novelists through the careful delineation of specific sites of play, work and torment, identified by street names, popular dance hall addresses, restaurants, and industrial spaces. For instance, the second chapter of Claude McKay's *Home to Harlem*, an important work of the Harlem Renaissance, opens with:

> Jake was paid off. He changed a pound note he had brought with him. He had fifty-nine dollars. From South Ferry he took an express subway train for Harlem. Jake drank three Martini cocktails with cherries in them. The price, he noticed, had gone up from ten to twenty-five cents. He went to Bank's and had a Maryland fried-chicken feed—a big one with candied sweet potatoes. He left his suitcase behind the counter of a saloon on Lennox Avenue. He went for a promenade on Seventh Avenue between One Hundred and Thirty-fifth and One Hundred and Fortieth Streets. He thrilled to Harlem. His blood was hot. His eyes were alert as he sniffed the street like a hound. Seventh Avenue was nice, a little too nice that night. Jake turned off on Lennox Avenue.[50]

McKay makes use of very specific urban markers throughout the novel. In this work, the reader is literally able to follow "step-by-step" the character's journey through the streets of New York City.

A number of scholars have remarked upon the ways in which the hip hop cinema of the late '80s and early '90s, variously termed "New Black Realism," "New Jack Cinema," or "rapsploitation" film, carries out the same tradition through the evocation of particular urban locales.[51] What has not been addressed is the way in which *Wild Style* and a host of other hip hop-oriented musicals appearing before the rise of ghetto-centric "New Black Realism" underscore the urgency of representing the actual contemporary topography of urban communities of color. The entertainment editor for the *Afro-American*, Ida Peters, made much of the fact that *Beat Street* was filmed entirely on location in New York City, and featured places that would have been notable and meaningful for contemporary communities of color "including an actual abandoned tenement building in the South Bronx, the Harlem campus of C.C.N.Y, and several subway stations."[52] She goes on to remark that "the popular Roxy dance club, which was the first Manhattan *discotheque* to spotlight hip hop music and break dancing, is the site of a climactic breaker battle."[53]

Wild Style also attests to the importance of specific urban locations by employing lengthy panning shots to emphasize the vastness of urban ruin in the South Bronx, and it utilized recognizable and meaningful inner city locations such as the Dixie Club, a famous party spot in the 1970s often presided over by "the godfather of hip hop," Grandmaster Flash, a local grocery store named Connie's Superette, and the immense expanse of the New York City subway system. Ahearn also made use of locations that had a particularly poignant meaning for specific individuals from the hip hop community. He notes that a pivotal scene in the film, the "Basketball Throwdown," was shot in a local Bronx park at Valentine and 183rd Street, the spot where Grandmaster Caz, who performs on the title track of the film "had played ball . . . as a kid, and had rocked that spot as one half of the DJ crew Casanova Fly and Disco Wiz the night the lights went out for the big blackout of 1977."[54] *Krush Groove* also made use of Upper Manhattan and South Bronx locations such as the Marble Hill Projects and Sal Abbatiello's legendary hip hop club Disco Fever.

Remarkably, *Beat Street* even gestures towards the innovative strategies of New York City's Sweat Equity movement. The film not only documented the devastation of the South Bronx and its deteriorating infrastructure, it also explored the effects of homelessness, poverty, and inadequate housing when Ramon the graffiti artist, his girlfriend, and their young baby are forced to take up residence in an abandoned housing unit. This space is initially unfit for habitation but Ramon's friends use their skills to obtain heat and light, and transform the ruined interior into a cozy domestic dwelling.

Like *Beat Street*, *Rappin'*, a musical that tackles gentrification and dereliction in Pittsburgh's communities of color, also makes housing problems and urban blight a principal strand of its narrative trajectory. Pittsburgh's Hill District never became a national spectacle and symbol of urban poverty on the same level as the South Bronx, yet it too was an impoverished black neighborhood that experienced a simultaneous decline in housing stock. While Ahearn was filming *Wild Style* amid the devastated urban ruins of the South Bronx, the Hill District was experiencing a similar crisis. William Robbins, a reporter for the *New York Times* writes of Pittsburgh:

> It is a city of neighborhoods and most, like its blue-collar South Side community and the Italian neighborhood around Larimer Avenue, are stable. But the city is losing more housing than it gains . . . Arthur Edmunds, executive director of the Urban League here, noted that it was the Hill District, a black inner city ghetto, that had suffered most from deterioration and that doubling up of families in black homes was increasing.[55]

Despite the appearance of dilapidated buildings and poverty plaguing the neighborhood in the 1980s, a middle class of vendors and professionals living in high quality dwellings characterized the Hill District community in the mid-nineteenth century.[56] Successive waves of immigration brought new ethnic and racial groups to the area, changing the character of the district as an influx of working-class Jewish, Irish, and black Americans brought their traditions and values to the community. According to the *WPA History of the Negro in Pittsburgh*, the area transitioned from predominantly white middle-class respectability (evidenced as late as 1887) to working-class poverty and immorality in the twentieth century. This document was part of the New Deal-era Federal Writers Project, and was the product of different authors throughout the 1930s. They write the following (and one can only assume that these observations are based on evidence gathered some time in the 1930s):

> On the Hill, 25,000 or almost half of the Negro people of Pittsburgh now try to live, fighting poverty, squalor, disease, crime, vice—every human handicap. Here thrive saloons and speakeasies, gambling houses and pawn shops, pool rooms, dope dens, houses of prostitution and assignation. The Hill is the symbol of the worst that a fiercely industrial city like Pittsburgh can do to human beings.[57]

At this time, it was recognized that black citizens in this area were threatened by inadequate housing, and the authors go on to describe the actual physical spaces of the neighborhood, remarking that "its dominant note is squalor."[58] They observe that

> narrow streets are lined with tawdry houses, dingy red, their scarred doorways and tottering porches often reached by crumbling wooden steps. Roofs sag. Walls lean. Window frames are rotted and patched.... No street on the Hill runs level for more than a quarter of a mile. Dozens of them, many of which are dirt and ash, gullied by open sewers, climb almost perpendicular.... Along the Hill streetcars side-swipe parked automobiles and trucks, and wait for the driver to push or pry loose his vehicle. Curbs are broken, cobbles dislodged.... Doorways and curbs are littered with paper; discarded boxes and crates inconvenience the pedestrian. A dead cat may be crushed against a curb. A man may lie bleeding in the angle of a house wall.[59]

Clearly, city space itself—the ramshackle structures and broken roads—are articulated as a threat to the bodily well-being of neighborhood residents. The Hill resident is endangered not only by the "moral ills" of working-class culture, but also by the physical hazards of poor industrial urban infrastructure. Even the streetcar, a service usually understood as a boon to poorer city residents, is described as a dangerous and potentially harmful menace to the urban pedestrian. The home, too, is ultimately depicted as a place that brings not salvation and comfort but physical harm.

Fifty years later, *Rappin'* showcases the poverty of neighborhood residents and inadequate housing as deleterious aspects of life in the Hill District. Through the conventions of the musical film, the community is able to unite in unique ways in order to overcome the danger inherent in their meager conditions. For instance, when nefarious real estate developers attempt to prevent heat from being delivered to the dilapidated structures, the neighborhood devises a plan to steal oil and heat their homes. Only through cooperative action can the community survive and keep its physical spaces safe for everyone (the neighborhood prostitute lures the gas man into her apartment while his fuel is pilfered by the residents). Rappinhood also performs many of the musical numbers with the neglected buildings and urban wasteland as a backdrop, further underscoring the constant struggle to infuse the impoverished landscape with positive energy.

While the Hill District has been a problematic site of urban development for numerous decades, and a neighborhood with a rich and varied

Fig. 1.2. John Rappinhood (Mario Van Peebles) and his neighborhood entourage rap and dance through the streets of Pittsburgh in *Rappin'* (1985); also pictured: Tasia Valenza. Courtesy of Photofest.

immigrant history, 1985 marked the opening of the first subway system for the city of Pittsburgh, and the years 1977–88 saw the implementation of the Renaissance II redevelopment project. This undertaking was a large-scale, public-private revamping of major urban areas, including several Hill neighborhoods. These major changes created a new set of problems for the residents of one of the historically poorest communities in the city. Even though the initial Renaissance project (1945–69) and its sequel sought to improve public life, urban historians argue that they also "disrupted neighborhoods and uprooted sizable numbers of people."[60] Gentrification, and the encroachment of white corporate interests into a historically black neighborhood—both problems that have plagued the actual Hill District—materialize as important themes in *Rappin'.*

To be sure, the moments in which Mario van Peebles executes his rather inadequate rapping abilities while dancing through devastated Hill District neighborhoods have provoked many groans. Nevertheless, the film makes a very provocative statement regarding the power that the inner-city performer actually wields in relation to urban space. Most importantly, *Rappin'* unequivocally suggests that the voice and body of

Rappinhood as performer acts as a catalyst for community action that portends very real change in the ownership and control of city space. This is most explicitly revealed in the courtroom sequence that occurs near the end of the film. In this scene, *Rappin'* shows us that the neighborhood voice, configured as a communal rap, can overcome not only problems of domestic inadequacy, such as cramped or decrepit housing, but can even challenge the law. Here, in the penultimate musical number of the film, Rappinhood enters a zoning meeting held to decide the fate of his neighborhood. The board rules against the local residents until Rappinhood begins his tale of communal values overcoming corporate greed. This number is a condemnation of Reagan-era capitalist values, and throughout Rappinhood repeatedly points his finger at the black executive Cedric, a lackey of the white-owned developing firm that attempts to destroy the neighborhood. As the courtroom audience (the neighborhood residents whose homes are under threat of demolition) becomes more unruly, they break into song and dance with Rappinhood. In fact, the song is so infectious, even the apparently hidebound board cannot resist the beat, and they join in the number as well.[61] After this exuberant outburst, the details of the zoning issues are magically erased. The film suggests through this series of events that the very act of participation by the board in the musical number seals the deal for the neighborhood residents. Only when the community comes together in performance, and deviates from the traditional channels of legal procedure, can they maneuver successfully in capitalist America.

This event in the film represents an inversion of performance traditions and social hierarchies. Civic officials are initially "performers" in the play of bureaucrat affairs as they orchestrate the course of events at the outset of the meeting. However, the audience gradually takes control of the space, and increasingly dictates the trajectory of the meeting, while the bureaucrats are eventually transformed into spectators. As this occurs, tenant and prostitute assert authority over city official and civic leader. When audience becomes performer and vice versa, social hierarchy follows suit and this spontaneous outburst reveals the ways in which the communal performance of hip hop just might activate and orchestrate social and political change. It is for this reason that the entire courthouse film sequence is a carnivalesque series of inversions.[62] Hip hop culture encourages and facilitates these reversals because the entire performance strategy is built upon the elevation of the quotidian and the forbidden to the status of artistic performance. Colloquial speech is transformed into rapping, and graffiti art emerges from a practice viewed by mainstream society as vandalism.

Interestingly, in 1985 the sensationalistic *New York Post* published an odious counterpart to this cinematic account of hip hop performance within the legal system. The title of the article, "Jailhouse Rock for Break Dance Muggers," suggests that mugging and dancing were related activities. But the text actually reveals that the accused teens were purportedly breakdancing in the courthouse during a trial in response to the alleged mugging of a 55-year-old man: "A group of laughing young punks callously break-danced in a Queens court corridor while a jury deliberated mugging charges against them."[63] The article goes on to note that "several relatives of the defendants who were sitting in the state Supreme Court in Jamaica also became disruptive and one of them, a woman, had to be subdued."[64] Here, breakdancing within the space of the judicial system is deemed callous—a display of the alleged criminals' insensitivity and lack of respect for authority—while the "disruptive" actions of relatives in the courthouse audience are disorderly and inappropriate. Most egregiously, the title attempts to link breaking in the street with criminal activity. The panacea of performance so enthusiastically rendered in *Rappin'* becomes a negative and inflammatory aspect of the *Post* article, even overshadowing the details of the initial crime. This news story reveals how conservative media sources attempted to demonize hip hop and expressions of youth culture in the 1980s. It also reads as an attempt to pathologize racially "Other" emotive gestures; in particular, the article sought to revive the trope of the unruly black audience—represented by the accused teen's relatives—in need of subdual.

Numerous examples from the history of the New York City tenant movement attest to the difficulty of waging successful neighborhood lobbying efforts in the service of staving off abandonment and tenant displacement.[65] Typically, the official channels of political discourse were closed off to fragmented tenant organizations. However, when these groups organized unconventional means of attack such as rent strikes, Sweat Equity programs, and the squatter movement, they were often very effective. Further, when they consolidated their efforts across city blocks and municipal regions to form large cohesive political entities such as the New York State Tenants Legislative Coalition, they were able to challenge rent decontrol and redefine lease contracts in Albany. *Rappin'* engages with the ethos of communal cohesion and unconventional activism that has characterized the largest and most visible American tenant activism in recent memory, and it moves musical performance and youth culture to the forefront of these transformative processes.

The Disappearing City

If *Wild Style* and *Beat Street* document the burnt-out tenements and razed city blocks of the South Bronx, and *Rappin'* emphasizes the inadequate housing conditions of Pittsburgh's communities of color, *Breakin'* and *Breakin' 2* make only vague references to actual urban spaces, and the city literally disappears from view in the first of the two Cannon films. Most of the breakdancing scenes occur on the Venice Beach boardwalk, and when jazz dancer Kelly supposedly ventures into the "hood" to visit Turbo and Ozone, her breakdancing mentors, very little of the surrounding neighborhood is actually shown. The camera sticks to tight shots of the breakers' home as it shows us a garage front converted into a bachelor pad for the two young dancers. Occasionally, a few children are glimpsed on a porch across the street, and a short sequence features Turbo teaching kids to dance in front of his home. Aside from this, however, there are no further attempts to link the performers to their neighborhhood. Thus, even when the breakers do dance in the street in *Breakin'*, it is not connected to any empowering social forces. The film clearly does not uphold the communal values of the folk musical. Even though it features breakdance and shares many features with several true hip hop musicals, the presence of a larger community is only very lightly sketched.

When the familiar iconography of inner-city neighborhoods—chain-link fences, abandoned cars, brick walls—finally does emerge in the film, it is in the form of the commodity, a final stage show with high production values and professional dancers. This final number is introduced with a shot of a looming marquee that boasts the "street names" of the film's three lead dancers, Turbo, Ozone, and Special K (Kelly). As we transition to the stage number entitled "Street People," performers leap out of battered garbage cans and dance on prop cars. The street dancers have clearly "made it" within the world of professional dance as their urban monikers preside over the exterior spaces of the theater. This incorporation into mainstream culture, however, is only predicated upon a complete theatrical simulation of the city that cleaves it from any tangible contemporary urban problems and returns it to the commodity form of the classical show musical.

The entire plot of *Breakin' 2* is concerned, unlike its predecessor *Breakin'*, with the relation between dance, neighborhood solidarity, and collective action. There is far more imagery of city streets and community members in *Breakin' 2* than in the original, and the narrative is directly connected to community empowerment through dance and performance. Even though the characters in the film never refer to hip hop culture by name, and displays of electric boogie and breakdancing are all simply described as street dance, the film does attempt to politicize the act of dance and performance as it relates to the fight for urban spaces.

The finale of *Breakin' 2*, however, comes together in a contradictory way that undoes some of the radical potential to be found earlier in the narrative. In this concluding neighborhood concert, the entire community unites for a performance, a charity show that is intended to save an important local resource, the Miracles dance center. Ozone dances atop the building under a sign that reads "Save Our Streets." The meaning of this phrase is somewhat ambiguous; it could be read as an appeal to improve the overall environment of the community, but it might also be understood as a plea to "save the streets" from idle youth as busy dancing young men might be less likely to commit crimes. Ozone then leads the community to a city zoning meeting (in a very similar manner to the scene described in *Rappin'*), yet their performance fails to convince the powers that be to save the neighborhood center from obliteration. Ozone and the rest of the group stage the show anyway to try to raise the money needed to repair the center and rescue the building from the hands of the developers. The film retains the familiar "let's put on a show" feature of the backstage musical, but the final extravaganza also allows for a somewhat ambivalent statement regarding communal empowerment through performance. Whereas the power of performance is all that is needed to save the community in *Rappin'*, the "kids" in *Breakin' 2* fall short of collecting the finances needed to save their beloved Miracles. However, in the final moments of the film, help arrives in the form of white wealthy conservative patrons, Kelly's parents, who have had their hearts softened by the sheer will and determination exhibited by the neighborhood kids to hang onto their community center. The parents are coded earlier in the film as very conservative Republicans who disapprove of Kelly's friends from "the street," yet in the end the father is convinced to pull out his checkbook and provide the missing funds to retain the neighborhood building.

This sudden act of generosity could be read as an attempt to show that poor communities must still rely on wealthy donors making charitable

Fig. 1.3. Ozone (Adolfo "Shabba Doo" Quinones) atop the Miracles Dance Center in *Breakin' 2* (1984). Courtesy of Photofest.

donations out of a sense of moral duty. The conclusion of *Breakin' 2* rings uncomfortably close to a demonstration of what is popularly known as the "trickle down" theory—Reagan-era economic policies that supported large tax breaks for the wealthy in the specious hopes of encouraging philanthropic endeavors, and further stimulating economic growth for the middle and lower classes.[66] As we know, this did not occur, and most of Reagan's economic platform worked towards absolving the government of responsibility for supporting its poorer citizens, arguing that capitalism was inherently self-regulating in terms of ensuring a redistribution of goods from rich to poor.[67] If this film is somewhat more progressive than the first *Breakin'* because it shows music and dance performance as a politicized communal activity that threatens the normative power structures of capitalist gentrification, the finale seriously undercuts the film's initial articulation of these activities as a real challenge to mainstream culture and the interests of corporate capitalism.

In a parallel strategy to *Breakin'*, the specificity of actual urban locations is almost completely obscured in *Body Rock*. This film made no attempt to accurately portray hip hop culture, nor did it reveal hip hop as a communal form of bonding. It also attached no significance to the actual spaces of New York City, and cinematic references to specific geographical urban locations are vague. *Body Rock*, however, does stress the poverty and dire social conditions of the main character, Chilly D. It emphasizes the extremely poor state of his home, and the only member of Chilly D's family to appear in the film is an uncaring bedridden mother. Even though images of interior domestic squalor appear in *Body Rock*, poverty is articulated as a personal obstacle to overcome and does not emerge as a systemic problem attached to other urban conditions. In comparison to other hip hop-oriented musicals, this film clearly shows little interest in addressing the issues and social problems that were affecting the communities of color who actually produced the images and sounds of hip hop culture.

Fast Forward, as noted in the previous chapter, is not technically a hip hop musical since none of the main dancers are hip hop practitioners but its appropriation of hip hop culture as a tool to revitalize more traditional forms of dance is worth noting. The energy of inner-city neighborhoods and street culture are not contrasted to the lure of fame, money, and conventional avenues of artistic success, the usual formula for the hip hop musical. Instead, this film features a group of racially mixed teenagers from Sandusky, Ohio, who venture to New York for a commercially sponsored national dance contest. When the teens arrive in the big city they are stunned by images of street breakdancers strutting their stuff in Columbus Circle. Eventually the group realizes that they need a new direction to infuse their dance routines and win the contest, and their style is reinvigorated through the adoption of breakdance moves observed in the street and in a number of club sequences.

As with the *Breakin'* series, the terms "breakdancing" and "hip hop" are completely avoided. All forms of hip hop culture are left off screen in *Fast Forward*, with the exception of one rival breakdance crew that serves as both nemesis and inspiration to the small-town kids. The terms of opposition that must be resolved in this film no longer emerge from the contemporary problems of urban life and impoverished inner city communities. Instead, *Fast Forward* is built around the contrast between small-town values and an urban environment that is characterized as both full of opportunities and riven with dangerous elements.

Any connection between racial identity, artistic production, and communal empowerment is lacking in this film, largely because New York City is reduced to the spatial parameters of Manhattan, with a brief sojourn into the upper-class milieu of Long Island garden parties. The two boroughs of New York City where hip hop culture actually emerged—Queens and the Bronx—do not materialize in *Fast Forward*. Thus, the appearance of a breakdancing crew performing for an uptown crowd in the middle of Manhattan does not reference the transformation of hip hop culture as it straddled geographical boundaries between communities of color in the outer boroughs and the mainstream cultural institutions, corporate events, and largely white crowds of tourists that Manhattan had to offer.

Fast Forward further erodes the progressive political and social aspects characteristic of the true hip hop musical because the film's main characters leave their community behind, severing the link between collective performance and communal empowerment so pervasive in most hip hop musicals. Moreover, the film privileges individual success over the concerns of the community, and reduces breakdancing to a set of skills adopted solely for the purpose of getting ahead in the world of showbiz, or utilized by a dance crew to make money in uptown Manhattan. The New York breakdance crew featured in *Fast Forward* is also not attached to any particular community, and none of the characters are even given names. Their only function in the film is to demonstrate to the group of determined small-town kids that they are out of touch with current dance fashion as they challenge them to a competition at the Zoo nightclub. The dancers from Ohio simply adopt some of the style of this crew, and use it to win an industry sponsored talent show, the Annual Shoot Out Contest. With the help of "real" urban street dance, small-town values and raw talent are able to triumph in the big city. The kids also get a helping hand from a wealthy white upper-class socialite who provides the final thrust of determination to send the Ohio teens on to victory.

It is not surprising, perhaps, that the three least "authentic" depictions of hip hop culture in the hip hop musical, *Breakin' Through*, *Body Rock*, and *Delivery Boys*, also greatly reduced the presence of black and Latino characters in their narratives.[68] Even though *Body Rock* featured Latino actor Lorenzo Lamas, the rest of his crew and legion of fans supposedly interested in hip hop culture are predominantly white. As the hip hop musical loses its racial and ethnic specificity, and attempts to draw a decidedly paler audience, the depiction of particular urban spaces and the connective understanding between those geographical regions and contemporary social problems is completely lost.

As a point of comparison, it is redolent that when the hip hop musical was resurrected in the early 1990s as a vehicle for Vanilla Ice (Robert Matthew Van Winckle)—the whitest rapper in history—mainstream cinema again failed to depict the actual geographic spaces of the city or have people of color at the center of the narrative. *Cool as Ice* (1991) stars Vanilla Ice as Johnny, the leader of an otherwise all-black motorcycle hip hop gang. While out cruising the highway, the gang is forced to stop in a small California town in order to fix mechanical problems with one of their motorcycles. This event sets in motion a predictable narrative trajectory in which the outlandishly dressed, free-roaming, but essentially "good" Johnny tries to win the affections of studious and conservative would-be college student Kathy, all the while fighting the conformist forces of the town, including dimwitted parents and Kathy's domineering boyfriend. The city from which the gang originates is never visualized in the film and is instead signified by an urban nightclub where Vanilla Ice performs. In the club numbers which bookend *Cool as Ice*, the city is completely elided and in its place we are shown a highly stylized dance performance in which a white rapper assumes both the role of star performer, and later on, the narrative center of action. Not only is Johnny the star of the nightclub, the romantic lead, and the head of the motorcycle gang, but members of the posse who obviously do come from urban communities of color are all but forgotten once the gang is forced to take up residence in the suburban periphery. City space in this later film is transformed into, and signified by, the performance of the white star and his ability to win over the residents of a small town—Johnny *is* the city.[69]

Furthermore, when Johnny attempts to woo his girl in a rather awkward romantic musical number, this is set against a backdrop of empty lots and homes under construction. If mainstream Hollywood attempted to avoid altogether illustrating the urban space of hip hop culture in this film, then it could find no suitable substantive site to fill this void. White suburbia might be a series of empty lots, but it is a space of construction, not destruction and neglect. The complete elision of African American city spaces in *Cool As Ice* is all the more striking given that this film emerges in the very midst of New Black Realism's insistence upon the visibility of urban communities of color. Released just a few months after John Singleton's visually explosive *Boyz in the Hood*—a gritty and remarkable depiction of the black community in South Central Los Angeles—*Cool As Ice* absurdly forces a white mainstream blonde, baby-faced entertainer to bear the burden of representing the ghetto-centric spaces that structured the narrative movement of contemporary hip hop cinema.

Even though I have primarily been concerned with the visualization of inner city neighborhoods in the hip hop musical, it is worth mentioning that the image of the urban skyline plays an important role in this cinema as well. To draw on examples from films previously discussed in this section, *Wild Style*, *Rappin'*, and *Beat Street* all incorporate an image of the city skyline to symbolically denote the "world out there" and the dream of literally making it out of the ghetto. In *Wild Style*, Raymond stares out of the window of an apartment belonging to a wealthy art dealer at a view of the Manhattan skyline at night. The city lights inspire him to paint an image on canvas, the initial step towards both the commodification of his work and potential flight from the South Bronx. Towards the end of *Rappin'*, John Rappinhood and his love interest, Dixie, stand on an elevated platform while the skyline of Pittsburgh appears as muted blues and grays in the distance. She attempts to convince him to rap professionally, a move which surely entails leaving his Hill District neighborhood behind. And in *Beat Street*, the city plays a spectacular role in the stage set of the final rap wake for graffiti artist Ramon. Set between two walls onto which images of the inner city and Ramon's graffiti are projected, a glittering Manhattan vista is the central backdrop of Kenny's hip hop show, his final performance extravaganza in which community and commercial success are both referenced. The heroes of the true hip hop musical are always firmly rooted in the spaces of their neighborhoods—breaking and rapping in its streets, and painting on its walls. When they travel to urban commercial centers, however, or when the narrative suggests a movement towards commercial success, the city appears literally as a picture to behold, a looming outline of buildings and car parks. This abstract image of the city floats in an unreal space, but it is a representation which suggests the possibility of an entirely other existence for our hip hop heroes, the promise of transcending community boundaries through artistic success.

The New "Music Man"

Several historians have attempted to understand the unique character of musicals made subsequent to the breakdown of the classical Hollywood system. This research, from a diverse range of scholars, including Jane Feuer, J. P. Telotte, James Hay, and Dave Kehr, has all but excluded hip hop musicals from the history of the postclassical era.[70] These scholars largely refuse to acknowledge the restructuring of racialized urban spaces inaugurated by the plethora of hip hop musicals in the first part of this decade, and they also overlook the racial dimensions of other postclassical musicals such as *Flashdance* and *Dirty Dancing*. Telotte curiously includes the

Prince vehicle *Purple Rain* (1984) and *The Wiz* (1978), a black-cast adaptation of *The Wizard of Oz*, in his discussion, without linking them to the history of black-cast musical film and the position of black performers in the Hollywood machine. He also mentions the way in which *The Buddy Holly Story* (1978) restages Holly's first gig at the Apollo as a harmonious meeting between blacks and whites. Feuer, for her part, discusses Spike Lee's *School Daze* (1988) and the racial issues present in John Waters's *Hairspray* (1988). She has also commented on the difficulty of applying certain aspects of genre theory to American post-1960s musical films.[71] For example, musicals made in the 1970s and '80s such as *Nashville* (1975) and *All that Jazz*—produced following the breakup of the studio system and the genre's golden age—critically appropriated studio-era themes, songs, and characters in order to deconstruct the mythmaking machine of the American musical. James Hay also argues that the "postmodern music men" of the "deconstructionist" postclassical musical

> are unable to orchestrate narrative resolution in their films because they are hopelessly driven by libidinal impulses.... They do not perform full, rounded roles as did their precursors, but rather complex characters whose darker natures are foregrounded and discourage intense audience identification or admiration.[72]

Indeed, the 1980s began with one of the fullest expressions of this intense critical treatment of the musical genre in *Pennies From Heaven*, a relentlessly dark film starring Steve Martin as an unsuccessful sheet music salesman who cannot achieve an ideal romantic relationship or a triumphant career related to performance, much less bring the two together.

In contrast, the subsequent wave of successful teen-oriented musical films from this decade promoted a distinctly different version of the genre. Feuer argues that many post-studio-era teen musicals of this period also conserved very traditional aspects of the genre and used historical quotation and conventional musical structures in order to reconstruct rather than deconstruct the genre.[73] The primary thrust of the teen "reconstructionist musical," as described by Feuer, is the resurrection of features from the classical musical such as narrative resolution, communal integration, and romantic coupling.[74] A film in this group is *Flashdance*, which concerns the romance of a working-class dancer and a wealthy business owner. The issue of class inequity is initially suggested by the disparity of the two leads' financial means, but this is magically erased through their eventual amorous union. Such a plot very closely follows the fairy tale musical pattern of the early classical sound-era as in the films of Maurice Chevalier and Jeanette MacDonald, produced in the 1930s, especially *Love Me Tonight*. As with its earlier prototypes, *Flashdance* divests the theme of class relations of any political content and even reverts to disturbingly regressive notions of class mobility and gender.[75] *Footloose* and *Dirty Dancing* follow the traditional musical structure even more closely by bringing together two ill-suited lovers through the power of music and dance. They both provide a final stage show in which romantic pairing and sexual energy are displayed through dance and musical performance, while also bringing the community together, transcending generational boundaries in the former and class boundaries in the latter.

Critics such as Telotte and Kehr have argued that the postclassical musical undoes one of the most consistent features of the classical musical, the integration between music and dance performance and plot advancement or thematic development within the film's structure.[76] The term "integration," an important part of the critical analysis of Hollywood musicals, suggests that performance numbers are inserted into the cinematic narrative on a relational axis to the plot or theme of the text. John Mueller notes that this can occur in a multitude of ways, from numbers which "contribute to the spirit or theme" of the film to those that directly "advance the plot by their content."[77] Of course, a musical performance may do both, and conversely it may also be completely irrelevant to the overall narrative development of the film. Classical-era musical film articulated the transcendent powers of music and dance as a realm of escape from the tedium of everyday life. Richard Dyer has described this thematic impulse of the classical Hollywood musical as a utopian configuration that is directed toward our desire for entertainment as an alternative and even superior reality to the one our contemporary quotidian interactions and social organization can facilitate.[78]

Telotte suggests that the postclassical musical emphatically inscribes limitations around the expressive power of performance by keeping the transcendent aspects of music and dance within the boundaries of conventional performance spaces.[79] Like the earliest show musicals, the postclassical musical film utilizes realistic spaces of entertainment—such as theaters, strip clubs, discos, and organized dances—to provide the narrative justification for the inclusion of music and dance numbers.[80] The hip hop musical film does follow this pattern and we witness breakdancers, DJs, and rappers performing at nightclubs, parties, and other theatrical venues.

74 The Case for the Hip Hop Musical

Fig. 1.4. Run-D.M.C. onstage in *Krush Groove* (1985). Courtesy of Photofest.

Fig. 1.5. The Fat Boys take to the stage in *Krush Groove* (1985): Mark "Prince Markie Dee" Morales, Darren "The Human Beat Box" Robinson, Damon "Kool Rock-ski" Wimbley. Courtesy of Photofest.

The Case for the Hip Hop Musical 75

Fig. 1.6. Busy Bee performs at the East River Park Amphitheater in *Wild Style* (1983). Courtesy of Charlie Ahearn.

Parallel to the movement of hip hop culture into "proscenium-oriented" spaces, however, spontaneous breakdancing and rapping numbers consistently occur on the street and emerge from everyday encounters, too. Both types of musical performances generally reinforce a broad thematic concern of the narrative, but it is the latter that have more potential to reference communal cohesion and activism. As the utopian thrust of the musical genre navigates the spaces of performance culture in the true hip hop musical and some surface hip hop musicals, it offers an alternate and progressive vision of political change and communal relations. Although films such as *Wild Style*, *Beat Street*, *Krush Groove*, *Breakin' 2*, and *Rappin'* might be said to use the "reconstructionist" framework of the musical, I argue that they turned the genre's hitherto conservative narrative structures towards a uniquely political, and in some cases, subversive form of cinema.

Hip hop musical cinema challenges Telotte's assumption that musical films from this era are "intent on reminding us that distinct boundaries separate musical activity from the 'real' world."[81] In fact, hip hop musicals radically counter his claim because they are structured around the impossible separation between music, dance, and the "real" world. These films *insist* that collective music and dance performance is an integral feature of quotidian life in the inner city neighborhood. For example, as I discuss more fully in Chapter 2, integrated musical numbers from *Wild Style*, the "Stoop Rap," and the "Basketball Throwdown" derive from everyday encounters in public spaces. *Krush Groove* also primarily uses actual concert spaces and recording studios to stage its numbers, but even this film features an integrated number in which teen rappers, the Fat Boys, take over their high school through the sheer power of musical energy. Musical and dance expression completely transcend the proscenium in these films *because* hip hop is explicitly about the interrelation between the everyday and collective public performance. These types of experiences permit the immediate pleasures of cooperative interaction between different groups of people and the potential attainment of future stardom outside of the community for hip hop artists.

Such encounters, which facilitate a pleasurable transcendence of barriers marked by race, class, and geography through performance, indicate a return to the utopian promise of the classical musical film in which the boundaries between musical expression and the everyday are indistinguishable. As if speaking directly to *Wild Style*'s unique reworking of this utopian premise of the musical film, Ahearn has referred to his hip hop opus as "a projection of our dreams."[82] He notes that

> there was nothing out there that showed all these artists together in one scene. It was only later that people began to look at it as some sort of documentary. But at first we were just projecting what we wanted it to be. It was our wildest dream of what could happen.[83]

Ahearn is speaking here specifically about *Wild Style*'s final concert scene. Even when the stage returns to provide a "realistic" space for musical performance, this venue still ties such expression to utopian desires. And, as noted earlier, the disused Lower East Side amphitheater symbolized the promise of newly organized city spaces that would permit more fluid interactions between different communities, an opportunity rife with the possibility of attaining "stardom" and a life outside of inner-city neighborhoods.

Kehr, in his 1984 discussion of the "new musical," suggests that the "implied rejection of the spectacle and artifice of the MGM-Broadway tradition" is exemplified in the teen-oriented films *Flashdance* and *Footloose*.[84] His work, unfortunately, does not take into account the range of hip hop musicals flooding the screens at this moment, with the exception of noting the use of breakdance in *Flashdance* and *Beat Street*, but he is acutely aware of the ways in which the postclassical musical, and indeed nearly all musicals, must pander to the tastes of popular music.[85] He also writes perceptively of the ways in which the demands of rock music posed numerous problems for the musical form.[86] Kehr notes that "rock dancing" is "too private, too self-directed" in terms of the demands of the musical genre, and that "its gestural range is too small to make a visual impression."[87] In light of Kehr's intriguing remarks about rock dancing on film in the early 1980s, it is curious that his only reference to the hip hop musical is reduced to a few lines in which he notes that the use of breakdance in *Beat Street* might be welcomed because it "draws on more theatrical traditions."[88] About the editing style in *Flashdance*, he also suggests that "if break dancing hadn't existed, the montage style would have invented it."[89] Kehr intimates that breakdance is important for its formal properties only, and downplays the significance of hip hop as a unique practice based around the expression of a communal identity. His conflation of montage and breakdance is particularly specious because he proposes that breakdance fragments the space of performance through abrupt movements and isolated gestures. I argue the opposite here. Breaking may lend itself towards a formal rupturing and deconstruction of cinematic space but the dance practice works towards achieving unity between all parts of the dancer and between different performers. Furthermore, it is usually a collective activity that encourages the interaction of a large group of people. Its tendency towards jerky, fragmented gestures does not imply a private world of dance whereby the individual is solipsistically absorbed in his or her movements. Since breakdance crews battle with each other, the dancer must have one eye on the competition (and the audience) at all times in case they "sabotage" his or her performance by jumping into the dance circle and mocking or challenging their last move.

These new hip hop–oriented performers of the postclassical era are also significant because they mark a transformation of the musical genre's male lead. Richard Dyer has argued that

> whites in musicals have a rapturous relationship with their environment. This may be confined to the utopian moments of the numbers, but then they are the reason why we go to see musicals. The potentially colonialist nature of this is suggested not only by the way whites stride down streets as if they own them (which in a certain sense they do) and burst all over other locales (which they don't), but also in the way the cultures of the colonized, as perceived by whites, are incorporated into the fabric of the numbers' music and dance.[90]

This apparent domination over the parameters of cinematic space is largely achieved through the classical "music man's" seemingly omnipotent control over the physical world through both song and dance. For example, when Dick Powell sings his affections for Ruby Keeler in *Dames*, his ardently amorous verse triggers the transformation of subway ads into the face of his beloved during the number "I Only Have Eyes For You." In other words, Powell's barely veiled sexual desires, which are expressed through song, are so powerful that they actually appear to alter the physical space that he and his darling occupy. Many of Gene Kelly's and Fred Astaire's dance numbers are also exemplary of this process, including Astaire's "Shoes With Wings On," a special effects extravaganza in which shoes dance on their own from *The Barkleys of Broadway* (1949), and his "ceiling dance" in *Royal Wedding* (1951). In the latter number, Astaire's body is no longer subject to the normative rules of gravity as he dances up the sides of walls and on to the ceiling. Gene Kelly transcends the threshold of realism in *Anchors Aweigh* (1945) when he engages in a dance number with Jerry the mouse, an animated character. In all of these examples, the normative parameters and rules of cinematic space are challenged and significantly altered through the dance performances of male lead characters.

Historically, the transformative potential of song and dance unquestioningly accorded to white actors has habitually been denied to African Americans and other performers of color in Hollywood musicals. As noted in the introduction, these entertainers have consistently been relegated to apolitical timeless rural settings in all-black Hollywood musicals, usually an idealized Southern past where blacks "knew their place," racially speaking, while their expressive power has been restricted to "legitimate" spaces of performance such as dinner clubs and dance halls. Such settings routinely mitigated the possibility of making a claim on space through the act of performance for African American entertainers.[91] In a related theme, James Snead has discussed the infantilization of Bill Robinson in numerous Shirley Temple films. Robinson, an adult black male, is paired with a white child in such films as *The Little Colonel* (1935) and *The Littlest Rebel* (1935), and this completely defuses the sexual energy of couple dances within the musical film, thus providing a non-threatening link between blacks and whites through cinematic performance.[92] If Gene Kelly and other white male stars of musical film transcend the proscenium of the stage and unleash the transformative power of music and dance in all facets of life, black performers in particular have been relegated to depoliticized evocations of rural all-black ghettos, the confines of the theatrical stage, or to the desexualized space of childhood.[93]

The hip hop musical explicitly confronts the historical constraints that have burdened performers of color in Hollywood cinema. In *Breakin'*

2, Turbo appropriates the classical-era "music man's" control of physical space and amorous influence as he moonwalks, spins, pops and locks up the walls and onto the ceiling of his home—a direct tribute to the aforementioned gravity-defying "ceiling dance" number that Astaire made famous more than three decades prior in *Royal Wedding*. A beautiful young girl appears to watch the final moments of Turbo's exhilarating routine and he confidently dances towards her to receive an affectionate embrace, underscoring the relationship between the dancer's ability to manipulate space and romantic success. In the first *Breakin'*, Turbo also references another Fred Astaire number in *Royal Wedding* in which he dances with a coatrack. Instead of a coatrack, Turbo picks up a broom as heads out of his place of employment to sweep the front sidewalk. The camera is tightly focused on his body as he dances and manipulates the broom in a skillful and comical manner while his ghetto blaster provides diegetic beats to keep him moving. His broom stands up on its own and even levitates when Turbo commands it to rise from the ground with some exaggerated hand gestures. This new "music man" combines work with "play," assuming command of his spatial environment. The background of a graffiti-covered wall and a few shots of passing cars in the sequence even remind us of the urban terrain that is otherwise largely absent from *Breakin'*. Turbo is invested with the power of traditional white male stars of the musical film because he asserts ownership over private and public space and seems to have control over objects (namely, his broom). Although Turbo's control over space through dance is never connected to contemporary communal problems or social issues in the first film, it nevertheless significantly reorients the racial dynamics of the Hollywood musical genre and, importantly, it is connected to such issues in the sequel. Some hip hop musicals of the 1980s, particularly *Wild Style* and *Rappin'*, overturn the racial power relations of the Hollywood musical by reinventing the "music man" or "music men" as a group of black and Latino youth who "stride down streets as if they own them." They are set firmly in the present, often in recognizable urban spaces. The new hip hop "music man" transcends a variety of social and physical spaces during his escapades within the city and negotiates these different sites via the performance styles to be drawn from hip hop culture. Through graffiti, rapping, DJing, and breaking, the hip hop "music man" inserts his subjectivity into a number of social and political spaces, which ultimately brings about diverse forms of individual or collective empowerment.

The hip hop "music man" also rejects both types of new "music men" theorized in current histories of the postclassical musical: Arthur Parker,

Steve Martin's ineffectual and miserable sheet music salesman who spectacularly fails to transform the world around him in *Pennies From Heaven*, and *Dirty Dancing*'s magnetic Johnny Castle (Patrick Swayze). As Feuer has noted, *Dirty Dancing* represents a conservative reconstruction of the musical genre, featuring elements of the fairy tale, show, and folk musical—including an alluring "music man" who fulfills a traditional generic role. The film, set in 1963, explores the cross-class relationship (an element of the fairy tale musical) between Johnny, a working-class dance instructor for an upstate New York resort, and Baby Houseman, an idealistic upper-middle-class Jewish girl. *Dirty Dancing* utilizes a folk audience and the appeal of the "amateur" performer, and features a final show number. While Feuer accurately characterizes the blending of subgenres within *Dirty Dancing*, she does not cut to the heart of the matter, so to speak. The narrative is about sexual awakening and desire. Baby, the film's conservative young Jewish "princess," is intrigued by Johnny and his ability to move, dance, and do what he pleases. When Baby first observes the erotic dance rituals of the working-class staff at Kellerman's resort while delivering watermelons to the kitchen, she is transfixed by a mass of bodies moving, gyrating, and "dirty dancing" to the Contours' original Motown hit "Do You Love Me." Not only is the scene of forbidden dance and unfettered sexual expression set to diegetic popular black music but the sequence also prominently features at least one African American couple "dirty dancing" until Johnny boogies through the door and becomes the center of narrative action. Baby takes on the role of spectator during this number as she gazes upon the rhythmic bodies paired with arched backs and glistening skin. In fact, it is clear that her sexual "awakening" commences the moment that she opens the door to this forbidden party. As she looks on with a transfixed gaze (a watermelon still clutched in her arms) at the raucous scene before her, she asks a resort employee, "Where'd they learn to do this?" He quickly answers, "I don't know. Kids are doing it in the basement back home." This offhand statement regarding the link between sexuality and dance squarely locates its origins with teenagers, popular music, and spaces of leisure outside the purview of regulated social encounters and parental surveillance. One suspects that such a relationship is also directly linked to the racial permeability of working-class social spaces since we are introduced here to black dancers in this otherwise nearly all-white resort, and the scene is set to a Motown beat. After her initial encounter with the erotic possibilities offered by "dirty dancing," Baby learns to dance and consummates her affair with Johnny.

Dirty Dancing's final stage number features a partner routine that expresses the fairy tale musical's cross-class desire between Johnny and his lover Baby. This performance, though, transcends the confines of the proscenium as Johnny leaps from the stage and beckons a willing audience—including upper-middle-class resort guests and working-class employees—to participate in the show. The peripheral black dancers return once again in the final show as the audience of white middle-class patrons begins to dance with each other and eventually the resort staff. Johnny's erotic appeal is undoubtedly linked to African American sexuality and music, however repressed within the film's narrative. Although *Dirty Dancing*'s finale gestures towards the powerful political dimensions of dance, and works to destabilize the boundary between performer and spectator, it is nonetheless contained within a space of fantasy and leisure—the vacation resort. Johnny remains a new "music man" who resurrects all of the erasures, repressions, and elisions associated with classical-era musical film, and the transformative power of music and dance is ultimately linked to white romantic desire rather than communal empowerment or politically progressive social relations. Alternatively, the hip hop "music man" appropriates the transformative potential of Gene Kelly's irrepressible verve and often redirects this energy towards political goals that are attached to specific urban spaces, communities, and ethnic and racial identities. The actions and potential of the hip hop "music man" in *Wild Style, Beat Street, Krush Groove*, and *Rappin'* appear even more radical when considering the ways in which this element of the genre was being reinvented and refashioned towards conciliatory and conservative ends in other contemporaneous youth-oriented musical films (like *Dirty Dancing*). When traditional aspects of the folk musical film, such as an emphasis upon community integration and expression, coalesced around contemporary impoverished urban neighborhoods in the early 1980s the notion of the "reconstructionist" teen musical as a conservative narrative force is considerably troubled.

My analysis here suggests that performance is overwhelmingly politicized in the first cycle of hip hop musicals through a variety of strategies that play with the expectations of the musical genre and the filming of urban spaces. The integrity of *Rappin'* and the *Breakin'* films is, however, undermined by the economic necessities of exploitation-oriented cinema. As I have stated previously, the inner city ghetto at this moment was a considerable site of contestation, and visualizing these urban spaces outside of negative news reportage was a gamble for film production companies hoping to draw a mainstream audience. David Zito, co-producer and co-screenwriter of *Breakin'*, laments that the film "did not live up to its potential."⁹⁴ He goes on to state, "I did go out and research the culture, the hip-hop scene and quickly realized that it was anything but a fad. I tried to stress that point as much as possible. Unfortunately, it didn't find its way into the movie. It's a shame, but Hollywood has a way of devouring culture."⁹⁵ Even though the first *Breakin'* was a financial success without stressing the politicized aspects of hip hop culture, Cannon Films released a sequel that significantly enhanced this aspect of communal music and dance.

As we compare the various ideological currents in this diverse group of films, from the independently produced *Wild Style* to the exploitation flicks released by Cannon, it becomes apparent that a great deal was invested in the cinematic representation of the inner city at this time. From the images of urban decay and abandoned housing stock in *Beat Street* and *Wild Style*, to the outright obliteration of the city in *Breakin' Through* and *Breakin'*, the hip hop musical reveals how black and Latino performance was consistently entangled with the production of urban identity as it negotiated contemporary issues such as the perils of gentrification and incessantly negative news coverage of inner-city communities of color.

Poverty and material devastation in the inner city was an unfortunate reality, as was the disproportionate news coverage of neighborhoods like the South Bronx in particular. Craig Watkins argues that during this decade the recently entrenched power of the New Right sought to gain control over all areas of representation that threatened the power of white middle-class Americans.⁹⁶ Such hegemonic representations, Michel de Certeau argues, literally flatten and colonize "real" places.⁹⁷ Indeed, the news coverage of predominantly black and Latino urban neighborhoods in the 1980s might be said to "map" over the actual everyday practice of space that formed the "real" conditions of existence for those communities. Like the maps of the early modern period to which de Certeau refers, news reportage compresses space while also functioning to "eliminate little by little the pictural figurations of the practices that produce it."⁹⁸ In other words, the effects of poverty, unemployment, and arson are revealed or expressed in condensed form but the conditions that produced the effects remain hidden to the viewer, and the circumstances of everyday life in the inner city, in both positive and negative forms, are reduced to data, statistical evidence, and dramatically composed images.

As a point of contrast, hip hop musicals such as *Wild Style, Beat Street, Krush Groove,* and *Rappin'* foreground the public interventions of hip hop culture, and in some cases even make visible hegemonic power structures facilitating urban blight and poverty, in order to remap the criminal backdrops and alien topographies evoked in newspapers, television reports, and sensationalist Hollywood productions such as *Fort Apache, The Bronx* (1981). The effect of giving voice and narrative (in the format of the feature film) to these communities who were silenced by the mainstream media evoked a variety of responses. In June of 1983, Harlan Jacobson, a critic for *Film Comment*, prefaced his interview with Ahearn by the following:

> There's something delirious about the camera as reporter, taking one into foreign waters, or behind enemy lines, or penetrating political curtains where the shape of the country on some schooldays map is the only image one has. True of China until 1972, true of Afghanistan until 1979, probably still true of Albania, and definitely true of the South Bronx today, twenty minutes from this typewriter.[99]

The temporal displacement may only be twenty minutes away for Jacobson, but it is the equivalent of a trip halfway around the world to the South Bronx of *Beat Street*, *Wild Style*, and *Krush Groove*. While the immense popularity of rap today has somewhat diminished the "Otherness" of such notorious and legendary hip hop locations as the aforementioned South Bronx and Queensbridge, as well as South Central Los Angeles' Compton, a review of *Beat Street* reveals the absolutely "foreign" territory these films introduced at this time. Jim Welsh, writing in 1984, avowed that "*Beat Street* is an agreeable picture once one gets over the culture shock, overflowing with a tremendous energy and inventiveness."[100] Jeff Millar, reporting for the *Houston Chronicle*, was even stronger in formulating his feelings of alienation in the face of hip hop culture and images of inner city urban life. "I am far, far away from the demographic ground zero of *Krush Groove* (rated R), far enough away that I felt I was watching an ethnographic film at the Rice Media Center."[101] "Ethnographic film," "culture shock," a trip "behind enemy lines"—these are strong words for productions that have acquired such a patina of benign mediocrity. As the true hip hop musical attempted to reveal the contemporary problems faced by inner city neighborhoods, as well as the creative means developed to combat such tribulations, it undeniably struggled to reclaim the images of urban devastation co-opted by mainstream media. The responses to these films demonstrate the ways in which such imagery immediately called to mind a foreign presence in the midst of one's own borders—neighborhoods that had been evoked as unknowable and alien in press descriptions and photography—but whose environs and inhabitants were now also being revealed as energetic and dynamic in their transformation to feature film musicals.[102]

Wild Style, Beat Street, Krush Groove, and *Rappin'* attempted to reorient negative news reportage of the inner city and "remap" its spaces by not only focusing on the innovative street culture that was redefining these neighborhoods, but also by resurrecting the traditional "music man" as a struggling black or Latino youth who, through his hip hop skills, was able to overcome social problems and connect in positive ways with his community. The hip hop musical repeatedly shows the communal audience, and the ways in which performance is completed by the spectator, when he or she becomes an active participant in the show. In many cases, this event is explicitly politicized, as in the penultimate performance of *Rappin'* where a communal rap forces a city zoning board to allow the impoverished residents of the Hill District in Pittsburgh to keep their homes.

For de Certeau, merely walking in the urban environment is a "spatial acting-out," an appropriation of space that may be considered as analogous to "what the speech act is to language or to the statements uttered."[103] He even speaks of the individual *style* of the urban pedestrian as a personalization of the act of appropriating space. Style, or the unique way in which one engages in hip hop culture—a signature "freeze" at the end of a dance routine, or a particular flourish in one's graffiti writing—is crucial to the language of hip hop because it asserts the distinctiveness of the individual even as it works towards an expression of communal solidarity and identity. Within the hip hop musicals of the 1980s, the consumer and producer of cultural capital are one and the same, and assertions of unique identity or style work to strengthen bonds rather than further stratify the social order. As these new "music men" and other communal participants set out to redefine the contours of their lived experience through music and dance, the hip hop musical frequently brings not only contemporary urban settings to the forefront of the musical film, but also makes the economic and political inequity of American culture pivotal to its story. Although *Breakin' Through, Body Rock,* and *Delivery Boys* utilize the structure of the hip hop musical to banal or even possibly nefarious ends, the need to purge specific urban locations and communities of color from these films to make them acceptable subject matter for Disney (*Breakin' Through*) and the twelve-and-under set (*Delivery Boys*) only emphasizes how powerful and contentious images of alternating urban blight or its political and social renewal actually were.

2

The Sound of the South Bronx
Wild Style Reinvents the Urban Musical

Wild Style managed to suggestively evoke aspects of hip hop culture through the negotiation of "real" urban spaces while, at the same time, largely conforming to the structure of the classical Hollywood musical. This is true of several other hip hop musicals, but it is the film's unique tension between documentary aspects and the musical genre that imparts it with an urgency and complexity worthy of a sustained discussion. Some critics have noted that hip hop musicals referred to the Hollywood musical genre through allusions to particular films and syntactic elements. In the case of *Wild Style*, more often than not writers have been oblivious to these generic characteristics. In his *New York Times* review of the film, Vincent Canby seems so befuddled by the ways in which the theme of city space takes center stage that he cannot discern the movie's show musical structure. He writes that *Wild Style* "is a series of random encounters of graffiti artists, rappers, and breakers, leading up to a giant rap-break concert in a Lower East Side band shell."[1] As I will show, Canby's "random encounters" actually consist of a romantic plot interspersed with a number of communal performances. All of these features tie *Wild Style* emphatically to the generic conventions of the musical film. The final stage performance, what Canby calls the "giant rap-break concert," is in fact the element of the film that satisfies a number of established film musical conventions through its incorporation of both a romantic union and a successful musical performance.

This chapter therefore has three broad aims. In the first instance, it looks at how *Wild Style* intervened in contemporary discourse about graffiti through the depiction of Raymond (Zoro). His journey follows the arc of traditional Hollywood "music men" and ultimately reveals him to be a thoughtful and complex artist whose creative growth has antecedents in other narratives of the visual arts, particularly the history of Abstract Expressionism. The chapter's second objective is to look closely at folk musical conventions operating in *Wild Style* as a means to deploy a radical and politically engaged cinema that reformed contemporary media visions of the South Bronx as a social problem riddled with crime and drug abuse. In doing this I open up a discussion of the notion of home in a wider context: its historical devaluation in urban communities of color, its significance to folk musical traditions, and its material condition in contemporary inner city life. Lastly, I turn to a discussion of *Wild Style*'s formal properties and narrative strategies. Here I address the film's reflexive tendencies in relation to the broader history of musical film and hip hop artistic practice, and the ways in which it dynamically harnessed the tension between two traditionally adverse modes of filmmaking, the documentary and the musical.

Graffiti as Performance

Although I am arguing that *Wild Style* is a musical, the two main characters are not musicians or dancers but graffiti artists. Nonetheless, *Wild Style*'s Raymond is a conventional "music man" in the sense that creativity is restored as a positive and utopian communal vision at the end of the film through the assistance of his artistic intervention, even though his main talent is neither singing nor dancing. The film worked to transform the stereotype of the graffiti writer from a destructive teenaged "hood" to a sensitive young artist intensely concerned with the integrity of his work, a process that was contemporaneously underway in black newspapers.

An article from the *Afro-American* referred to graffiti as a disease in 1972, while the *Chicago Defender*, another widely circulated black newspaper, decried the presence of graffiti in a series of articles from February of the next year, with such titles as "Let's Stop Killing Our Communities" and "Vandalism: Who are the Victims?"[2] The latter opens with a quote from an angry fifteen-year-old writer who states, "I hate the man's world . . . we gotta let him know it wherever we are."[3] In response, journalist Carolyn Fortier asks whether or not "he really hears(s) you when you write on walls and destroy the community where YOU-not-HE-have to live?"[4] The article examines graffiti as part of a larger vandalism explosion in black Chicago communities allegedly stemming from young people's apparent lack of respect for public and private property, a problem that the piece ultimately attributes to parental failure and neglect. Accompanying the text is a photograph of a Woodlawn apartment façade in which words such as "Mighty Falcons" and "Sundown" are scrawled across an entranceway flanked by Corinthian Columns. Classical art is under attack since "intricately designed pillars hold up the dying claim to beauty" and "the rampant abuse by vandals has scarred a magnificent structure."[5]

A little over a decade later, things were entirely different. The editors of the *Afro-American* chose to print a picture of graffiti writer Dominique Philbert (Ero) with the caption, "From Subway to Fame," as they noted his rise to international renown in the art world. Philbert appears in the photograph with one of his graffiti-on-canvas works at New York's Fun Gallery. Later that year, the newspaper printed a "Hip Hop Glossary" and defined the "Graffiti Writer" as "an artist who works in the spray can paint medium, creating works of art on public surfaces, such as walls and subway cars (and sometimes canvas)."[6] In just ten years, a directionless angry youth looking to spurn "the man" was transformed into an intelligent painter who selects the medium of spray paint to articulate his artistic intervention.

The initial hostility of the black press (and, in particular, the *Afro-American*) to graffiti is understandable given that the nation's oldest environmental campaign, The Clean Block Program, was initiated in 1935 by Francis L. Murphy, daughter of the newspaper's founder. Murphy's program was resoundingly successful, and in 1939 the *Afro-American* boasted that it registered over 8,000 entrants and 500 city blocks in an annual contest.[7] As the publication remarked on the specific transformations that had taken place during the campaign it noted that "whole rows of houses were painted by landlords. Hundreds of yards and back alleys were cleaned, back fences white-washed or painted, yards beautified and fronts literaly [sic] made to look like flower gardens or little parks."[8] Later, this environmental program would also align itself with national concerns. The 1941 campaign, for instance, emphasized hygiene and cleanliness in line with wartime initiatives to keep disease at bay as America prepared for battle. A tag line from an article about the contest in May of that year forgoes any mention of flower gardens and freshly painted fences but includes the subheadings "Clean Blocks First Line of Home Defense" and "Disease and Dirt Must Go."[9] The program grew in prestige and financial sponsorship as it consistently emphasized cleanliness, urban gardening practices, and civic duty. It reached out to the

Holding its own...
Intricately designed pillars hold up the dying claim to beauty of this apartment building in the Woodlawn community. The rampant abuse by vandals has scarred a magnificent structure. Children passing on their way from school are unaware of the demise of what was once a lovely home. (Daily Defender Photo by Bobby Sengstacke)

Fig. 2.1. Classical architecture under threat from the "Graffiti Disease," Feb. 24, 1973. Courtesy of the *Chicago Defender*.

community through luncheons and workshops and rewarded hard-working residents with block parties, tickets to sporting events, and movies.[10] Even though the program's initiatives often dovetailed with more radical grassroots campaigns to improve life for inner-city neighborhoods, it is easy to see how the presence of graffiti seemed to disrupt the decades-long mission of the Clean Block campaign—a tidy, well ordered urban vista free of garbage, dirt, and peeling paint. Without a doubt, the impulsive scrawls found in and around public spaces in Chicago and New York in the early 1970s, such as those pictured in Fortier's article, were very different from the intricate and premediated large-scale works that began to dominate the urban landscape a decade later. *Wild Style* gave narrative form to a detectable change in attitude in some black publications, one that positioned graffiti practitioners as artists who could be identified by their particular medium, and had the potential to exhibit on the

Wild Style Reinvents the Urban Musical 89

Fig. 2.2. Graffiti as Communal Revitalization: Production still from *Wild Style* (1983) featuring a graffiti mural on Connie's Superette. Photographer: Cathy Campbell; courtesy of Charlie Ahearn.

international art circuit. If the Woodlawn apartments' façade struggles to bear the weight of a hideous disfigurement, the paint bombs thrown in *Wild Style* are intended to invigorate the architectural squalor and bring new life to its moribund surfaces.

Ahearn's film actually opens with an image of the word "graffiti" executed in the new "wild style" of urban script that supplanted the somewhat softer and more readable bubble style letters of the late 1970s. We then see a rope thrown down an outdoor wall with the figure of Raymond (Lee Quinones) scurrying down. The camera cuts to a close-up of the face of this young artist as we hear a subway train screaming by, and the soundtrack breaks into a chunky hip hop beat. These shots evoke the clandestine and dangerous nature of graffiti writing, or "bombing," at night in the city. Subway noise permeates this scene (and the entire film), attesting to the omnipresence of trains in the South Bronx. Most of the illegal graffiti writing in the film also takes place in train yards at night, echoing these first few scenes.

In *Wild Style*'s prologue (these images precede the credits) Raymond's art making is clearly defined as an outsider practice. He must paint covertly at night, and the film underscores the romantic aspect of Raymond's work and persona somewhat forcefully as an opening shot frames his face in the darkness behind the grid-work of a chain-link fence. The shadows play on his face and the connection between urban spaces and his identity are not only revealed in his bodily performance, but are literally inscribed on his face by the chain enclosure of the train yard.

This sequence also introduces us to the film's romance plot as we witness Rose (Sandra Fabara) writing her name on a wall beside Raymond's graffiti signature. Like Quinones, Fabara plays a character based on her own experiences as a young graffiti artist. Documentary aspects of this film, while largely related to emergent hip hop culture, also chronicle the actual relationship between the two lead actors in the film. The couple appears together in this initial sequence, yet once we are inside the narrative space of the film we learn that they have recently split. As such, the initial shots in *Wild Style* function as a thematic introductory episode that is somewhat narratively disconnected from the film. It tells the viewer what the film will be about rather than locating any specific diegetic incident.

The ensuing credits are part of an animated sequence including both colorful words and images pulsating to a hip hop beat. This credit sequence, which will be discussed in detail later in the chapter, announces the tone of the film as somewhat playful. It also locates the urban as a space of performance, one which will be reimagined many times as the film constantly reconfigures the environs of the city through various modes of creative representation.

After the credits, we are made aware of Raymond's graffiti *nom de plume*, Zoro, since he paints an enormous image of the famed masked marauder on a subway car and we also see several Zoro images and tags around the city.[11] The signifier of his secret artistic presence encapsulates many representational strategies—from an animated, purely pictorial graphic image of the character Zoro to multiple forms of the written word, which display varying levels of intricacy and decipherability. His confidant and would-be promoter/manager, Phade, played by recording and graffiti artist Fab Five Freddy, knows the real identity of Zoro because he used to paint with him; a large part of the narrative involves a plan to unmask Raymond as Zoro by both Phade and a reporter (played by Patti Astor). This happens in various ways, including the introduction of a white, predominantly female, and somewhat predatory New York art world. Raymond's secret identity will come to play a major part in the narrative of the film, attaching itself to conventions of the Hollywood musical. For instance, his veiled identity is linked to both communal and romantic dissonance, a common threat to stability in the narrative of the classical musical. Raymond's unmasking will be followed by his incorporation into the larger community, a plot turn symbolized by his "appearance" within the final stage number of the film.

Although I have analyzed this portion of the film in relation to the commodity status of the final number in classical musicals in the previous chapter, it deserves further examination here with respect to art historical precedents. In this final number of *Wild Style*, Raymond performs as a gestural artist in painting the stage backdrop for the film's concluding rap concert. Raymond uses his whole body to paint, and this performance follows in the tradition of American mid-century Abstract Expressionists who were often referred to as action painters or gestural artists.[12] These earlier painters, such as Jackson Pollock, Willem de Kooning, and Franz Kline, often used expansive broad strokes to cover their large canvases, which served as reminders of the bodily movement required to create such bold and assertive works. Both graffiti writing and Abstract Expressionism require a constant and dynamic physical effort on the part of the artist that is not common in other painting traditions. Ahearn himself understood graffiti writers to be the natural inheritors of modern art practice and he has suggested that there is a direct line from Fauvism and Abstract Expressionism to graffiti:

> (I)f you do something that's aesthetic—graffiti is entirely—it's like Vlaminck and the Fauves. Vlaminck used to say, "They throw bombs, I paint pictures." In other words, the whole idea of the modern artist as a rebel, someone making some kind of social statement coming out of himself rather than a committee, and the idea of the modern artist as an outlaw—all these things have twisted around Pollack, [sic] and in a way have come out in the most natural form in this whole graffiti movement.[13]

Interestingly, Ahearn here emphasizes the "outsider" nature of *avant-garde* artistic progression in the twentieth century even though his film also works to incorporate the outlaw artist within the collective. The enormous images of painterly play in the amphitheater undertaken by Raymond are followed by the final rap concert. During this show Raymond perches atop the amphitheater while the entire community participates as performer and audience at the same time. This act of social cohesion represented through performance also coincides with Raymond's eventual romantic reunification with Rose. Thus, the process of unmasking or redirecting a concealed, false, or troubling identity found in such classical-era musicals as *Love Me Tonight* and *Top Hat* is employed in *Wild Style*, like its antecedents, to satisfy the genre's expectations for successful romantic pairing and integration of the couple within the social body.

As in most backstage musicals, a winning show is equated with romantic partnership and the amorous couple almost always appears together on stage by the end of the film in at least one production number.[14] *Wild Style* reworks this ending, although Raymond's involvement in the show entails painting the "set" of the disused amphitheater rather than singing and dancing. Raymond's painting of the stage is captured by Ahearn as a performance, a solo act in the space that will become the final hip hop show of the film. Initially, Raymond is unhappy with his creation, a composition that evokes themes of artistic alienation. Rose and Raymond come together to discuss the direction of this present work, and she convinces him that "it's not about you, it's about the performers." With this in mind, Raymond repaints the space with a design anchored by a large emblematic star in the center of the stage in order to represent the future stars of the show. He shifts the focus to the community, rather than expressing his own personal frustrations as an artist. The concluding show with his new backdrop is a raging success, and when perched on top of the amphitheater during the concert, Raymond is cleverly integrated into the spectacle of performance without literally being on stage.

As noted in the previous chapter, Altman has argued that the musical film genre works to hide all of the labor necessary to produce the final show (i.e., set construction, lighting design, etc.), yet *Wild Style* significantly inverts this dynamic. In fact, the camera lingers on not one but two different attempts to paint the abandoned amphitheater (the "set" of the show) in preparation for the final rap concert. Additionally, it is the actual "star" graffiti artist of the film, Zoro, not a crew of unnamed and unseen workers who performs this task. There is a deliberate sense of leveling here between various echelons of performance. Set painting, which is typically associated with manual labor, or at best craft production (part of the labor of musical production referred to by Altman), is equated with art, authorship, and the "star" of the film, and it is the vigorous bodily actions of Raymond that most forcefully signify the artist at work.

Raymond has been transformed into his alter ego Zoro through multiple and sustained acts of tagging and repeating this name and image throughout the urban environment. The rope thrown over the wall in the opening shots signifies the breaking into and getting out of a prohibited space. This action defines the artistic practice of graffiti, perhaps even more so, than the writer's finished work and *Wild Style* makes it clear that performing *is* inscribing oneself into social space. The contemporaneous documentary film *Style Wars* (1982), directed by Tony Silver, also provides ample evidence to support this statement. *Style Wars* features young men—Ahearn's defiant modern artists—scurrying down to the shadowy depths of the ancient subway tunnels to perform their work, "bombing" New York City trains before they rush towards throngs of anxious passengers. It also visualizes the efforts of the city—chemical washes and ineffectual anti-graffiti advertising campaigns—to stop this cycle of creation and destruction. Intercut between these scenes of perpetual urban "play," *Style Wars* allows the writers to have a voice. For example, a young graffiti artist named Skeme is interviewed in his apartment with his disapproving mother at his side. Skeme notes that he participates in the subculture because he wants other writers to know his name. Another goal for this young artist is to go "all city"—which refers to having his tag, "throw up," or larger piece on every line in the subway system. Other writers in *Style Wars* discuss the alluring smell of resting trains in the yard and the pleasure of navigating unfamiliar subway tunnels at night. Like the earlier generation of Abstract Expressionists, practitioners of hip hop culture in *Style Wars* and *Wild Style* value the act of artistic creation as much as the resulting product of that endeavor. And, for this emerging generation of artists, it is the repetition and proliferation of the name that is a sign of the performance and act of creation—it is evidence of the body at work.

Herbert Kohl and James Hinton have argued that the ability to rename the self, facilitated by the practice of graffiti, takes on an urgent political dimension for urban youth. In graffiti culture, refusal of the given or family name, and the adoption of a self chosen name, or one selected by peers, insists upon a radical repudiation of the authority of the parent generation. More specifically, according to the authors, it is also a negation of the oppressive social and political conditions historically offered to black

Americans in the U.S., since most African American names bear traces of the slavery system and attest to the naming of slaves by white masters.[15]

Many graffiti names also specifically challenged the constraints of contemporary urban life. For instance, an early acknowledgment of graffiti as something other than vandalism by a mainstream media source was a *New York Times* article entitled "Taki 183 Spawns Pen Pals," which included an interview with the infamous writer.[16] His moniker, the writer explains, is a combination of a diminutive of his given name, Demetrius, and his street number.[17] The name asserts his ethnicity, but also proclaims his urban affiliation with 183rd Street. An appendix from Norman Mailer's *The Faith of Graffiti* shows that the use of numbers in one's graffiti name to denote an urban location or street number was common practice in the early 1970s. The list provides an extended catalog of graffiti names inscribed in and around New York City, several of which are followed by a number. (A small sampling of this list includes Rafi 179, Dynamite 161, King Super Kool 223, 113 Hellcats, B. J. of 118 St and Keep it cool 153.) This form of "naming" is no less a politicized act than Kohl and Hinton's example. Because adopting a graffiti identity often entailed the appropriation of one's street address—a signifier of the immobile place—while unfixing it and literally spreading it all over the city, the act of graffiti itself can be read as a reaction against the constraints of the urban environment and its arbitrary systems of division and order.[18] For Taki 183 and a host of others using a similar graffiti identity, it seems that the urgency and political aspect of "bombing" the city with a moniker that bears one's own city address lay in the desire to initiate an interpenetration of spaces, communities, and people that was unavailable in the current urban milieu. The subway cars moved names and identities throughout the topography of New York, modifying the traditional boundaries of the municipality, and transforming its threshold spaces.

Although the ethnic, social, and financial stratification of the city was deeply disturbed by outlaw graffiti culture, some institutions that were eager to co-opt this new urban script welcomed the art form. In *Wild Style*, the potential transformation of hip hop culture into a commodity form is largely dealt with through an exploration of the relationship between street graffiti and the lure of the New York gallery. Young street artists, short on cash and tired of having their words and images covered in a matter of days, did, in fact, accept commissions to make graffiti artwork on canvas (as we see Raymond do), thereby diminishing many communal or performative aspects of the piece.[19] This tense relationship between gallery work and the street artist takes up one of the most important themes of very early backstage musicals—success in the popular arts at the cost of personal, familial, or communal loss. I would suggest that *Wild Style*, *Beat Street*, and *Rappin'* capture the very problem of the founding text of the backstage musical, *The Jazz Singer*. Like Raymond, Jakie Rabinowitz (Al Jolson), star of *The Jazz Singer*, is torn between being successful outside of his community and remaining true to an "authentic" cultural role as a performer bound to a geographically located space of practice. For Jakie, the pull of communal obligations is strongly connected to his family and also the Jewish religion. His family, especially Jakie's father, anticipates that the talented youth will use his abilities to honor the Jewish faith by performing traditional melodic chants such as the Kol Nidre. But Jakie (who changes his name to Jake) has other plans. He leaves Manhattan's Lower East Side and its devout Jewish community in order to follow the path of stardom into the world of vaudeville theater and nightclub shows where he performs as a "jazz singer." These two spaces of culture—the urban Jewish community and the musical theater circuit—seem irreconcilable, but through performance their differences are in fact magically erased in the final live concert scene. For Jakie, the appearance of his mother in the audience of his successful "jazz" act attests to the potential integration of "authentic" regional performance and popular culture, while the final "rap convention" of *Wild Style*, involving the South Bronx neighborhood putting on a show in a downtown space, brings the regional together unproblematically with the potential for integration into popular entertainment in an explosive outdoor party. At the end of Ahearn's film, we are unsure whether or not Raymond will continue to paint in the street or be lured by the glamour and monetary promise of the gallery, but the final scene, by involving the local collective and a prospective way of "being heard" and "getting seen," seems to suggest that you don't need to choose between success and the community: you can have it all. A reviewer for *Artforum International* in 1984 noted that

> like the classical Hollywood musical, *Wild Style* is about everyone's desire to be a star, which, as is ironically acknowledged, is impossible to realize without validation and promotion by the mainstream culture, and consequently, exposure to the risk of exploitation; so far rap and break dancing have not been incorporated into white style to the extent of graffiti art.[20]

While folklorist Sharon Sherman remarked that "the graffiti artists and breakdancers ... in all of these films ... find their way into the heartland of America, selling McDonald's hamburgers and Pepsi-Cola, and turning glorified music videos into box office hits," the hip hop musical often works towards achieving a complex balance between maintaining "authenticity" and "getting paid" for members of the performing community—a process that is unquestionably linked to urgent political and social issues.[21]

Raymond is a Latino youth but his dilemma encapsulates the tensions between individualism and the community in ethnically and racially distinct populations of the United States more generally under the twin pressures of capitalism and assimilation. Jakie Rabinowitz struggled to "sing jazz" without alienating his traditional Jewish roots, and this same tension has permeated films about contemporary communities of color. In an excellent analysis of recent African American cinema dealing with college life, Lesley Speed suggests that films like *House Party* (1990), *House Party 2* (1991), and *Higher Learning* (1995) explore how the desire for personal advancement can be effectively balanced with a responsibility towards the larger black community. She notes that the *House Party* films, in particular, use popular musical forms and entertainment to engage a youth audience as they explore social and political issues relevant to African Americans.[22] In a similar way, *Wild Style* contributed to an ongoing discussion in American culture regarding how an individual might participate in the pleasures offered by assimilation into the larger social order without abdicating their personal responsibility to a minority community.

A New Community, A New Home—Reworking the Folk Musical

Wild Style's crews or teenaged gangs traverse the city like the train cars decorated with their graffiti art, and they compete with each other through breakdancing, rapping, and athletics. These competitions happen in many different city spaces: the club, the street, the basketball courts, as well as the train yard. This theme of competition and performance structures nearly every aspect of the film, and it is negotiated through the conventional aspects of both folk and show musicals.

Altman writes that the folk musical is characterized by its emphasis on "family groupings and the home."[23] He also goes on to argue that "in many cases the action of the film is entirely limited to the type of town where everyone is a neighbor, where each season's rituals bring the entire population together."[24] Community or family audiences within the diegesis are central to the structure of the folk musical because they provide a model for spontaneous performance. The entire neighborhood assembles to hear Judy Garland sing in her own living room during the party scene in *Meet Me in St. Louis* (1944) while several members of the rural community in *Cabin in the Sky* surround Ethel Waters as her character, Petunia, delivers the title track of the film in a forest setting. In this film, too, a delivery man joins Waters and her husband, Joe (Eddie "Rochester" Anderson), for the impromptu song and dance number "Taking a Chance on Love" in the couple's home.

According to both Feuer and Altman, the folk musical values the quality of the amateur over the professional and imbues everyone in the community with the ability to perform.[25] Being a spectator in the folk musical is a participatory practice that erases the boundary between artist and audience. The essence of the folk musical seeks to tap into the desire that everyone can be a performer. Thus, the constant permeation of performance space by the diegetic audience attests to the fact that the barrier to professional theatrical talent is in fact irrelevant. Feuer makes this argument about nearly all classical-era musicals and suggests that the porous border between audience and entertainer in these films addressed the tension between the loss of live performance in theater and the "dead" celluloid space of film. According to Feuer, "The Hollywood musical as a genre perceives the gap between producer and consumer, the breakdown of community designated by the very distinction between performer and audience, as a form of cinematic original sin."[26] She goes on to argue that "the musical seeks to bridge the gap by putting up 'community' as an ideal concept."[27] In the case of *Wild Style*, however, communal presentations of music and dance are not idealized as a way to compensate for the absence of live performance in the movie theater. Rather, these events are complex strategies of collective empowerment that function either literally or symbolically to safeguard against the contemporary social conditions that undermined the familial and communal structures of inner city neighborhoods. As I note in the previous chapter, the South Bronx was a site of unprecedented contemporary urban squalor. The communities in this region had been victimized by increasing crime, unemployment, poverty, inadequate housing, and a spate of devastating arson-related fires. Under such obviously detrimental material conditions, the concept of community resides in the possibility for random productive encounters with one's neighbors when no designated neighborhood centers or spaces exist, and the amateur performer has the potential to facilitate a strikingly politicized role in creating and nurturing communal bonds.

For example, Ahearn stages an integrated musical number on the front stoop of a home that clearly derives from a casual street encounter. We see the spontaneous song of the golden-era folk musical transformed into a rap performed by members of Double Trouble. Rather than the traditional nuclear family grouping found in the folk musical, the number includes two adolescents and a young boy whose familial and filial connections are unclear except for the fact that they are all part of the same South Bronx neighborhood. In this scene, the boy is casually walking in the street and then stops to listen to Double Trouble's rap. The number begins with a very tight close-up shot of the two rappers. In the following medium shot, our performers appear to be perched on a front stoop with metal banisters framing their lanky teen bodies, which are casually arranged on a set of concrete stairs. A young boy walks into the left side of the frame, snapping his fingers. He is shot from behind and his figure is present throughout the entire rap, providing the audience for their doorstep performance. The camera focuses closely on the faces of the rappers for most of the scene, but also cuts to the child, *our* audience, dancing while continuing to contribute to the number by snapping his fingers, keeping the beat. This young boy functions as a surrogate audience member for the film spectator. His presence provides a point of entry into the scene that is similar to the standard filming techniques employed in classical Hollywood backstage musicals during the depiction of musical numbers that take place in an actual theater. This type of shot sequence utilizes a camera position that approximates the actual distance and lateral positioning of an ideal spectatorial position—an imaginary third-row center seat. The shot pattern often gives the film spectator the impression of being part of the diegetic theater audience shown on screen by panning back from the stage floor, and gradually revealing increasingly more space of the theater, and with it the rows of audience members seen from the backs of their chairs.[28] In Ahearn's film, the boy is filmed from the back as stated, alluding to this previous tradition and suggesting that the viewer may casually step into the boy's audience position after he leaves the scene to become a member of the street audience. The point, however, is not to recoup the loss of live entertainment endemic to every musical film, but rather to suggest that this new kind of encounter between performer and audience is random, quotidian, and an important element of communal bonding and expression within the community depicted on screen.

Fig 2.3. Rap duo Double Trouble in *Wild Style* (1983). Courtesy of Charlie Ahearn.

During Double Trouble's rap we hear the musical percussion of the young boy in addition to the sounds of the city. Not only does the diegetic audience literally become a performer, but the city also participates in the number since its sounds—a barking dog and the groaning of the subway—permeate the scene, underscoring the fusion of documentary and musical elements in the film. This number presents a reconstruction and reworking of the folk audience and the traditional locus of the folk performance—the home. Instead of the private and semi-private spaces of small-town middle America (such as the local fair or living room parlor) or the expanse of black rural Southern neighborhoods where American film folk musical numbers have traditionally been staged, the locus of communal performance is drastically reconfigured to reflect vastly different forms of collective bonding rituals found in inner city neighborhood of the 1980s.

Double Trouble's number shares, but also highlights, the folk musical's characteristic emphasis on generational relations and the passing down of traditions to young people.[29] Rap, and hip hop culture more generally, was a new mode of performance but one that initially included a positive emphasis on children and the community. Rapping is closely related to older forms of African American rhyming games such as "the dozens," and the Jamaican born tradition of toasting. Even though rap may be understood as a manifestation of traditional African American and West Indian customs, hip hop culture is also youth culture, and is, in a sense, far enough removed from previously established forms of African American and Jamaican oral play to be considered new. Thus, rap is a Janus-faced practice, one that simultaneously looks back to established performance traditions, such as toasting, and forward to new representational forms, such as commercial hip hop music. Furthermore, scholars such as Andy Bennett have suggested that hip hop culture has its roots in the eighteenth and nineteenth century slave trade since it works to unify the African diaspora uprooted from their traditional homelands. Thus, hip hop links West Indians in England with the concerns of black Americans in the United States through the notion of a pan-African identity.[30] This may be true for some groups. However, when American rap music in the early 1980s raised social and political issues, they were usually related to national if not local concerns. Astute contemporary observers like music critic Robert Palmer also argued that that the emergence of rap music reflected a wider interest in talking (rather than singing) for the music industry evidenced by the 1978 recording of Linton Kwesi Johnson's poetry read against a background of improvised music, the success of Laurie Anderson's 1982 album *Big Science*, which featured talking rather than singing, New York City performance artist Julia Heyward's experiments with talking and chanting in her shows, and Jamaican toaster Yellowman's record deal with Columbia.[31]

In the scene from *Wild Style* discussed above, both the rappers and their audience are drawn from the street. Nearly all the neighborhood members are shown to be talented at some aspect of performance in the film, and in the same way all residents of the community provide an audience for collective performance, from nighttime graffiti writing to rapping and breakdancing. The communal audience appears in most of the performance-oriented scenes in the film, including two extended club sequences featuring breakdancing, two integrated musical rap numbers (the scene including Double Trouble described above and the "Basketball number," which will be addressed later in this chapter), numerous graffiti writing exploits, and the final stage show. Ahearn continually shows us that, as one breakdancer or artist steps out of the limelight, he or she immediately becomes a member of the audience. Indeed, this permeable border is in fact integral to *Wild Style*'s depiction of the breakdancing circle filmed in the Roxy nightclub. As one member leaves the circle, another one enters, creating a continuous flow between performer and audience.[32] We even see Raymond and Rose, the "stars" of the film, as just two of the numerous clapping and cheering spectators in this scene. Performance in *Wild Style*, both in the club and on the street, is made possible through a continual regeneration and replacement of the community-based audience.[33] Likewise, *Beat Street, Breakin' 2, Krush Groove,* and *Rappin'* all feature some depiction of the participatory communal audience as they significantly transform and politicize the relationship between performer and spectator within the folk musical. Let us recall, for instance, the final sequence of *Rappin'* in which Rappinhood walks through the streets rapping with his crew while neighborhood grocers, moms, street vendors, and even prostitutes contribute to the number with their own rhymes.

As noted earlier, numerous scholars have either directly or indirectly noted that the structure of the folk musical has habitually been used to romanticize or neutralize the history of racial struggle in the United States. It depicts happy and apolitical African American sharecroppers, slaves, or the general rural poor whose joy comes from their love of nature and fervent religious beliefs.[34] Alternately, the folk musical can also evoke an all-white culturally homogenous utopian space of familial and communal harmony. The hip hop musical, by contrast, is a jarring intervention in this history. In the true hip hop musical, folk culture is actually used in a critical and political manner. There is also no point of absorption and re-presentation of Americana in the hip hop musical—no reworking of

American historical mythology. These films present black and Latino culture in its contemporary context without the patina of historical romanticism. Importantly, rituals of performance refuse to simply speak about "timeless" and benign aspects of communities of color. Every integrated musical number in *Wild Style* includes a young man boasting his name and abilities, and this turn facilitates both the recognition of individual talent as well as a representation of communal identity through music and dance.[35] In fact, as early as 1980 emerging recording star Kurtis Blow expressed the importance of rapping to the poverty stricken inner-city community. He noted that "rapping is a way of life to lower income people. . . . In Harlem each square block has its own rapper DJ who does battle with the other rappers."[36] Blow suggests that rapping in urban communities of color is historically and inextricably tied to collective representation and regional "dialogues" within the neighborhood.[37] These regional dialogues coalesced into a broader discourse of communal solidarity and political leverage when the track "King Holiday" was produced in 1985 by Mercury/Polygram to honor the first observance of Martin Luther King Day.[38] The song was a musical collaboration by rappers such as Run-D.M.C., Whodini, and the Fat Boys, as well as other performers like Kool and the Gang, Lisa Lisa, and Whitney Houston. King's son, Dexter Scott King, who oversaw the project "specifically wanted to make a rap-based record because he wanted to reach the audience that has come of age since his father's assassination."[39] In the 1980s, rapping was a form of collective representation that was able to deftly maneuver between the local inner-city block and the national political stage. *Wild Style* suggests as much a few years prior to the release of "King Holiday" by using hip hop performance strategies and the communal audience of the folk musical to engage with broader contemporary social issues.

Just as Ahearn reworks and redeploys the traditional folk audience of the musical, so too does the conventional setting of the home undergo a radical transformation in *Wild Style*. As we have seen, according to Altman the focus of performance in Hollywood folk musicals often takes place in a country setting or within the home. Altman argues that within these films

> the family residence, whether farmhouse, mansion, or humble flat, thus takes on a symbolic value, for it serves not only as the stable and constant backdrop of the folk musical's action, but also as a permanent reminder of the strength and stability of the American family and home.[40]

In *Wild Style*, however, it is the street and other public spaces of the South Bronx that function as "home," the community's central locus for communication, socialization, and performance. We rarely see the interior of any actual residence. The domestic has instead been replaced by the street and other urban locales—spaces that provide the backdrop for communal expression and bonding. Children play in the streets, people meet, converse, and perform on front stoops, groups convene to play ball on neighborhood courts, and an abandoned amphitheater is taken over by the community to be used as a performance space for amateurs.

In an early scene, after we first see Raymond painting his Zoro logo, the camera follows our graffiti hero walking at night and then tracks up slowly to reveal the shadowy façade of a brick tenement building. Raymond then climbs into his home through a window, and encounters his brother Hector (a military man) who greets him with a gun as he condemns the state of his graffiti covered room. Thus, even when we do glimpse the spare interior of Raymond's apartment it, like the street and the trains, has been covered with graffiti. Hector refers to Raymond's art brought indoors as "fucking garbage" and advises him to "stop fucking around and be a man." Here we witness a conflict between two brothers, yet Hector clearly displays a paternalistic tone toward his younger sibling, disciplining Raymond in what appears to be a home without a father.

This sequence reinforces the theme of entering prohibited spaces by recalling the opening shots of the film in which Raymond breaks into a subway yard, transgressing spatial boundaries. As Raymond enters his bedroom like a cat burglar through the window frame, he is literally apprehended and admonished by his older brother in military garb. Even though Raymond is in fact entering his own residence, this domestic space promises none of the comforts of the family home found in the folk musical, and it is monitored by an authoritative figure who resists the socially progressive artistic interventions that graffiti has to offer.

The conflict between Hector and Raymond is staged as a "showdown" between a figure of parental authority and a teenager, referring to the stereotypical problem of teenagers and their perpetually untidy rooms. This scene uses a cliché found in many representations of parent/youth relations (in sitcoms, television ads, and countless teen films) in order to open up a radical and suggestive premise regarding the transformation of space through artistic intervention. The "garbage" to which Hector refers is of course a radical reworking of domestic space, an intervention that seeks to resist the conformity and limitations of inner-city tenement housing.

It is worth pointing out that the camera prevents us from seeing the entirety of Raymond's cramped room. Ahearn only focuses on small sections of the space, dividing it up into artistically abstract components that isolate and emphasize the graffiti rather than the domestic function of the room. Susan Stewart has argued that

> graffiti make claims upon materiality, refusing to accept the air as the only free or ambiguously defined space. The practice of graffiti emphasizes the free commercial quality of urban spaces in general, a quality in contrast to the actual paucity of available private space.[41]

Ahearn's *mise-en-scène* underscores the unstable and permeable border between the inside and outside, between legal and illegal spaces, and, most dramatically, between the functions of "home" and street.

Other rap musicals of this era do not undertake such a drastic reconfiguration of "home" as a locus for communal interaction, but in most of these films it is still the street (rather than the domestic interior) that provides the focal point of communal gatherings and rituals. Interestingly, what cultural anthropologist Melvin Williams wrote of the impoverished African American Pittsburgh neighborhood Belmar is relevant here:

> "Home" for the "genuine" Blacks in Belmar is "just a stopping-off place." It is a "motel" where you sleep, eat, and "hide, if you have to." But it is not one's "hearth," "castle," or showplace for entertaining. The street corner, the tavern, the "speakeasy," a favorite stoop, or the neighborhood "greasy spoon" are where people, especially men, "hang out." This variation of location is referred to as "down the way," "up the way," "hit the street," "over the way," and the "avenue." Most "genuine" Blacks have never had the consistent resources to furnish and maintain a home, so they spend most of their interactional time out of the house. Part of the mystique of out-of-home interaction is the potential for including large numbers of people. One of the techniques is loud communication. Thus, all within hearing distance are welcome to interact and respond to "what's going on."[42]

Wild Style showcases the domestic squalor and transformation of a Latino home in particular, but the observations made by Williams in the 1970s about a black community in Pittsburgh seem to ring true for the inhabitants of the South Bronx in Ahearn's film as well, regardless of their race. Thus, the function of hip hop for communities of color is partly an extension of organizational structures that ensured the largest potential for public participation in political and social rituals. This model for collective communication and interaction described by Williams shows how multiple public spaces in less prosperous urban black communities replaced the importance and centrality of the family home found in the classical-era folk musical, and indeed the heart of white middle-class American mythology. As he notes, "home" (one's actual domestic living quarters) functions more like a place where one fulfills necessary duties (like sleeping and eating) instead of providing a nurturing space of social interaction for the black residents of Belmar. Likewise, all of the important actions and rituals that bring people together in the hip hop musical occur outside of the symbolic confines of "home." Williams's observations are about a specific black community, yet they are important here because they illustrate the ways in which many facets of hip hop culture are in fact coping mechanisms for life in an impoverished inner-city region. Neighborhood spirit is not gauged by displays of domestic exterior extravagance, a common measure of communal pride in suburbia. Rather, exhibitions of individual creativity that are fleeting, ephemeral, and within public view, such as graffiti murals and impromptu dance numbers, displace the physical presentation of suburban neighborhood pride so neatly evoked by the imagery of the perfect white picket fence. Even through historically the *Afro-American* Clean Block Drive encouraged urban blacks to emulate postwar suburbia's fascination with uniformity, orderliness, and superficial perfection in their communities, these goals, perhaps, seemed less important and less within reach given the rapid decline of inner-city housing and other infrastructures in the early 1980s.

It can be said that the representation of "home" in the hip hop musical is structured in two different but related manners. Firstly, the true hip hop musical reveals how the family residence is no longer a productive site for social bonding. For instance, *Wild Style* and *Beat Street* point to the failure of governmental bodies to maintain the infrastructure of inner-city communities by visually documenting the actual dilapidated housing of the South Bronx. When domestic spaces are revealed in *Wild Style*, they become sites of confrontation used to underscore the inadequacy of housing structures in disadvantaged urban neighborhoods. *Rappin'* is largely about the need for better homes and domestic services in an impoverished urban locale, and Rappinhood, the "music man" of the film, becomes a community activist on his journey towards romantic success and stardom. In this film, the home is an actual menace to the health of poor citizens as the community nearly freezes to death waiting for heat that has been turned off by a greedy landlord. In *Krush Groove*, musical bonding rituals occur almost entirely in public spaces, while we see very few domestic interiors. In contrast, the classical-era folk musical usually featured one or more musical numbers within a domestic setting that brought the family and extended family of neighbors together within a neatly proscribed space of social ritual, representing a positive symbol of familial and communal spirit. The true hip hop musical inverts this spatial norm in order to reveal how the family home has in fact become non-nurturing, claustrophobic, and even life- threatening for certain populations.

Secondly, the representation of "home" is reduced or completely elided in some examples drawn from the surface hip hop musical. In *Breakin' Through* and *Delivery Boys*, this omission can be explained by the fact that poverty and problematic living situations of inner-city neighborhoods are not important aspects of the films. In the case of *Body Rock*, as noted earlier, we do witness the impoverishment of the main character's living quarters, yet there is no link between his indigence and the plight of the rest of his community. *Delivery Boys* and *Breakin' Through* simply avoided any polemic or socially charged material, and the absence of a black or Latino inner-city household in a film supposedly about hip hop culture functions differently across the spectrum of early hip hop cinema.

The displacement or absence of the actual home in the surface hip hop musical, and the complete transformation of it in *Wild Style*, are radical reconfigurations of the conservative exchanges, values, and rituals that signified "home" in the classical folk musical. Contested notions of "home" invoked a volatile and troubled discourse for the nation in general at this time, and specifically for inner-city neighborhoods. I have discussed in the first chapter how the massive failure to provide adequate housing for many of the nation's poorest urban communities had been exposed in national news media following President Carter's widely publicized visit to the South Bronx in 1977. Just a few years later, President Reagan vowed to transform this devastated area through tax incentives and the involvement of private industry, but his policies achieved the opposite effect; the gap between the wealthiest and poorest citizens widened and the number of people living in poverty—particularly black and Hispanic children—increased.[43] Granted, poverty rates had risen during Carter's presidency, but social programs had been created or buttressed in the 1970s rather than reduced or eliminated. The Reagan administration, in contrast, endeavored to roll back spending or eliminate altogether a number of programs related to child abuse, neglect prevention, as well as juvenile delinquency.[44] African American families became more vulnerable on several fronts when changes to governmental policy, which reduced or eliminated programs that had previously protected the rights of minorities, took effect during the early 1980s.[45] Under Reagan, federal assistance programs across the board were dismantled or significantly reduced.[46] This was particularly troublesome for black families because they (even those whose members were working) have statistically been more reliant on government assistance than nonminority families, and their income levels actually diminished in the first few years of the decade compared to other sectors of the population.[47] Even when relatively sympathetic mainstream media attempted to assess the status of African American families in the mid-1980s, the results were less than admirable. "The Vanishing Family—Crisis in Black America," a CBS report helmed by Bill Moyers, was met with vitriol by the black community because it appeared to repress the institutional roots of black poverty and the reality of diminishing access to public programs in favor of what historian Manning Marable decried as a "'blame the victim' thesis of black poverty."[48] In fact, the year that *Wild Style* was completed marked the highest poverty rate for black children in America since the U.S. Census Bureau began compiling and recording poverty statistics. While trying to find a neat and conclusive correlation between statistical data and cinematic production is certainly not the goal of this argument, it is significant that this film emerges at a time when children of color, their families, and the material infrastructure of urban communities were considerably destabilized, rendering the search for meaningful articulations of "home," family, and community increasingly urgent.

According to Altman, the folk musical often called up a distant past in order to expurgate all of the unpleasant aspects of that earlier historical period. He notes that the classic Hollywood folk musical used various aspects of American regional popular culture, and that this "lens" of folk culture helped to romanticize and cast a mythic glow upon American history.[49] Although earlier black-cast folk musicals such as *Hearts in Dixie* and *Cabin in the Sky* often reveal music and dance to be the most important cohesive activity undertaken by the rural black community, group performance frequently only laments personal failings. The threat to collective harmony comes from within the group rather than outside.[50] One of the first all-black cast films by a major studio, *Hallelujah!* (1929), is exemplary here. In this film, the organization of labor that allowed for the systematic exploitation of black rural cotton pickers is not scrutinized as a problem for the community. Instead, the moral weakness of one man, Zeke, is responsible for all of the hardship and suffering. He loses six months wages earned by the entire family, refuses the affections of a morally respectable girl from his community, and causes the death of his brother. Thus, poverty, familial grief, and neighborhood tensions are attributed to the actions of the individual rather than the systemic racial exclusions and inequities of the hegemonic social order and economy.

In contrast, *Wild Style* documents urban poverty without romanticizing the living conditions of inner-city residents and it highlights communal solutions rather than focusing solely on personal weakness as a destructive force for the collective. As noted earlier, *Beat Street* even explores the plight of a family who is forced to squat in an abandoned building because there is no adequate affordable housing. While there are occasionally "bad" individuals in these films (such as the character Spit in *Beat Street* who covers other graffiti artist's work), the use of folk musical devices in several hip hop musicals, such as an emphasis on the neighborhood as socially inclusive, and the demonstration of communal cohesion and values through amateur performance, facilitates creative and productive responses to oppressive material conditions rather than focusing on individual shortcomings.

Reflexivity, Animation and Social Critique in *Wild Style*

Ahearn filmed one of the most successful sequences of *Wild Style* as a tribute to Robert Wise and Jerome Robbins's *West Side Story* (1961).[51] However, instead of presenting the problem of urban divisions as violent warfare between racial groups (represented by the white working-class Jets and the Puerto Rican Sharks in Wise and Robbins's film), Ahearn constructs a city space of performance that frequently crosses racial divides. This cinematic tribute, shot in an inner-city basketball court, features rival crews Cold Crush and Fantastic Five engaging in a competitive rap session while performing a stylized dance inflected basketball game. The references to *West Side Story*'s opening shots of New York's Spanish Harlem are very specific, from the use of urban basketball courts to the decisive snapping of fingers that anticipate the number. Furthermore, the inscription of gang territory is marked in the earlier film by graffiti as well. These two films, however, differ radically in their appraisal of the sublimation of violence into performance. In *West Side Story* the initial friction between the Sharks and the Jets is represented through dance but this rivalry later culminates in a violent, ultimately lethal rumble at the end of the film. Conversely, the competitive performance aspects of *Wild Style* suggest that the potential for youth gang conflict can be fully diffused through its redirection into creative forces.

A decade before Ahearn's film was released, graffiti and gang culture in New York City sometimes shared a close relationship as rival gangs waged war on each other through violence as well as competitive tagging. Graffiti writers without gang affiliations were occasionally subject to harassment and beatings when they ventured into unfamiliar municipal regions.[52] To secure their safety, a gang of Brooklyn-based graffiti writers, the Ex-Vandals (short for Experienced Vandals)—whose only purpose was writing—emerged in the early 1970s.[53] A decade later, the desire to transform the brutality of youth gang interactions into non-violent and creative entities is largely how hip hop culture developed, according to most sources. Afrika Bambaataa and other former gang members created the Bronx-based Zulu Nation, "a loose organization dedicated to peace and survival," and promoted performance and hip hop as creative ways to end strife between youth gangs in inner-city neighborhoods.[54] David Toop writes that early venues for hip hop culture such as community dances "helped bring former rival gangs together. In the transition from outright war, the hierarchical gang structure mutated into comparatively peaceful groups, called crews."[55] *Wild Style*'s basketball rap is an example of this potentially radical diffusion of violence into competitive performance, uniquely situating this utopian aspect of inner-city youth culture within the generic boundaries of an integrated musical number.

There is little statistical data on gang violence in inner-city regions at this time, nor could one really attain accurate numbers relating to the escalation or lessening of these incidents. Sally Banes, in her review of the breakdance manual *Breakdancing* (1984), is skeptical of the arguments made on behalf of breaking as an alternative to gang violence. After an unfavorable evaluation of the manual, she tersely quips "And, the book claims that as a result of breaking, gang warfare has stopped in the Bronx (!)."[56] On the other hand, in July of 1984 *Newsweek* reported that a Denver high school was embracing breakdance as a successful strategic alternative to gang violence:

> At North High School in Denver, where fighting erupts regularly between rival gangs, kids have begun to break-dance in the hallways between classes.

"It's a way to be No. 1 without blowing somebody away," says Pierre Jiminez, director of a Denver juvenile-delinquency program who pushed for a city-sponsored break-dance contest.[57]

Boston Globe reporter Ethan Bronner also noted that

on a recent Saturday afternoon at radio station WMBR in Cambridge, two black teen-agers with a long-standing rivalry nearly came to blows as they waited for disc jockey Magnus Johnstone to interview them. Seeing trouble through the glass of his studio, Johnstone intervened, asking "Do you want to battle with the beef or the word? If with the word, let's do it on the air." The two aspiring "rap" musicians accepted his offer. Using rap's driving boastful idiom, they fought it out on the airwaves through a formalized singsong duel of rhymes each had written, mirroring similar "battles" held in parks and on street corners throughout Roxbury and other black sections of Greater Boston.[58]

Mandalit del Barco, writing in 1984, asserted that "by all accounts, break-dancing has become a substitute for violence."[59] She backs up this claim with the words of Lorenzo "Kuriaki" Soto, a member of Rock Steady Crew:

Instead of fighting, we break against each other.... If I was dancing and somebody were to say, "You're whack, man. You don't even got the good moves," I'd tell him instead, "Well, I'll battle you." Right there, instead of me coming up and hitting him, I'd say, "I'll battle you, see how good you are." Whoever has the most moves wins.[60]

Interestingly, *Delivery Boys*, the juvenile hip hop musical parody, ridiculed this serious and potentially progressive aspect of hip hop culture. During this film's final show number, the Brooklyn Bridge Break Dance Contest, the event's corporate sponsor extols the virtues of breaking's ability to circumvent violence. In fact, he even refers to this practice, and hip hop culture in general, as a "new hope for the young people of our nation's inner cities" and a "new way of settling difference." However, not long after the contest begins, increasingly aggressive dance moves between the rival crews (the Devil Dogs and the Delivery Boys) degenerate into an all-out gang brawl. Competitive performance, the very heart of hip hop culture, is shown to be the catalyst to gang violence in this film. *Wild Style*, in contrast, maintains hip hop's utopian promise of channeling conflict into dance through organized competition.

It is difficult to argue convincingly that competitive rap and breakdance contests in the early 1980s indisputably stemmed gang warfare, but hip hop culture's push to assemble complex grassroots inner-city organizations dedicated to solving an urban problem is in itself a momentous and laudable achievement. Without a doubt, many youth who were pulled towards hip hop crews interested in developing skills rather than fighting were positively affected, learning to cope with anger and frustration through means other than violence.[61] As a testament to the continuing relevance of this facet of early hip hop culture, the sublimation of physical conflict through dance has continued to be explored in youth films of the later 1980s and into the 1990s, including *Rooftops* (1989) and *Only the Strong* (1993).[62]

Ahearn's *West Side Story*–influenced "basketball number" brings dance and athletics together as two opposing teams or "crews" battle each other through rhyme and choreographed movements, all the while chasing the ball across an inner-city court. This number makes reference to a specific iconic musical number but it also neatly brings the relationship between violence and performance to bear on the concept of integration within the musical film genre. As noted in the opening chapter, the term "integration" refers to the myriad ways in which a musical number relates to the overarching thematic concerns of the narrative. Musical film numbers generally conform to two modes of performance—spontaneous musical outbursts derived from an everyday encounter and song and dance numbers confined to the actual space of the stage proscenium. The first instance often transcends the boundaries of realism to offer a spectacle of utopian artifice while the second usually consists of a realistic use of sound and space.[63] Although both types of musical numbers may relate to the plot or theme of the film, the former is usually more closely linked with revealing thematic or emotional plot information because it arises directly from situations and speech contained in the film narrative. Thus, the naturally occurring musical performance is most closely associated with the concept of the integrated musical number within the genre.

In *Wild Style*'s basketball throwdown, the transition from speech to song as a natural occurrence arising from the plot is certainly in place, unavoidably so, since rapping is already directly derived from everyday speech. Individual members of the crews answer back and forth to one another in increasingly challenging rhymes directed both at individuals and the gang as a whole. Because crew competition is one of the overarching themes of *Wild Style*, by the time this number occurs, the motivation for the scene is in fact already inscribed in the film through many prior displays of creative rivalry.

The competitive theme of this musical number is highlighted by the lyrics of the rap because the names of the two opposing crews—the Cold Crush Brothers and Fantastic Five—are repeated throughout the performance. Members of the two groups also state their own individual names during the rhyme, emphasizing the unique components of each organization. The initial movements of the number are choreographed to match the competitive boasts asserted by the rappers who physically challenge one other as each new crew member is introduced. Camerawork in this sequence utilizes both rapid editing and sustained long takes that follow the ball through the air as it travels between players and the net. In the latter instance, the movement is so quick that the resulting images often resemble a blur of outstretched arms and leaping torsos while the two crews vie for possession of the ball. When the camera directly follows the actual movements of the basketball this underscores the escalating confrontational "dance" of the two crews by imitating the conventional style of filming sports games for televised broadcast. Thus, the musical content, dance expression, and camera movement of the number all work towards conveying a central concern of the film: the competitive configurations of hip hop culture that developed from organized youth contests.

As the camera enthusiastically follows the basketball, it also brings into view the surrounding spaces and faces of the inner city and shows us a chorus line of young female rappers commenting on the two crews. The edge of the cinematic frame reveals a vibrant picture of inner-city life as it captures other ball games, graffiti-laden walls, tenement blocks, and onlookers. Documentary images of street life in the South Bronx are completely fused with the spaces of a musical performance in this sequence. A sustained focus on the rappers movements, rather than preventing documentary aspects from entering into the screen, actually facilitates their inclusion.

Wild Style is not only a musical, but also a dramatized documentary or docudrama.[64] As such, it complicates any traditional discussion of reflexivity within the musical, and also helps illuminate a central contradiction of the documentary film: the form attempts to heighten the realistic experience of the film world for the spectator through its exploration of actual events and persons, but paradoxically its employment of non-trained

Fig. 2.4. Basketball Throwdown in *Wild Style* (1983): Rival MC crews from the Bronx, The Cold Crush vs. The Fantastic. Photographer: Cathy Campbell; courtesy of Charlie Ahearn.

actors also functions to fracture the illusionism of the cinematic diegesis. Ahearn based *Wild Style* on his own observations and experiences of the South Bronx community in the 1980s. The main protagonists and the supporting cast were not professional actors but part of the community that the film attempted to capture and present as a fictionalized narrative loosely based on actual events. Thus, the "quality" of acting does not conform to mainstream Hollywood expectations. It is important to note here that many documentaries made before the innovation of compact and easily portable sound and visual recording equipment were, to a large degree, dramatized documentaries. Technology did not permit the filmmaker to record spontaneously until approximately the mid-twentieth century. Before this time, most approaches to documentary filmmaking concerning living people closely conformed to Ahearn's method: the subjects would be studied and these observations were then organized and narrativized by the filmmaker. The subjects of the film would subsequently participate in the reconstruction of certain "truths" about their culture or particular situation by "acting" in the resulting film, which was, by all contemporary accounts, considered a documentary.[65]

Writers like Ellin Stein enthusiastically detailed Ahern's use of hip hop practitioners and art gallery mavens to play roles based on their own personal experiences in New York City.[66] Other hip hop musicals also made use of talented dancers, rappers, and performers who were important figures within the subculture. For instance, *Krush Groove* featured "real" rappers and "authentic" talent such as LL Cool J, Run-D.M.C., the Fat Boys (the Disco Three), New Edition, the Beastie Boys, Kurtis Blow, and Russell Simmons. The film, which fictionalizes the story of Russell Simmons's record label Def Jam and his relationship with Run-D.M.C. and Kurtis Blow, cast Run-D.M.C. as themselves (Blair Underwood played the role of Russell Simmons). Simmons was also involved in the writing of the film's screenplay. *Beat Street*, likewise, has been lauded by critics for attempting to realistically capture ghetto life while using experienced hip hop practitioners.[67] Additionally, the extras hired for club scenes in the film were actual patrons of the Roxy, a move that enhanced "the film's authenticity," according to the *Afro-American*.[68] To gauge the importance of "authenticity"—location shooting and actors culled from hip hop subculture—when these films were first received, consider dance reporter Kevin Grubb's enthusiastic (albeit overstated) account of *Beat Street*'s "documentary impulses":

> There are no studio sets in the forthcoming feature film *Beat Street*. The "set" for the movie, one of the first to focus on break dancers and rap musicians, is the urban landscape of New York: the crumbling tenements of the South Bronx, traffic-thronged city streets, dressed-down hip-hop clubs. In this authentic environment, *Beat Street*'s cast is right at home, for most of them have grown up here. Their dance and their music are products of an inner-borough upbringing, an outgrowth of a society that grudgingly condones subway graffiti, ghetto blasters, and head spins on the sidewalk.[69]

While Grubb accurately characterized the setting of *Beat Street*, the film's "music man," Guy Davis, was the son of renowned actor, playwright, and activist Ossie Davis, and female lead Rae Dawn Chong, daughter of actor Tommy Chong, was Canadian. The film, however, did feature other cast members who grew up in impoverished inner-city New York communities and were directly involved in hip hop culture. Moreover, even the most commercially-oriented hip hop musicals, like the *Breakin'* films, included emerging hip hop talent such as Ice-T.

The hip hop musical as a subgenre is inconsistent in this respect since rapping could be performed by someone without experience in such vocal stylings, and graffiti might also be simulated by a film crew (as was the case in *Beat Street*) rather than using the available urban milieu and actual inner-city writers. A convincing depiction of breakdancing, however, must involve the casting of actual performers schooled in this style of dance. For this reason, even though breakdance-oriented films were the most commercially saturated of all hip hop cinema, these productions paradoxically had to utilize actual hip hop practitioners. Despite the garish costuming and repression of graffiti culture in the *Breakin'* films, they were firmly linked to "real" hip hop talent through the casting of urban dance innovator Adolfo "Shabba Doo" Quinones, who had previously appeared on *Soul Train* and *Saturday Night Live* with his groundbreaking dance group the Lockers, and rising electric boogie dance star Michael "Boogaloo Shrimp" Chambers in leading roles. Quinones was quick to emphasize his "street cred" in interviews with the African American press. Shortly after the release of *Breakin' 2*, for instance, he told the *Afro-American* that "being from the streets, I can assume all kinds of characters, based on what I saw in the ghetto in Chicago."[70] Quinones also contributed to *Breakin's* script.[71] Likewise, as noted earlier, Ahearn's film takes us closer to "real" characters and spaces through the use of location shooting and the employment of amateurs connected to the actual events of the film.

Wild Style also inserts animation sequences into the live-action portions of the film, causing a further disruption of spatial continuity and narrative flow. These strategies can usefully be considered instances of reflexivity—a process by which a text acknowledges its medium of production, specific intertextual references, and in some cases, its reception and authorship.[72] *Wild Style* makes use of several reflexive devices—lack of naturalism in acting style and the insertion of animated sequences within a live-action narrative—which function to demystify the cinematic text and allude to its status as a crafted object. Paradoxically, these moments of fracture and demystification, which are closely tied to experimental and avant-garde filmmaking strategies, are also strongly connected to the overall structure of the film as an exploration of hip hop culture.[73] For instance, the animation that punctuates the film recalls the act of graffiti writing not only because the two are closely related forms of visual expression—they are both graphic arts—but also because many of these initial animated sequences include images of graffiti-style writing. Robert Stam suggests that animation and the musical film are linked by their shared tendencies towards anti-illusionism.[74] Characters in both types of cinema are usually endowed with the magical ability to transgress the parameters of the physical world and transcend corporeal limitations, such as when

Fred Astaire dances on ceilings and walls and when the Roadrunner survives numerous head on collisions with highway traffic.[75]

Both animated sequences that occur in *Wild Style* are set to music and feature, respectively, the words of the opening credits and a scene of sexual exploration at a late-night hotel room party. In the latter animation sequence, Phade, Raymond, and rapper Busy Bee attempt to seduce a trio of girls at the Alps Hotel, after a club competition victory by Busy Bee. The girls, who are lured to the local hotel after being promised a night at the Hyatt, are initially disappointed. However, they soon warm up to the three men and we witness an intense and rollicking party scene as rapid editing captures the revelers passing joints, sharing beer, and throwing around the money Busy Bee earned from the evening's performance. This is intercut with animated images of sexually explicit acts and a live-action shot of lacy red bras falling to the hotel floor. Throughout this party sequence, the spectator is acutely aware that the animated figures, to some extent, are blocking the view of "actual" sexually explicit material. The cartoons are crudely drawn, distinguished by a bright but minimal palate, and each figure is rendered in only one color with a consistent black background. In this sequence, the sexual desire of the characters on-screen is transposed onto a group of drawn images instead of being articulated through a live-action performance number—the typical vehicle for expressing amorous desire in the Hollywood musical. These animated figures acknowledge the particular history of the musical genre, which although steeped in sexual tension, rarely visually articulates sexually explicit images.[76] Such deliberately unsophisticated cartoon images of sexuality transgress the limits of the musical genre with their highly erotic content while simultaneously upholding its prudish antecedents by visually hiding the "real" scenes of explicit sexual content.

The opening sequence of *Wild Style*, which conveys the film credits through animated words, deserves special attention. Artists began working on the animation sequence in the summer of 1982, and the unique result was a collaboration between graffiti artist Zephyr (who plays Zroc in the film), Revolt (animation student Joey Ahlbum), and Becky High.[77] It was intended to be a representation of the graffiti writer's "black book," described by Zephyr as "bound sketchbooks that we'd fill with 'pieces' or 'styles,' that we'd execute with thin black Flair pens and colored alcohol markers; Design markers were our favorite."[78] Graffiti artists carried their books with them so that their work was always available to be seen by other writers. Zephyr also notes that these books functioned as a conduit of influence between graffiti writers, and as a secondary circuit of

Fig. 2.5. Animation cell from *Wild Style* (1983) by Zephyr. Courtesy of Charlie Ahearn.

movement, which distributed the artist's work throughout the urban environment.[79] The film sequence, which was created with paper and colored markers—the same materials writers used to create their "black books"—included words such as "BREAK," "POP," "WILD STYLE," and "RAP," an image of the New York skyline, stars, and a moving subway car. Words dominate the opening credits. For instance, the sequence begins with an animated image of the word "GRAFFITI" exploding to unleash the rest of the visual material. Subsequently, a human figure emerges from the letter "O" in the word "POP" after it appears on screen. Words appear first in this animated sequence and they give rise to pictorial forms and human figuration as the segment progresses. *Wild Style*'s animated words are also very different from typical animated opening credits. The words found in the film's opening sequence seem to dance across the screen in perpetual motion, pulsating with movement; they truly are *animated*. This treatment of the text as image incorporates the perceived sense of movement accorded to the word within the particular style of graffiti referred to as "wild style," which the film showcases. As Ahearn notes, the graffiti writer makes letters dance; he or she animates them.[80]

Wild Style's initial animated sequence expresses this attribute of graffiti by equating the word with movement, a quality not usually associated with film credits or other conventional forms of writing. Letters dance just as people dance in musical film, and in this way the words of graffiti are conceived of as central characters in the film's narrative. This opening gesture therefore ties the practice of graffiti, and the animation of the word, to the tradition of the Hollywood musical, a form that relies on the centrality of dance to express emotional states and plot advancements. Subway trains, perhaps the most famous urban canvas for graffiti, also suggest a perpetual "dance" throughout the city.

As the opening credits demonstrate, the word becomes image in graffiti writing; it is the center of visual interest and it displaces the primacy of the pictorial image grounded in mimetic principles. In Western art history, the pictorial image has traditionally been the center of artistic expression. This was challenged somewhat in the 1960s and '70s with the rise of conceptualism, a practice that frequently presented the written word or a set of words as the center of artistic focus.[81] In these projects, the formal rendering of the word was usually not an exercise in the display of artistic virtuosity. The text suggested an idea to the spectator, and the idea itself was the important aspect of the piece rather than the skill used to craft and fashion the actual object located in the gallery or museum. This institutional art shared a key concept of the urban vernacular of graffiti, which came to prominence at roughly the same time. In both practices, the word literally became the center of visual interest, yet graffiti maintains very traditional values that run almost counter to conceptual art. In fact, graffiti places a high value on artistic displays of virtuosity—an aspect forcefully absent in conceptual art—with the most intricate and skillfully executed textual images garnering the highest accolades in the subculture. Although such a traditional veneration of formal skills is apparent in the rapid development and proliferation of distinct styles in the early 1980s, graffiti culture also permitted a more democratic route to fame in that a writer who was prolific could command respect even if his or her tags and "throw ups" were hastily rendered and poorly executed.[82]

Graffiti also returns language to the "primitive" form of the pictogram, a type of visual representation in which the signifier was closely wed to the signified.[83] This kind of written communication was supplanted by the alphabet system, a form that is premised upon the "effacement of the signifier."[84] These histories of written language are particularly relevant to the painted image of Zoro we see in the film—a literal representation of a well-known character's profile. The signifier bears a mimetic relation to the signified, yet meaning is deferred because the signifier relates not to the original character Zoro, but to a young artist who has co-opted his image as a signature. In contrast, it would seem that the word Zoro—and indeed all wild style forms of graffiti in which an artist's chosen name is rendered through a highly stylized alphabet—is an intensification of the later historical development of the alphabet whereby written language is transformed into an arbitrary system in which the link between signifier and signified is completely broken. This assessment is complicated, moreover, by the fact that each graffiti artist is generally associated with a particular and distinct visual style. Therefore, the population of graffiti writers, and others in the community in general, would be able to decipher the *meaning* (the identification of a particular work with a specific person) of a piece through its stylistic characteristics or unique flourish. Thus, the word or signifier constituted through an arbitrary language system returns to the realm of the pictorial, but this return is only partial since the decipherability of the image is dependent upon a certain familiarity with the practice of graffiti culture. The circulation of graffiti images in the film, both in its live-action portions and animated sequences, challenges the threshold between pictorial and arbitrary signification.

Julian Stallabrass has argued that graffiti travels a parallel history with advertising culture in terms of the relationship between signification and referent. He notes, "Graffiti fails as a symbol because of the mismatch between real identities and the tags which are supposed to stand in for them but only end up representing themselves."[85] In his effort to show that graffiti mimics the aims of modern advertising—the repression of the commodity's actual conditions of manufacture and the fact of its discrete material components—Stallabrass emphasizes the apparent erasure of the body at work in graffiti culture.[86] He insists that the written name or tag becomes a meaningless form of branding whereby "identity is a progressively disappearing point, discarding all qualities behind the mask of the sign."[87] In contrast, I have been arguing that this is something Ahearn's film implores us to see—graffiti culture is precisely about the presence of the body and the process of creation as a work of art. Ubiquitous tags and large graffiti pieces were not emptied of meaning as they invaded the urban environment in the 1980s. To the contrary, they participated in a dialogue in which spatial terrain was a constantly shifting and highly politicized arena of social "play." Stallabrass's evocative essay ends with an eloquent articulation of the historical processes of graffiti, what he describes as the overwriting of the graffiti surface—a cacophony of multiple voices that long for recognition as they crumble into one another.

This unintentionally radical result is, for Stallabrass, a "comment on fragmentation, the loss of meaning, and the decline of writing under commercial culture."[88] As romantic as this vision is, it does not account for the historical specificities of voices that were part of this archeologically embedded dialogue. Further, Stallabrass does not relate graffiti to other tenets of hip hop culture and his essay works to tie this practice closely to the repetitious nature of advertising rather than explore the dichotomy of individualism and collectivity that characterize graffiti as an art form in the United States.

In contrast, as noted earlier, *Wild Style* sought to unite a romantic individuated persona of the graffiti artist with communal cohesion, as well as historical *avant-garde* art practice. This connection to twentieth century art history extended not only the content of the film but also to Ahearn's formal strategies. The director has remarked that he was hoping to achieve a cubist strategy of editing within the film. His original commitment to this approach was somewhat undercut by the demands of his editor, but the finished work retains a disjointed and often abrupt quality. Ahearn notes that his initial intent to connect the overall artistic effect of the film to various aspects of hip hop culture was tethered to an understanding of hip hop as being intimately related to earlier twentieth century *avant-garde* movements. He writes that

> the aesthetic of the DJ back-spinning a record relates to a kind of cubist idea of cutting up and rearranging the original. A lot of scenes I had arranged to music would have shown up visually like a record you're back-spinning, so that they would run forward, backward, and recreate in a visual medium what is going on with the rap artists and the breakdancers. I wanted to spin the images on themselves.[89]

He has also described the practice of the hip hop DJ, graffiti writer, and breakdancer in terms of "kinetic cubism" whereby bits of records are rearranged, manipulated, and recombined by the DJ, while the breaker and graffiti writer use a highly stylized and original approach to manipulating the compositional figurations of the body, and the established linear forms of the letter.[90] Cubism and Futurism's interest in fracturing the spatial plane, Fauvism's appropriation of bright non-naturalistic colors, and Abstract Expressionism's embrace of everyday materials and broad muscular gestures structured Ahearn's vision of hip hop culture. Thus, the aesthetic quality of the film's various reflexive characteristics—disjointed editing and the intrusion of animation into the live-action format—are actually related to *Wild Style*'s attempt to fully represent the artistic sensibilities of hip hop as the inheritor of modern art strategies.

In *Wild Style*, the historical presumptions of reflexivity within the musical are vastly complicated by its link to the musical and performance strategies of hip hop. The film's reflexivity is different from the variety associated with Hollywood musicals of the 1930s, which often included a knowing wink to the camera or an exaggerated gesture meant to reveal the personality trait of a character. These cinematic flourishes of the classical era, while disrupting the transparency of the medium, nevertheless worked towards an overall cinematic harmony.[91] They also united spectators within a shared cinematic fantasy, and are generally considered to promote feelings of incorporation within the diegesis of the film for the spectator rather than fracture or disjuncture. When Maurice Chevalier winks or smiles directly into the camera during *Love Me Tonight*, for instance, he acknowledges the presence of the camera but simultaneously invites the film spectator to be in on the joke. In contrast, *Wild Style* fosters an ambivalent spectatorial experience. On the one hand, the narrative is held together by the established conventions of the Hollywood film musical and therefore works toward narrative coherence. On the other, the various elements of reflexivity I have described—animated sequences, disjunctive editing practices, and non-naturalistic acting—disrupt the flow of continuity and fracture the narrative space and coherent diegesis of the film.

Furthermore, if *Wild Style*'s basketball number can be considered a traditional integrated number, it nevertheless challenges the narrative links assigned to the integrated musical performance by Altman.[92] Altman argues that the musical number functions to reconcile two mutually exclusive terms introduced in the plot of the film, usually the male and female leads. But how do we account for a musical film in which none of the "stars" are musical performers? *Wild Style*'s romantic leads are also not even present in two of the main musical numbers, the "Basketball Rap" and the "Stoop Rap." The two stars of the film might not be musical entertainers, but like the typical folk musical, the concept of amateur performance suffuses every aspect of the film. Living in the inner city is described *as* performing for the teenagers and young adults in Ahearn's film (the same can be said of *Beat Street*, *Krush Groove*, and to some extent several characters in *Rappin'* and the *Breakin'* series). The differences between Raymond and Rose, and everyone else in *Wild Style*, are somehow significantly reduced because, according to the film, everyone can be captured as a performer.

This attenuation of distance between "stars," supporting actors, and spectators further enhances the documentary aspect of the film. Even though *Wild Style* was a totally scripted documentary drama, Ahearn's camera spends a great deal of time filming urban spaces that don't necessarily further the plot. The street and the everyday encounters of urban life are also in many ways the "stars" of the film.[93] Thus, the two main integrated musical sequences entirely leave out our protagonist, and at moments the power and space of the street totally encroaches on the narrative trajectory of the film. In fact, *Wild Style* deliberately democratizes performance spaces, creating a productive generic tension. The ostensible discord between the musical genre's utopian impulses and documentary cinema's aspirations toward social critique has permeated criticism of this film. For instance Jean Fisher writes that

> in some respects, despite its assembly of original and articulate talent, *Wild Style* represents a missed opportunity to establish an "alternative" movie in the spirit of its own subject matter, or to open up a serious debate on the impulses that generate a subcultural network of codes and on their ambivalent relation to a wider cultural context. With the exception of a few panning shots of the semi-derelict landscape of the South Bronx and passing references to the origins of subway graffiti, *Wild Style* does not attempt to function as social documentary.[94]

I am not sure what the "missed opportunity" referred to here is since the film showed occupants of a notoriously oppressive social space responding positively to the challenges presented by this harsh urban environment. It is precisely the juxtaposition of "semi-derelict landscapes" with images of vigorous and creative responses to poverty and social constraints that thrust the film into the realm of social criticism. Moreover, all of the images of graffiti in the film—not just the "passing references to the origins of subway graffiti"—function as social critique. This is especially true given that part of the rhetoric of graffiti writing in the 1980s was, contrary to the views of most mainstream culture, communal beautification. Of the public's initial reaction to his crew's first full graffiti car, Lee Quinones notes that "they probably didn't know it was graffiti; they probably thought the city was doing something good for a change. They probably thought they paid some muralist to do it."[95]

If documentaries have historically been concerned with everyday life and the exposition of various unusual, problematic, or unacceptable social conditions, the musical has been largely concerned with spaces of fantasy, imagination, and utopian desires.[96] *Wild Style* brings these two approaches to filmmaking together by using documentary strategies in an inventive way that imagines a progressive social space of performance with the power to transcend the particular problems of inner-city life. Even if Ahearn received some criticism for what was seen as the "whitewashing" of certain negative aspects of the South Bronx—namely, heroin and violence—this enabled him to capitalize on the most important theoretical aspect of the musical: to imagine what an idealized community might feel like, or at least what it might look and sound like.[97] In response to this type of criticism of *Wild Style*, Ellin Stein notes that Ahearn is not "oblivious to these problems but he feels that this is usually the only side of ghetto life presented in the media."[98] The majority of true hip hop musicals function in a similar manner—as a positive and affirmative counter to the tremendously pessimistic media coverage that plagued inner city communities at this time.

Wild Style overwhelmingly celebrates the power to be found in noncommercial spaces of creativity associated with hip hop culture in the early 1980s—the painterly gestures of graffiti production, the art of creating innovative rhymes, muscular "kinetic" dance moves in breakdancing, and cutting up a record. Most importantly, it suggests that the ever-present image of graffiti art offered a means to transform the "real" geographical spaces of the city and that youth culture more generally occupies a prominent place in the progressive reordering of communal relations.

Hip Hoppers and Valley Girls
The Economic and Racial Structuring of Youth Cinema in the 1980s

The Teen Film: An Overview

Young people have been captured on film since the birth of the medium, yet the development of what is now identified as a coherent genre, the teen film, has been heterogeneous and contested. Timothy Shary notes that children rather than teenagers seemed to dominate the image of youth in the 1920s, although some later films featuring adolescents (such as *Port of Missing Girls* [1928]) attempted to exploit adult fears about teen sexual desire.[1] Indeed, the parent culture's anxiety about both juvenile delinquency and adolescent sexuality have consistently framed youthful representations on screen with significant entries from both mainstream production companies (*The Wild Ones*, 1953; *Rebel Without a Cause*, 1955) and smaller exploitation-oriented enterprises (*Teenage Crime Wave*, 1955; *Teenage Gang Debs*, 1966).[2] Prior to these mid-century productions, Warner Bros. and Universal also made a number of "social problem" films dealing with crime, juvenile delinquency, and poverty throughout the 1930s. Adolescence was consistently defined negatively in relation to delinquency during the early part of the twentieth century, and it was a category largely invented in order to monitor and "correct" the undesirable behavior of teenaged persons.[3] If adolescence was "invented" as a problem to be investigated by medical doctors and social scientists at the turn of the twentieth century—most notoriously in G. Stanley Hall's *Adolescence: Its Psychology and Its Relations to Physiology, Anthropology, Sociology, Sex, Crime, Religion and Education* (1904)—the cinema provided a space that dramatized these contemporary concerns about young people in a highly ambivalent manner.[4] Juvenile delinquency films such as *The Road to Ruin* (1928; later remade as a "talkie" in 1934), exploited cinematic language in order to highlight the pleasurable aspects of reckless teen antics as they simultaneously disavowed deviant behavior by dealing their youthful protagonists fates that were often shockingly disproportionate to the social transgressions depicted on screen.

In contrast, the cinema has also produced a vision of teen life that has been most aptly characterized by Thomas Doherty as the "clean teen," which refers to the representation of youth as generally good, mildly and innocently sexual, and keenly interested in music, dance, and other rituals of youth culture.[5] Exemplified by Annette Funicello and Frankie Avalon, the stars of American International Pictures' cycle of beach party films from the 1960s, this characterization was rooted in productions from the 1930s and 1940s such as the Mickey Rooney–Judy Garland musicals *Babes in Arms* (1939) and *Strike Up the Band* (1940). Young characters in these earlier films were interested in having a good time but they also used music to express their own unique identities and prove themselves capable of overcoming obstacles as they transitioned to adulthood. The narrative thrust of the films was ambivalent, however, with teens working to please not only themselves, but also parents, school administrators, and other adults, as they explored music, dance, and dating rituals. Likewise, the cycle of musicals featuring pint-sized operatic crooner Deanna Durbin, made during the 1930s, displayed a significant amount of intergenerational appeal. Throughout these films the adolescent Durbin used her remarkable voice to appeal to adult authority figures in order to solve social and familial problems. She saves the family unit in her debut feature *Three Smart Girls* (1936) by exposing her father's new fiancée as a gold-digging opportunist and reuniting her estranged mother and father, and in *100 Men and a Girl* (1937) she finds employment for destitute musicians (including her father) by creating a new orchestra at the height of the Depression. Adult figures significantly shape the desires of Durbin's youthful characters as she works towards upholding community and the family.

Such intergenerational harmony in the movies was significantly refashioned during the mid-1950s as the motion picture industry consolidated attempts to lure a youthful audience into theaters with the release of several cheaply made films concerned expressly with teen life and adolescent interests. Audience research had revealed that young people already made up a significant percentage of filmgoers at mid-century, and productions such as *Rock Around the Clock* (1956), *Don't Knock the Rock* (1956), and *Shake, Rattle & Rock* (1956) were calculated attempts to exploit teenagers' growing interest in rock 'n' roll music and dance.[6] Along with youth-oriented horror and science fiction, and diverse excursions into the nature of teen delinquency, these films were part of a much wider recognition of the consumer power of youth. Radio and television became increasingly teen focused, while cosmetics producers and clothing manufacturers scrambled for soda-shop wages. In truth, young consumers had been recognized and targeted even as early as the twenties and thirties, but postwar plentitude brought progressively methodical and research-oriented approaches to the process of fashioning and promoting teen products.[7]

The rock 'n' roll flick appealed to young people by making their music, fashion, and dating rituals more central to film narratives than ever before. Nonetheless, these adolescents were not the promiscuous tragic figures of *Road to Ruin*, and many rock-oriented teen films still insisted on some degree of conciliation and understanding between parent and youth culture. Cute young rock 'n' roller Lisa Johns, for instance, marries a former big band promoter twice her age at the end of *Rock Around the Clock*, and Dad snaps his fingers to the beat of Alan Freed's *Rock 'n' Roll Jubilee* lineup from the comfort of his living room chair while his teen daughter and friend shake and swoon in a segment of *Rock, Rock, Rock!* Amid superficial attempts at generational conciliation, these films addressed related, but much more pressing matters. As noted earlier, they participated in a discourse that encouraged white teen social practices, representational spaces, and music culture to embrace young black musicians in the midst of growing anxiety over African American civil rights and cross-racial socializing.

The late 1960s witnessed the emergence of films diametrically opposed to the "clean teen" beach productions and other innocuous fare of the early part of the decade, with drug tripping exploitation extravaganzas such as Roger Corman's *The Trip* (1967) and youth-oriented biker flicks such as *The Wild Angels* (1966), *Devil's Angels* (1967), and *The Born Losers* (1967). These films responded to increasingly sensationalistic accounts of young people in general, especially bikers and the "hippie" generation. The 1960s also offered a sprinkling of more thoughtful dramatic portrayals of young people's emotional expectations and sexual desires with films such as *Last Summer* (1969).[8]

After a significant absence of teen cinema in the 1970s, the 1980s proved to be an enormously successful decade for the youth-oriented film.[9] This era is defined for many critics and observers by the John Hughes hit machine, which presented an enclosed and racially homogenous version of white middle-class life staged in the Chicago suburbs in *Sixteen Candles*

(1984), *The Breakfast Club* (1985), *Weird Science* (1985), and *Pretty in Pink* (1986).[10] One must also include here the aforementioned trio of wildly successful teen-oriented musicals *Flashdance, Footloose,* and *Dirty Dancing.* The 1980s also gave birth to an inversion of the safe and squeaky-clean Hughes world in the form of the teen slasher film, which presented a terrifying and unstable suburban terrain where middle-class life was no longer an idyllic haven. To be sure, these subgroups are unique and important developments in the history of teen cinema, and scholars have given them their due. What has been overlooked is how the cycle of youth-oriented hip hop musicals set in black and Latino neighborhoods, which emerged in the early 1980s, also played an important role in the development of teen film.

Teen cinema has historically offered little in the way of racial diversity, so these films are important not only for their transformation of the musical genre detailed in the previous chapters, but also for the way that they challenged the racial homogeneity of the teen film genre—a corpus consistently focused on white families and adolescents. Firstly, I will show that cinematic fantasies of teen life in the 1980s were critically defined through the delineation of both urban and suburban terrain. Suburbia is comprised of school hallways and classrooms, comfortable domestic interiors, and most importantly, the shopping mall in the films of John Hughes and other middle-class suburban tales. In complete contrast, the hip hop musical shows us youth culture against a backdrop of streets, clubs, recording and dance studios, and a multitude of exterior locations. More specifically, hip hop musicals confronted the values of white suburban teen cinema by evoking a cultural economy that attempted to resist the standardization and consumerism symbolized by "mall culture." Secondly, this chapter argues that hip hop musicals directly addressed the contemporary crisis of the vulnerable African American family unit and utilized performance culture in order to map an alternate set of filial practices and relations to support inner city communities, especially young people. The altruistic actions and public performances of this collective culture directly countered the emphasis on private spaces in the suburban teen film and its incessantly negative portrayal of the familial structure. Finally, this chapter looks at the history of audience participation and teen violence during screenings of *Krush Groove* at multiplex theaters across the country. Multi-screen theaters courted a mixed audience of inner-city youth from communities of color and young suburban whites when hip hop musicals were shown in tandem with teen comedies or "slashers" at shopping mall venues. I suggest that this conflict is related to anxieties about both the permeability of racialized geographical boundaries and the post-industrial unraveling of suburbia.

The Economies of Teen Film in the 1980s

Delinquency, generational conflicts, and participation in consumer culture (or resistance to it) are three of the most enduring aspects of teen culture represented in American film. Indeed, mainstream teen films of the 1980s are often explicitly about consumption and commodification as distinct markers of a desirable and autonomous adolescent identity or subcultural affiliation. Youth participation in consumer culture came to the fore in teen films of the 1980s in a particularly politicized manner. Their narratives directly engaged with the legacy of failed postwar social and economic structures marked by distinctly racialized demographic shifts and a harrowing legacy of poverty for inner-city communities of color.

The relation between the spatial geography defined by white-oriented mainstream teen film and the hip hop musical conforms to the history of large-scale population shifts that occurred in the postwar era. As discussed in the introduction, white residents fled metropolitan areas for outlying bedroom communities, and black Americans migrated to Northern urban capitals.[11] Postwar demographic shifts ushered in the birth and rapid proliferation of the suburb and the perceived decline of urban centers as more people of color moved in.[12] Thirty years later, this racialized dichotomy formed the very basis for the representation of American teen life in the movies. Youth-oriented cinema from this decade reproduced a racial schism that identified white middle-class life with small-town suburban settings and black familial structures with an urban lower-class milieu. Of course, many black American families are rural and suburban, while large numbers of white families occupy city spaces. The National Census Bureau even reported an increase in the movement of black families to the suburbs during the 1970s.[13] Yet black newspapers interrogated this claim in 1981 by avowing that "behind the raw data indicating more blacks in suburbia lurks the ugly reality of a dual housing market and the segregation of blacks to predominantly black suburban neighborhoods."[14] Citing Robert W. Lake's groundbreaking study *The New Suburbanites: Race and Housing in the Suburbs*, the *Afro-American* warned its readers that black movement away from cities was restricted to upper-class and professional families who settled in older towns close to large African American urban populations. As this transition occurred, white families moved from these established suburbs into newly developed outlying areas that proscribed black ownership and created new racially homogenous enclaves.[15] Thus, black Americans, especially working-class and indigent families, were still denied access to upwardly mobile white suburban development and this process only magnified the continuing racial inequity of urban development in the United States. A detailed report from the *American Journal of Sociology*, "Racial Segregation and Racial Change in American Suburbs, 1970–1980," which evaluated black suburbanization in different regions, also showed that the most effective indicator of black suburbanization was a nearby African American urban presence. This type of suburbanization—"a process described as 'spillover' from the central city"—favored a movement towards inner rather than outer suburbs for black Americans.[16] Television, mainstream news media, and the rebirth of the teen film in the early 1980s continued to reinforce a racialized urban/suburban dichotomy.

Teen cinema was not only revived in the 1980s, but also transformed by the rapid proliferation of malls and their attendant multi-screen venues. According to Shary, "The mall became a scene of teen congregation where arcades and food courts replaced the pool halls and soda fountains of the past."[17] Elayne Rapping suggests that the mall was the primary setting of the mainstream teen film of the 1980s because this site progressively became a symbol of the principal way in which life was experienced in the suburbs. It was the space where one not only shopped, but also socialized. Rapping writes that

> malls are the prototype of a social formation which increasingly characterizes contemporary life. They are the community centers of the white middle classes who have fled urban decay and its problems for a Ryan-built haven from a heartless world. From ten in the morning till nine at night, you will see couples, older people, and young mothers strolling past the fake palms, waterfalls, and stone benches, under the enclosed, climate-controlled, security-safe auspices of the mass market-place. The [*sic*] seem often in a semi-daze, absorbed in the spectacle of endless consumer goods, displayed in numbing repetition, window after storefront window.[18]

I agree with Rapping's argument on one level, but she does not adequately explain how the ethics of consumption characterized by mall culture are actually represented in teen cinema. Nor does she acknowledge the racial bias of her selection of films by choosing to discuss only those concerned with white communities.[19] Furthermore, Rapping pays no attention to the racial issues that are intertwined within the enclosed suburban world of the mall. In the introduction to his engaging study of teen film from the 1980s, *Generation Multiplex: The Image of Youth in Contemporary American Cinema*, Shary stresses the importance of the mall as a catalyst that led to the resurgence of teen cinema at this time.[20] However, he is more concerned with how American teen film has utilized and developed a "codified system that delineates certain subgenres and character types within the 'youth film' genre," and thus does not analyze how the films themselves explore themes related to the economic and social shifts wrought by the birth of suburban mall culture.[21] In what follows, I will describe in detail how mainstream teen cinema revealed the extent to which aspects of social life were wedded to the economic system of exchange symbolized by the mall and the ritualized practice of conspicuous consumption. The purpose of this discussion is to demonstrate the ways in which the hip hop musical of the same era offered a stark contrast to the "mall economy" so pervasive in white suburban teen films.

Imagery of suburban shopping centers and the explicit relation between consumer power and social status were two of the most prevalent features of mainstream teen film during the 1980s. From *Valley Girl* to *Risky Business* (1983), youth-oriented cinema was habitually concerned with the ways in which consumer capitalism and displays of symbolic wealth structured the lives of predominantly white suburban-dwelling high school students.[22] The actual space of the mall figures prominently in many of these films (including *Fast Times at Ridgemont High*, *Valley Girl*, *Weird Science*, and *Can't Buy Me Love* [1987]). Even when the literal space of the mall is left off-screen, most mainstream teen cinema from this period evokes, and to a large extent is even structured by, the logic of consumer capitalism with its emphasis on standardization and conformity.

The precursor of the modern-era mall first dotted the American landscape following a large-scale flight of predominantly white, aspiring middle-class families to suburbia in the postwar era.[23] These shopping configurations—clusters of stores united by a single parking area located strategically to serve expanding residential regions—were designed to meet the consumer needs of a family-oriented generation with an unprecedented amount of buying power and numerous automobiles.[24] Since this time, the modern shopping mall has transformed into a fully enclosed retail space with restaurants, entertainment, and an expansive car park. These enormously successful enterprises proliferated in the United States in the late 1970s and into the 1980s, with 16,400 built by 1975, and a jump to 22,750 by 1981.[25]

Contemporaneous with the establishment of modern consumer culture and the growth of the mass media at mid-century, sociologists, philosophers, and other intellectuals discussed the impact of these large-scale changes on American social life and behavior. David Riesman, writing in the late 1940s, suggested that

> it is obviously impossible to separate the media from their wider cultural context, just as it is impossible to separate the messages of advertising in the media from the "messages" carried by the goods themselves, displayed in the stores, the streets, and the home. We still believe that the long-run impact of the media on the style of perception, the understanding (or, more often, the misunderstanding) of life, the sense of what it means to be an American boy or girl, man or woman, or old folk, is immense.[26]

Other intellectuals, such as Marshall McLuhan, remarked that American consumerism and the mass media had the potential to unify disparate groups of people, providing a sense of community and a common language to an aggregate nation. He writes that

> the multi-billion dollar, nation-wide educational programmes of the ad-men (dwarfing the outlay on formal education) provide a world of symbols, witticism, and behavior patterns which may or may not be a fatal solvent for the basic political traditions of America, but which certainly do comprise a common experience and a common language for a country whose sectional differences and technological specialisms might easily develop into anarchy.[27]

McLuhan's cautious, yet positive remarks regarding the impact of modern mass culture and consumerism on quotidian life are striking in comparison to Paul F. Lazarsfeld and Robert K. Merton, whose views stressed the detrimental effects of mass culture on the general population. The latter were concerned with a perceived deterioration of aesthetic taste in the general public, as well as the "narcotizing effect of the mass media."[28]

Recently, scholarly attention has turned to the development of suburban communities and the spatial topography of leisure in American postwar culture. James Farrell even suggests that the increasingly concentrated shopping areas of newly established suburbs were the "most significant post war innovation" in American life.[29] He goes on to argue that by the 1980s consumer culture and its most prominent space of exchange, the suburban mall, had changed life so drastically that American community in the late twentieth and early twenty-first centuries could be said to be defined by "life-style" choices—a concept of identity negotiated and enacted within spaces of the modern shopping center. He writes that

> values have been around a long time, but life-style is a relatively recent word, invented to describe the lives we make for ourselves as consumers. In the past, people had a life, but not a life-style. Some living people had style, but style wasn't deemed essential to life. People admired character and competence, who you were and what you could do. They didn't care particularly what car you drove, or what clothes you wore, or how many appliances you owned. Over the course of the twentieth century, however, character and competence were increasingly challenged by personality and personal style.[30]

Mainstream suburban teen cinema of the 1980s highlighted the cohesive aspects of consumerism as a "life-style" for American youth, revealing the ways in which social difference could seemingly be transformed through economic means.

In films such as *Fast Times at Ridgemont High*, *Valley Girl*, *Weird Science*, and *Some Kind of Wonderful* (1987), the realization of successful social relations with peers, and a demonstration of mature adolescent identity is either directly linked to the accessibility of goods and "life-style" described by Farrell, or these films imply that social status is explicitly connected to buying power. Most importantly, the attainment of goods in mainstream teen cinema is related to conformity and the standardization of behavior. Riesman's assertion that what one buys, as well as *how* one buys, has a profound affect on the individual's sense of identity is demonstrated in many mainstream teen films from this era.

Even *Pretty in Pink*, a John Hughes film that at the outset seems to value an individual non-consumerist style over displays of wealth and conformity, in the end suggests that for young girls and women the only way to succeed in capitalist America is to acquiesce to normative standards of beauty and fashion. The entirety of *Pretty in Pink*'s romantic plot revolves around class inequity. As it follows the budding romance between Andie

Fig. 3.1. Class differences dramatized through style and clothing in *Pretty in Pink* (1986). Pictured: James Spader as Steff and Molly Ringwald as Andie. Courtesy of Photofest.

(Molly Ringwald), a kid from an impoverished single parent home, and Blaine (Andrew McCarthy), an upper-middle-class "richie," the film continually reinforces the incongruence between lower-class and upper-middle-class teen experiences. The disparities between the rich and the poor in *Pretty in Pink* are located in differing attitudes toward life, friendship, and personal success, but most spectacularly in displays of personal style via clothing, transportation, and home.

An association between style-oriented group identification and wealth is underscored in an early classroom scene in which Andie is ridiculed for her offbeat thrift store outfit. Two well-heeled "richies" ask Andie if she got her clothing at the "five and dime" as the teacher gives a lesson on the New Deal era. Clearly, any benevolent behavior on the part of the rich has been forgotten in the era of accelerated capitalism. *Pretty in Pink* even opens with a shot in which the metaphor "wrong side of the tracks" is literalized. As the title song by the Psychedelic Furs plays, a row of poor housing—small structures with white clapboard siding nestled between unattended yards—is revealed. The motion of a street cleaner cuts through the center of the scene, pulling the spectator's attention towards the cracked, uneven pavement. When the cleaner moves away from the camera, more of the surrounding squalor comes into view, and a dissolve follows in which a set of train tracks appear. After the preceding image has faded from view and train tracks are the main focus of the scene, the camera glides rapidly over them to continue its documentation of domestic poverty. Next a series of abandoned and dilapidated buildings are shown, as the camera finally fixes on the home of the film's lower-class heroine. Even before Andie emerges from her room in dime store vintage, her social and economic position has been forcefully presented to the spectator through the opening shots.

Although *Pretty in Pink* is reputedly a romantic teen comedy, it also chronicles the stylistic transformation of Andie and her older friend Iona (Annie Potts), who sports punk, new wave, and retro fashions throughout the film. In fact, *Pretty in Pink* suggests that romantic success for the two women is contingent upon giving up their individualized sense of style, built around recycled vintage clothing, the ability to sew, and references to a multitude of subcultures. The film reveals the two women to be resourceful, stylish, and significantly hipper and more interesting than the wealthy characters in the film who dress in standard preppy garb—pastels, suit jackets, and perfect blond tresses. In order to cement a romantic bond with men who will ultimately guarantee a step up the socioeconomic ladder, however, both Andie and Iona must transform into "softer," more conservative women. For Andie, this is signaled by her appearance at the senior prom in a pink taffeta dress, while Iona loses her Cleopatra eyeliner, spiked tresses, and blond wigs in favor of a string of pearls and a blazer in preparation for her date with a small business owner. Even though contemporary critics were acutely aware of the simplistic and heavy-handed treatment of class differences in the film, rarely did the relation between gender and social mobility enter into this debate. For instance, Thomas O'Connor, who interviewed John Hughes for the *New York Times*, noted that "*Pretty in Pink*, while a traditional, upbeat tale of a romance that must hurdle obstacles of social class, also raises for young viewers serious, adult issues about taking responsibility for one's choices and the obligations of friendship."[31] *New York Times* reviewer Vincent Canby suggested that

> audiences who go to this movie know better, but they still like what they see anyway. *Pretty in Pink* is selling dreams in which a social order still means something. A world made of of [sic] "richies" and, I assume, "poories," holds promise. At least, if you're poor you can aspire to be rich.[32]

While Canby's hostile review aptly captures many of the film's flaws it never questions or investigates how the simplistic delineations of class boundaries are shown to actually impinge upon the lives of men and women differently.[33]

Weird Science, another John Hughes teen film, deals with two male nerd characters, Gary (Anthony Michael Hall) and Wyatt (Ilan Mitchell-Smith), who create the "ultimate woman" with their home computer. They are mercilessly tormented by a group of "cool kids" until the arrival of Lisa (Kelly LeBrock), their newly manufactured playmate. While the two teens create a beautiful girl to boost their image with peers, they also give her immense intellectual abilities—signified by Gary and Wyatt feeding images of Einstein into their computer during her creation, as they siphon power from a military computer system and an electrical storm. Lisa, however, largely solves their teen angst woes by providing endless consumer items such as new clothing and flashy cars, while she works to improve their popularity and help them acquire girlfriends.

Weird Science reveals images of the mall in only one sequence, and these scenes forcefully underscore the importance of the shopping center as a communal focal point for suburbia. They also foreground the centrality of consumer goods as a barometer of one's social value in a film primarily concerned with improving social status. The mall sequence opens with Gary and Wyatt at the perfume counter trying to impress a young saleswoman. When she recognizes them as "the ones that got beat up at the homecoming game," they immediately offer to purchase a bottle of perfume for her after being "outed" as nerds. Clearly public humiliation and buying power are linked in this sequence, and the pain of being recognized as a social outcast can only be countered with an attempted display of consumer power.

Moments later, Gary and Wyatt are seated on a bench on the lower level of the mall while the "cool kids" are glimpsed perched over a balustrade on the upper concourse level, giving them a perfect bird's-eye view of the two hapless teens. Throughout the scene, the camera cuts to the viewpoint of the "cool kids" from the upper level as they prepare to dump the contents of an enormous slushy cup on the unsuspecting "uber-geeks" Gary and Wyatt. After the two teens are covered in red goo it appears as though every patron in the entire mall has come to observe the scene and have a laugh at the expense of the two nerds. The repetition of point-of-view shots from the perspective of two confident male teens and their entourage as they look down upon the unfortunate duo appropriates and transforms the usual dynamics of the gendered gaze in Hollywood cinema.[34] While mainstream teen films typically adhere to the precedent of classical Hollywood cinema by identifying the voyeuristic gaze with men and the object of the gaze with women, *Weird Science* attempts to express Gary and Wyatt's social ineptitude by identifying them with the cinematic coding usually reserved for women and girls.[35] Not only do they become the object of a sadistic gaze, but their bodies are associated with the abject products of the feminine body—blood—as they are drenched in thick red goo. Furthermore, the film undercuts our sympathy for the affront suffered by Gary and Wyatt because it weds the spectator's point of view to the look of the dominant male who dumps the slushy and emasculates the teen nerds.

The mall concourse is presented as a space of social ritual—a stage upon which one is literally seen by others—and it functions as a spectacular arena in which to deride those males who do not conform to acceptable notions of masculinity. Scopic drives within interior consumer spaces in the film are related not only to social exclusion but also to sexual desire and the quest for potential sexual partners. For instance, an intense exchange of glances on the mall escalator between Lisa and Ian (Robert Downey, Jr.) and Max (Robert Rusler)—two bullies who have been making life miserable for the films' protagonists—prompts the tormentors to chase after Gary and Wyatt's perfect older woman through the mall in erotic anticipation.

Although the specific architectural configuration of the mall concourse facilitates a spectacular recognition of social ineptitude in *Weird Science*, the shopping center is also the site in which the "cool kids" are forced to reckon with the sudden attainment of wealth (expensive car) and status (attractive older woman) by Gary and Wyatt. The mall is an environment of social surveillance where the community excels in recognizing social undesirability and humiliating those who do not conform to acceptable notions of identity. At the close of the mall sequence, however, Gary and Wyatt (still covered in red slushy) are able to partially counter their initial mortification through a remarkable display of affluence as they are seen leaving the shopping center with a Porsche and a beautiful woman. Although the mall allows for an inversion—the "cool kids" chase a desirable woman into the parking lot only to find out that she "belongs" to the nerds they had humiliated earlier—this is possible only through an incredibly sexist delineation of female subjectivity whereby a beautiful woman is the ultimate consumer item. Lisa is a computer-generated product, but one who is also shown to be a highly intelligent, caring individual, yet she is nonetheless articulated solely as a commodity. She exists for the

Fig. 3.2. "Val Girls" in the mall, *Valley Girl* (1983). Starring Elizabeth Daily as Loryn (second from left) and Deborah Foreman as Julie Richman (second from right). Courtesy of Photofest.

dual purposes of giving male pleasure and imbuing others with social status—the most important quality a commodity can offer—and her "value" is most explicitly and complexly defined in her movement through the space of the mall.[36]

Fast Times at Ridgemont High opens and closes with images of the mall, and uses it as a primary space of narrative action (although this film is markedly different from other teen films because it focuses on the sexual frustrations and desires of two young girls, thus it is from a female point of view that the look is cinematically constructed).[37] *Valley Girl* also opens with an aerial shot of the San Fernando Valley as the credits roll to the beat of Bonnie Hayes & The Wild Combo's "Girls Like Me." The camera reveals a vast expanse of green dotted with suburban outposts and housing, until it finally fixes upon an image of the Sherman Oaks Galleria. This massive, windowless mall structure was the official home away from home of the "valley girl," a consumer-oriented teen made famous by the Moon Unit Zappa song "Valley Girl." We then see images of young girls in a buying frenzy, as shoes are inspected, clothing racks ravaged, credit cards swiped, and purchase totals revealed.

The film is very explicit about the relationship of consumer culture to the lives of the Valley teens. At one point in the narrative, typical "Val Girls"

Fig. 3.3. Promotional poster for *Valley Girl* (1983). Courtesy of Photofest.

Julie and Stacey are convinced to hang out at a Hollywood club by Fred and Randy, would-be suitors from (gasp!) Hollywood High. The girls' disapproval of city life is strongly registered as a dislike for things that do not come from the mall and are outside of the purview of consumer capitalism. In this club sequence, Randy asks the girls, "What do you do over there that's hot?" Julie replies, "We go to normal parties, go to normal places . . . we *buy nice new clothes*." Thus, we are reminded of the opening images, and the space of commercial retail that the film repeatedly associates with "Val Girls." Later in the film, Julie is shown in the mall with Randy; the film closes with a shot of the Sherman Oaks Galleria neon sign at night; and promotional material (fig. 3.3) even included the mall in the background.

This film, like *Fast Times at Ridgemont High*, is completely oriented around mall culture. Both films are also actually bracketed by images of malls. Even though these productions do launch some critiques at the value system associated with suburban mall culture, they also show us that the structural basis upon which suburban life is built remains embedded within the pleasures offered by the social spaces of the mall and the gratification of consumerism as a lifestyle.

One glaring exception to my assessment of the predominance of consumerism and conformity entrenched within mainstream teen cinema of the era is *Pump Up the Volume* (1990). This film features an underground DJ, Happy Harry Hard-On, who broadcasts his teenaged angst over the radio to a population of misunderstood white suburban teens, fomenting social upheaval and so-called delinquent behavior in the youth population of his small town. Although made in 1990, it is relevant here because it is the only white-centered mainstream suburban teen film from this era that articulates alternate and non-consumerist methods of expression and communication as triumphant and viable options for youth. Happy Harry Hard-On is arrested at the end of the film because authorities believe that his clandestine broadcasts are responsible for aberrant behavior and possibly even suicide among the town's youth population. However, as we transition to the credits a cacophony of teen voices is heard on the soundtrack. This veritable symphony of pirate radio transmissions suggests that even though Harry is literally contained by authorial forces, his broadcasts have produced a revolutionary tidal wave of teen dissent.

On the whole, then, there is a tendency in mainstream teen film of the 1980s to evoke, if not the mall itself, then the ethics of consumer consumption associated with suburban mall lifestyle and the standardization of social values. When threatening others enter the pristine conformist spaces of suburbia and the confined cleanliness of mall life, they often come from the city and/or the lower classes. They also frequently exhibit a sense of personal style that is not congruent with expressions of conformist values that are linked to commodity consumption and display within mall culture. Overwhelmingly, characters that are initially defined as non-conformist and anti-consumerist are incorporated into the dominant social order through romantic unions. These mergers usually necessitate a visual transformation towards the second half of the film whereby the threatening other is remade into a more acceptable identity, one that is compatible with clean, dominant consumer culture values. This happens, as just discussed, with *Pretty in Pink*, but the most literal representation of this kind of transformation occurs at the end of *The Breakfast Club*, in which John Bender, an impoverished irascible thug, is given a diamond earring by Claire, the film's spoiled rich girl. Their attraction for one another is only acceptable once she has conferred upon him a symbol of wealth, her large diamond earring, which Bender places in his ear at the end of the film. *Some Kind of Wonderful* ends with a romantic union between two poor teens whose quest for acceptance by their upper-class peers is symbolized by a pair of diamond earrings purchased at the mall. In *Valley Girl*, punk city dweller Randy appropriates symbols of wealth and status—a limo and driver rented for the prom by Julie's former wealthy suburban boyfriend—as the film closes with the aforementioned image of the Sherman Oaks Galleria sign in view.

Community and romance for the suburban teens in these films is largely centered upon the negotiation of social class and wealth. For young women, transformation usually involves a "makeover," or complete reinvention of the self, while young men need only adopt the symbols of material wealth to transcend their apparent social boundaries. Since the ascendance of teen cinema in the 1950s, the life choices available to young women have, of course, been different than those of young men, depending on the specific historical moment of each film's release. Mainstream teen cinema in the 1980s (especially the John Hughes films) offered a particularly regressive view of gender relations and class barriers in American culture as it simultaneously screened out racial and ethnic diversity.

Hip Hop Cinema: The Symbolic Exchange of Style

The hip hop musical of this same era explicitly confronts the sensibility of consumption and uniformity, and the notion of buying style or "lifestyle" found in mainstream white teen cinema. For the protagonists of the 1980s hip hop musical, it is not about what you own or the potential buying power you possess, but about what you create. Style is a personal quality that exists outside the mall economy of consumer capitalism. The emphasis moves from purchasing symbols of cultural value (in the mall) in white-centered suburban teen cinema to inventing them yourself (on the street or in the club) in the inner-city musical.

Within hip hop culture of this era, the display of personal style even deliberately counters capitalist delineations of space and ownership. Graffiti, for instance, defies demarcations of spatial possession. This practice constructs new concepts of ownership (even if only fleeting) that do not depend on monetary exchange in order to lay claim to a city space. One may assert "ownership" over a city wall or train car through the act of tagging or graffiti writing rather than pay for use of that space, as in the purchase of a billboard or the rental of a public venue. Tony Tone, a member of the South Bronx hip hop crew Cold Crush Brothers featured in *Wild Style*, has remarked that "hip hop is being free. Feeling like I'm free. It's mines to keep, and mines to share."[38] Thus, for Tony Tone, hip hop culture as a practice connotes ownership, yet paradoxically it is offered as free cultural goods to the larger community in block parties, subway graffiti, and street dancing. In the same way, DJ Kool Herc, the "father of hip hop," can lay claim to inventing (and to some extent owning) the extended break beat through the manipulation of two records and turntables, yet this innovation was soon copied and dispersed throughout the hip hop community. It has also been well documented that hip hop DJs achieved fame in the '70s and '80s through an entirely underground cassette tape market in which their performances at parties were recorded and sold for a fairly hefty price ($15 a tape on average). However, no stipulation was enforced as to how many copies of the tape could be made.[39] Again, paradoxically, the idea of ownership and freedom of distribution coexist in this example.

Several hip hop musicals are structured around the desire to resist corporate culture and standardization, hallmarks of suburban mall value systems. These films present hip hop as an alternative economy to the values of mainstream consumer culture that are celebrated in white-centered teen cinema. In *Krush Groove*, a local Queens-based record company of the same name initially attempts to represent Run-D.M.C. until they are scooped up by the much larger, white-run Galaxy records. The lure of money convinces the rap trio to abandon their independent label, yet Krush Groove continues to find black talent to represent. Both the local and the corporate succeed, perhaps somewhat uncomfortably, in promoting black musicians in this film. Undoubtedly *Krush Groove* gestures towards initial African American ventures into the music recording industry such as the emergence of Black Swan Records in 1921, also a New York-based independent endeavor. This earlier business shuttered its doors in 1923, partly because performers of color were attracted to mainstream white-owned companies with larger distribution circuits and more lucrative prospects.[40] Krush Groove's "real-life" counterpart (Def Jam) continues to promote black talent to this day but it has been significantly transformed by industrial alliances with large corporate entities.

As mentioned previously, *Breakin' 2* envisions a struggle between the sensibilities of a hip hop-based economy and the machinations of corporate capitalism. In this film, white corporate developers attempt to dismantle Miracles, a minority neighborhood dance center, in order to make way for the construction of a new shopping center. Miracles is a concrete manifestation of the values that a hip hop economy represents because the film suggests instruction is given there freely by members of the community that it serves. Community interaction is based upon the dispersal of skills throughout the neighborhood rather than through the rituals of consumerism encouraged by mall culture. The film presents a crude scenario in which a hip hop economy (represented by the Miracles dance center) is literally threatened by the forces of capitalism and gentrification through the construction of an actual shopping mall. The communal and free aspect of alternate and non-commercial forms of culture is always shown to be under attack, in some sense, in the majority of hip hop musicals—by a white-owned record label in *Krush Groove* and a rapacious New York art scene in *Wild Style*.

One of the most interesting examples of this aspect of the hip hop musical occurs in *Beat Street*. In this film, Lee, a child breakdancing prodigy, first experiences the lure of commercial interests in the form of a racially diverse professional Manhattan dance company which includes Tracy, an Upper West Side wealthy black dance choreographer/music composer who is also the love interest of the film's "music man." We are introduced to her character in the Roxy nightclub as she scopes the venue for new dance talent. Later, we follow Kenny and Lee from the Bronx to her dance rehearsal in Manhattan in order for Lee's "street moves" to be presented to the dancers in her show. The performance is taped as Lee ascends the stage, surrounded by the ranks of trained professional dancers. At the conclusion of this dance sequence, Kenny becomes angry that Lee has not been asked to perform in the show and he retrieves the tape to take with him as his crew leaves the stage. Kenny accuses the professional black dancers and producers of discovering and exploiting their own "nigger." In fact, he reproaches them for making a spectacle of blackness by videotaping Lee and then showing him the door. This scene articulates the difficulties of negotiating a meeting ground between wealthy Manhattan enclaves and the impoverished inner-city neighborhoods of the Bronx. Interestingly, the film takes great pains to show that all spaces of New York City are characterized by a pan racial, multiethnic diversity, and it would be a mistake to characterize the threat to "authentic" culture, and the alternate economy of hip hop, in these films as always a vehicle of white appropriation and exploitation.

Hip hop musicals are also rife with the possibilities of circumventing, even if only momentarily, the hegemonic economic, social, and political configurations that structure mainstream white teen cinema. The films privilege public venues over the private and semi-private spaces of mainstream teen film at a particular moment in American political culture when the prevailing currents of conservative doctrine demonized most public institutions, services, and space. In truth, the hip hop musical's communities of color frequently represent the inverse of the suburban teen film's economic and social systems of exchange and influence.

One could argue that both spaces of cultural signification and negotiation—the mall and the inner city—offer the potential for utopian transformations through the recognition of shared communal values but the utopia of the mall in white-centered teen cinema is built around the premise that anyone can buy and display the goods that procure social acceptance. Paradoxically, the mall offers only a false promise of public utopian space and democratic social exchange. Jean Baudrillard notes that within consumer society "the 'status' system . . . has the virtue of rendering obsolete all the old rituals of caste or class, along—in a general way—with all preceding (and preclusive) criteria of social discrimination."[41] He argues that this system of value does not imply any true sense of democratization because it relies upon a "perpetually renewed obsession with hierarchies and distinctions" whereby "new barriers and exclusions have arisen in the realm of objects: a new class or caste morality is thus enabled to colonize the most material and hitherto unchallengeable of spheres."[42] In American culture, the mall has been the primary space of mobilization for this new ethic of "status" predicated on changes in the postwar economy. It has been duly noted that the automobile and its attendant "car culture" are immensely important aspects of this postwar system of social hierarchy. The space of the mall, too, with its multiple stages of consumer "play"— food courts, elevated store-lined concourses, and glass elevators—allows a vastly complex set of social rituals to occur. Significantly higher levels of impoverishment among black and Latino communities in the 1980s, however, would have rendered people of color at a great disadvantage for achieving "status" within the supposedly democratic system of consumer culture. Moreover, Anne Friedberg suggests that the mall is not "completely a *public* place," rather it functions as a "contemporary phantasmagoria, enforcing a blindness to the range of urban blights—the homeless, beggars, crime, traffic, even weather."[43] Freidberg does not specifically mention race, but the term "urban blight" within an American context demarcates a cityscape of communities of color within the national imaginary. The Sherman Oaks Galleria in particular has even been described as a "white windowless box that turned its back on the local community."[44] When interior mall scenes appear in mainstream cinema, the Galleria's white façade is echoed by racially homogenous spaces teeming with white middle-class youths and their families. The emergence of mall culture points to the ways in which postwar white flight was largely premised upon the desire to create enclaves of racial uniformity that were disconnected from the conditions of urban life and its communities of color.[45]

Intriguingly, the shopping center also functions in a similar way to Altman's assessment of the traditional show musical, with its emphasis on entertainment as commodity and spectacle, and simultaneous denial of the physical labor needed to produce a seamless performance. As Friedberg observes:

> The mall becomes a realm for consumption, effectively exiling the realm of production from sight. Like the theme park, the mall is "imagineered" with maintenance and management techniques, keeping invisible the delivery bays or support systems, concealing the security guards and bouncers who control its entrances.[46]

Of course, the suggestion that modern spaces of entertainment and leisure depend upon a concealment of the actual conditions of production can be traced back to Marx's writings on the nature of the commodity within industrial capitalism. He argues that within this system of exchange human labor is abstracted, thus transformed into a common unit of currency, which obscures the unique and varied character of particular production practices.[47] In other words, in order for the value of an object to become apparent as an exchangeable commodity, it must be severed from its particular conditions of production. The mall intensifies the status of the commodity as something dependent upon the concealment of its material production by providing a space in which this process becomes the foundation for contemporary forms of socialization. Suburban malls, both in film and actual historical instances, succeeded in generating a pleasurable vision or "phanstasmagoria" of racial exclusion in tandem with the erasure of visible forms of blue-collar work on a variety of levels. This conjunctive process is suggestive of two larger historical facets of American culture: the persistent refusal to recognize the labor extracted from African American people under slavery, and the struggle for wage equity among different races in industrial and service jobs.[48] As white families moved away from urban centers in the postwar era, they succeeded in creating spaces of social and racial exclusion whereby their material wealth could not be contrasted to images of poorer communities of color. When the mall emerges as a central symbol of social interaction for young white teens in the 1980s, this potentially utopian space dramatizes the false promise that American capitalism offers, and has always offered—a democratic system of social hierarchy.

In marked contrast, utopian impulses in early hip hop-oriented cinema were linked to the empowerment of inner-city communities. The true hip hop musical reveals the actual spaces of impoverished urban neighborhoods and in doing so signifies the "homeless, beggars, crime, traffic"—all of the elements so neatly ejected from the space of the mall. Perhaps most importantly, the economics of hip hop are delineated as fluid, and able to move throughout a variety of public outdoor spaces, encouraging the community to participate in the production of neighborhood entertainment. In mainstream white teen cinema, conversely, there is no emphasis on large-scale cultural production through public performance. Communal exchange and bonding in these films is often a passive activity that occurs within rigidly defined semi-private and private locales such as the mall and the home.

Notably, the producer and consumer are one and the same within the hip hop musical. The theme of active spectatorship and consumption in all aspects of hip hop culture has been explored in a previous chapter. This facet of hip hop was more that simply a *subject* of the films that explored this particular inner-city culture, as journalistic accounts of audience behavior during screenings of these films reveal. For instance, *Washington Post* reporter Rita Kempley writes that "*Wild Style* celebrates its roots. It's a ghetto-box blast, a film made mostly for partying. With its visual anarchy, it inspires audience anarchy. And, that's the best part, the break dancing in the aisles."[49] *Wild Style* also opened in Washington, D.C., with a multimedia event that featured live breaking and rapping in addition to a film screening. Richard Harrington notes that "300 folks waited for those packed inside to signal surrender to the heat and the pulse. There was a slow substitution of new bodies for exhausted ones—and they were just the watchers."[50] Ahearn has even suggested comparisons between *Wild Style* and cult film's most famous participatory ritual, *The Rocky Horror Picture Show* (1975).[51]

Wild Style has consistently been discussed in relation to its energetic and exciting imagery and sound instead of its narrative structure. *Krush*

Groove, on the other hand, was a far more traditional musical with a very conventional and clearly defined narrative progression. Yet Schultz's film also opened with a series of audience related activities, although this time the exuberance of youthful spectators apparently degenerated into violence. In what follows, I explore and contextualize the infamous events surrounding the release of *Krush Groove* in order to elucidate the profound connections between race, audience, and geographical space in 1980s teen film.

When the film was screened in small, predominantly white communities on Long Island such as Franklin Square, an Italian working-class enclave in Nassau County, neighboring African American youth from New York City boroughs attended these suburban showings.[52] At least two large-scale violent confrontations between local white youth and visiting urban black teenagers occurred in the Long Island area during initial screenings of *Krush Groove*. The first, which took place in Valley Stream during November 1985, involved an unbelievable 500 teens while police indicated that the later Franklin Square episode implicated approximately 225 youths.[53]

Journalistic coverage of the events plaguing the film's theatrical release often characterized the spectators of *Krush Groove* as brutal teen thugs. Although a *New York Times* article reporting the disturbances asserted the benign content of the film, it nevertheless subtly suggested that black spectators were to blame for the incident since they were transgressing their urban boundaries and entering suburban territory. The article quoted two teenagers from the white Long Island communities and did not present the viewpoint of any black teens involved in the confrontations. It also only reported injuries sustained by the white teenagers and the attending police while neglecting to mention whether or not any African American filmgoers were hurt during the event. This has the obvious effect of locating reader sympathies with the suburban teens since we only hear their personal opinions, experiences, and viewpoints. We read that "Scott Lund, a 17-year-old from neighboring Elmont, was thrown through a window and required more than 200 stitches before being released from Franklin General Hospital yesterday."[54] The first teenager quoted in the article, Gino D'Angelo, clearly places blame on African American teenagers and states of the film that "it's attracting a black crowd to a white town.... That means trouble, especially because they come out of the movie all psyched up."[55] By contrast, black cinema-going youth were reduced to the status of members of "a group of more than 500 young people [who] stormed a theater in Valley Stream, L.I., after doors were closed to a showing of the film."⁵⁶ White victimhood is personified while the experience of black youth is reduced to an amorphous angry mob.

Interestingly, the youths who allegedly clashed with black *Krush Groove* spectators were reportedly at the Franklin Square Quad Cinema to take in the teen slasher *Nightmare on Elm Street* (1984). This film was the inaugural installment of a horror series that critiqued suburban life while simultaneously longing for the promise of a "safe" middle-class, small-town haven. The setting of *Nightmare on Elm Street*, Springwood, Ohio, is characterized as a menacing place to children. Rows of perfect, serene, and affluent houses encased in white picket fences become looming symbols of terror as child killer Freddy Krueger invades all aspects of this delicate idyll, slicing though the dreams of sleeping children and the walls of domestic security. The *New York Times* article presents more than one viewpoint which suggests that black teens were possibly "stirred up" by what they saw on screen while attending *Krush Groove*.⁵⁷ However, no mention is made of the fact that white teens were possibly deeply affected by images of suburbia in ruin at the hands of Freddy Krueger, the super-violent, dark-faced monster who terrorizes young people in the *Elm Street* series.

Moreover, the site of the largest riot mentioned in the article, the Sunrise Multiplex in Valley Stream and the adjacent Green Acres Mall, was a notorious space of racial contestation, which bordered the African American neighborhood of Laurelton in Queens and the predominantly white working- and middle-class communities of Nassau County. Franklin Square theater, the site of the other incident, straddles the border between Nassau County and predominantly African American neighborhoods in Queens such as Cambria Heights and Hollis, the district that produced Run-D.M.C. as well as LL Cool J.

Although the Valley Stream multiplex catered to a diverse clientele, young people undoubtedly made up a large part of their audience due to its proximity to a large suburban mall, the presence of arcade machines in the lobby, and a steady run of teen-oriented films such as *Roller Boogie* (1979), *Airplane* (1980), and the aforementioned *Nightmare on Elm Street*.⁵⁸ Unfortunately, youth-related violence continued to plague the locale as evidenced by a lively conversation thread on the *Cinema Treasures* website, a space dedicated to the discussion and preservation of movie theater culture. One online poster identified as Nova writes that

148   The Economic and Racial Structuring of Youth Cinema in the 1980s

> I was at the adjacent Green Acres Mall with a friend just killing time in the arcade before going to see *Nightmare on Elm Street 4* at the Sunrise Multiplex. We started to play the old USA-Russia hockey game, when an all-out massive fight broke out between rival African-American and Latino gangs and spilled right into the arcade. I remember it clear as day. My friend and I both hid under our video game the whole time, scared as sh*t. After the movie I remember thinking that no Freddy movie seemed as frightening as that one, though I suppose it was brought on by the pre-show action rush at the mall.[59]

This event must have occurred in 1988—three years after the *Krush Groove* riot—since that was the year the fourth installment of the *Nightmare on Elm Street* series was released. Throughout the thread, many references are made to "a certain Queens element" that was supposedly having a detrimental effect on the theater and surrounding area. For instance, the opening writer Chris Connolly notes that "for a while (early to mid-80's), this was THE place to see a movie if you lived on the western south shore of Nassau County on Long Island. . . . But the theatre's proximity to some less than desirable neighborhoods just over the Queens line in NYC began to have it's [sic] effects on it."[60] Connolly not only dates the decline of the Sunrise Multiplex theater to the mid-1980s but also cites the *Krush Groove* incident as the defining moment that prompted him never to return there.

Krush Groove also sparked unrest in other parts of the country. For instance, when the film was later screened in Boston at the Pi Alley theater, a riot involving over 1,000 teenagers ensued, resulting in injuries, cancelled screenings, and damage to the theater and other property.[61] Fights also broke out in movie houses in Los Angeles and Las Vegas at approximately the same time.[62] The screening in Las Vegas was accompanied by rival gang disputes involving over 400 people fighting both inside and outside the theater, and was only subdued when dozens of police officers arrived to quell the violence.[63] Canada even heard the rumblings from New York and took extra security precautions when the film opened at the Palace Theatre in Montreal.[64] While *Krush Groove* sparked tremors throughout the country (and even the continent), I have chosen to focus on the events in New York since they so clearly illuminate the important role that perceptions of geographical boundaries play with respect to community identity and racial harmony in the United States. The increased potential for interactions between racially and geographically defined adolescent crowds has hitherto remained unexamined in studies of teen film from the 1980s. Clearly, the racially marked urban—suburban dichotomy perpetuated in teen cinema from this era became visible through the format of the multiplex when both white-oriented suburban youth films and inner-city hip hop musicals focused on communities of color were screened at the same location.

White fears of "black engulfment" have always been represented in popular American film—grandly and spectacularly with *The Birth of a Nation*'s (1915) racist and paranoid imagery of black political and sexual machinations and more subtly with preclassical cinema's appropriation of theatrical blackface minstrelsy's obsession with the mouth as a site of immense and grotesque consumption. In the 1980s, black urban neighborhoods increasingly became a symbol of the threatening expanse of racially "Other" Americans who had the power and numbers to transform topographical spaces. While these spaces signified poverty and governmental incompetence to most Americans, they concurrently evoked deep-seated fears about racial transformation. As we have seen, inner-city regions were often described in mainstream journalism as an alien or war-torn landscape—a trope that stressed the social "Otherness" and instability of these areas. If communities of color had taken over American cites in the postwar era, could the boundaries of white suburbia also incorporate black life into their midst? The simultaneous screening of vastly different films in one location offered by the multiplex format drew youthful crowds from racially divergent neighboring communities. Resulting confrontations recorded in the popular press seem to speak directly to this question, but regrettably these events only magnified the perceived racial antagonism between urban black teens and neighboring white suburban youth in the New York area.

The anxieties that these meetings produced continued to escalate in this area in the years following the *Krush Groove* disturbances, and the Sunrise Multiplex remained a site where the urban-suburban racialized divide seemed to materialize in concrete form. In December of 1990, a fatal shooting occurred at the venue during a screening of *The Godfather Part III*. A barrage of bullets was unleashed upon the audience as members of two rival gangs opened fire on each other after an argument, wounding three spectators and killing a teenager.[65] Prior to this event, police indicated that there had been at least eight "serious incidents reported in the last five years" around the theater.[66] A *New York Times* article from March of 1991 was brave enough to address the underlying tensions and racial issues that such violence in suburban communities tends to nurture:

As more black residents of Queens and Brooklyn have crossed the city line to attend a theater that they say is much better than those at home, Nassau County whites have all but stopped going. Race has something to do with it, though no one wants to say so publicly. Instead, many of the whites who shun Sunrise put it a different way: it is city people who are causing the problems they say.[67]

Blacks who attended the Sunrise patronized the venue because movie houses in their own neighborhoods were either disappearing or declining, and the local theaters still in operation there were "small, dirty and tend[ed] to show unpopular movies."[68] The city multiplexes that did exist, such as King's Park in Brooklyn, were "overcrowded with people and cars" and had "a much worse atmosphere than Sunrise."[69] Sunrise patron Mekita Coe, who was a resident of Rochdale Village, Queens, was more upfront: "This theater is clean and well kept up because it's in a white neighborhood. . . . They don't have any nice theaters in black neighborhoods."[70]

The violence and criminal activity at the Sunrise was overwhelmingly associated with black urban youth by Nassau residents and city officials. This viewpoint was seemingly validated when all of the people arrested in connection with the *Godfather III* shooting were African American residents of Queens—a reminder, according to Jack Sharkey, a former village trustee, that "the entire western border is a worry and concern because of the happenstance of people coming across the border, committing crimes and then running back over."[71] Even though most black patrons came to the theater because their neighborhoods failed to provide an adequate venue for film viewing, the shooting, unfortunately, seemed to lend credence to the racist vein running through the Nassau communities, and to accredit all crime in the area and even the general foreboding environment of the theater to black urban dwellers. After the shooting, security increased at the Sunrise multiplex, with the presence of metal detectors, cameras, and a stringent policy that would only allow people into the lobby once they had purchased tickets. While some politicians such as Democrat Bruce Nyman felt that it was a "calculated overreaction" and an example of "classic Nassau County Republican politics: keep the problems on the other side of the line," most city officials continued to avow that "the problems came from an unsavory element of the out-of-town crowd who were giving Valley Stream a bad name."[72] Local residents appropriated the same rhetoric, for instance, when Michele Raiola, "an office manager from Lynbrook," made note of the distasteful environment in the theater—"people were smoking marijuana, there was verbal abuse"—she remarked, "I don't think it was people from the neighborhood; it was people coming over from Queens."[73] Paul L. Covington, president of the NAACP's local chapter, responded: "When they talk about 'those people,' meaning those from outside Nassau County, frequently they're using it as a euphemism for blacks.... The people who are in positions of authority in Nassau County want to think of this as a nice lily-white suburb."[74] He acutely identified the submerged racism that was permitted in the slippage between racial identity and urban geography throughout the Nassau Country responses listed in the article. In an environment with an overwhelmingly white demographic (98.83 percent as of 1980)[75] that is hemmed in by neighboring urban regions with a nearly all-black population, it is indeed difficult to read this as anything other than a problem with black people on the part of white suburbanites.

It is no accident that the cinema itself became a site of contestation for young spectators divided by spatial environs and ethnic traditions, and later an arena to wage political battles, which turned on the trope of suburbia in peril—an enclave of racial homogeneity threatened by some nebulous and vaguely defined "city element." With postwar white flight, black urban residential areas lost local amenities, including entertainment venues, which they were now forced to seek out in white neighborhoods. An article from the *New York Times* explains the historical importance of performance culture and access to theatrical venues for inner-city Latinos in the South Bronx. The neighborhood's Teatro Puerto Rico was a "Hispanic equivalent of the Apollo Theater in Harlem" that featured "famous singers, dancers, comedians, and musical groups from every corner of Latin America and the Caribbean."[76] Historically, the theater was a cultural center for the Latino community, a place to experience Spanish music and dance and to maintain language traditions in spite of the "city's overwhelmingly 'Anglo' environment."[77] Shuttered and dilapidated in the 1970s due to the decline of the surrounding neighborhood, the Teatro Puerto Rico was purchased in 1984 by local Latino developer James Sanchez, who had attended the theater in the 1940s and '50s as a child to see live acts and films with his family. Sanchez installed new movie theaters in the building—one Spanish and one English—to update the cultural function of the historical landmark and to bring different generations together. Sanchez noted, "We've tried to set it up so that we can offer a night out for families that don't want to go all the way down to 42d [*sic*] Street for a movie."[78] He went on to state that "the older folks can go see a Cantinflas movie at the Spanish theater, and for the kids we'll have something like *Krush Groove* at the English one."[79] Local families would no longer have to travel so far outside of their neighborhood or even the borough to see a film. Sanchez was a developer and certainly meant to turn a profit in this endeavor but the impetus to restore the theater seems to be motivated by sincere and even altruistic intentions since the Teatro Puerto Rico was a historically important cultural center for the Latino community, and in its rehabilitated form it was to provide a local cinema experience when there was a dearth of theaters in the South Bronx region. The project also proposed to serve the existing population, not move in a new, more affluent one. Even more importantly, it ostensibly offered a spectatorial experience that would nurture familial bonds and intergenerational socialization by screening Spanish language and current popular youth-oriented Hollywood films together.[80] Film studios had given up on the "family audience" decades before this. Sanchez's vision was therefore both novel and financially risky given the widespread notion that cinema culture was unwaveringly youth driven. After four months of family-friendly business, Sanchez indicated that the theater was a success and remarked that "we have no graffiti and no ripped out seats."[81] The revival of the Teatro Puerto Rico was short-lived, unfortunately, and it became ensnared in lawsuits and financial troubles in the 1990s, ultimately defaulting on rent in 1996.[82] Even though its rebirth was truncated, this innovative venture draws attention to the importance of ethnically specific cinema, communal audiences, and "intergenerational" social spaces for inner-city populations ravaged by urban decay and alienated by conventional cultural forms. Moreover, Sanchez specifically names *Krush Groove* as a film that would be appropriate for the resurrection of local youth cinema culture in the South Bronx. This is significant considering that it was already notorious as a catalyst for violence and audience unrest. Clearly, the developer saw *Krush Groove* as a film that would inspire social cohesion and communal pride in his South Bronx community despite its history of audience-related conflicts, which had been reported in mainstream news publications for at least two months prior to Sanchez's statement.

The "Intergenerational Gap": Race and Family Structure

The urban musical of the 1980s worked to define hip hop culture in opposition to the consumer capitalism of mainstream teen cinema. These films maintained an ambivalent, if not contradictory, relation to their status as teen films in other ways as well. As Rapping notes, popular white-centered teen cinema of this era is predominantly focused on the world of teenagers, while the role of younger children and adults is usually minimized, ridiculed, or otherwise deemed incompatible with the teen universe.[83] Hip hop musicals, by contrast, tend to incorporate "intergenerational" meetings between teens, children, and young adults far more frequently than mainstream teen cinema. Even though these films often feature a group of teens or young adults, the true hip hop musical emphasizes the links between different generations in a variety of ways. While both suburban-oriented teen cinema and inner-city musicals registered anxieties over the wane of traditional familial groupings, the latter films attempted to construct alternate social groupings, which functioned as surrogate filial structures.

These films include a broad spectrum of the population and often highlight harmonious relations between different age groups. Such an emphasis on alternate forms of social bonding undoubtedly speaks to the dramatic rise in divorce rates initiated in the 1970s, which peaked between the years 1979 and 1981 before beginning a slight but steady wane in 1985.[84] This fact, in conjunction with a wide range of Reagan-era government initiatives, put minority families at risk in the ways detailed in the previous chapter. The family structure is a point of crisis found in several examples of urban cinema focused on communities of color during the 1980s and '90s, including both "New Black Realism" and hip hop musicals. Many white-centered teen suburban films from the 1980s also explore themes of familial discord. However, the evocation of parent culture and the ways in which teens respond to familial disintegration in these two forms take on markedly divergent dimensions. Parents are either stupid, uncaring, or absent in the majority of innocuous suburban teen flicks from the 1980s (such as *Sixteen Candles* and *Better Off Dead* [1985]), while representations of grossly misguided parental guardianship are taken to the extreme in predominantly white-centered teen slashers (such as the *Nightmare on Elm Street* and *Friday the 13th* franchises). The bulk of these films envision a world in which parents and other forms of authority are acutely dangerous to the well-being of the younger generation. Yet teens in this middle-class environ still have comfortable bedrooms and other interior private spaces from which they can ward off the evil entities and spirits that their parents are helpless to protect them from. In contrast, young people in the true hip hop musical have no safe middle-class enclave in which to reconstruct social relations in the absence of traditional families. Instead, the public spaces of collective performance constructed around hip hop culture provide alternate milieus of familial bonding.

The representation of such an inclusive community suggests that the true hip hop musical is structurally different from mainstream white suburban "teenpics." Even within surface hip hop musicals such as *Breakin' 2*, children are often featured in communal dance sequences. And while a review of *Breakin'* from the *Baltimore/Washington Afro-American* found the film to be "silly, amateurly acted, and badly directed," the writer nonetheless praised the breadth of the film's cast and talent of its dancing stars. The author writes that

> the real stars of *Breakin'* are the amazingly supple moves of "Boogaloo Shrimp" Chambers and the film's other breakdancers, which include children and a parapalegic breaker who spins on both his crutches and his head to the steady stream of hot rock steady street music.[85]

Further, a large advertisement for the film that appears beneath the article proclaims that it presents "the hottest break dancers in America," including Shabba doo, Boogaloo Shrimp, and "the amazing 9-year old sensation Coco."[86]

Krush Groove features both teenagers and young adults as it follows the exploits of teen rappers the Fat Boys (formerly known as the Disco 3) as well as older, more established artists, including Run-D.M.C., Kurtis Blow, and Sheila E. The film even deliberately references its ambiguous status as teen cinema by staging a stock teen musical number that takes place in the enclosed world of an urban high school. In this sequence, the Fat Boys cut biology class to entertain the whole school with their rhymes. The scene opens with the camera surveying a bored science class performing a fetal pig dissection. As the teacher turns her body towards the chalkboard, she drones on about the importance of the assignment while drawing a diagram of the pig's internal organs. To her surprise, as soon as her back is to the class, beats and other percussive noises fill the room. The culprit is Buffy, the Fat Boy's human beat box. However, all three members of the group claim responsibility for the aural disturbance and are promptly ejected from class. When the bell rings the trio is perched atop a set of stairs, awaiting the flow of students through the halls who provide an audience for the their impromptu song and dance number, "Don't You Dog Me." While the entire school participates in the number by singing,

Fig. 3.4. The liberating power of teen music: musical pandemonium erupts in the school hallways when the Fat Boys perform "Don't You Dog Me" in *Krush Groove* (1985). Courtesy of Photofest.

dancing, and clapping, the teacher resurfaces in the chaotic hallway to shake her head in disapproval.

This is the only school sequence in the entire film. The Fat Boys become successful after they ditch school, and the rest of the narrative takes place in streets, clubs, and record studios—the consistent locales of the hip hop musical. *Krush Groove*'s initial school sequence seems to acknowledge the potential relation of the film to mainstream teen cinema. For example, this performance encapsulates the founding twin dynamics of the postwar American "teenpic"—music and delinquency—an intersection that proved to be both volatile and popular in the early years of teen cinema. The initial furor over *Blackboard Jungle* (1955), the archetype of the school youth flick, stemmed largely from the fear that teens viewing the film in theaters may actually be motivated to commit violence not only because of the representation of juvenile delinquency, but also because these actions were set to the beat of Bill Haley and the Comets' "Rock

Around the Clock."[87] While the Fat Boys don't commit violence on screen, they are clearly disruptive in class (from the perspective of adult authority) and through their subsequent musical performance in the hallway they are shown to propel other students towards behavior that is viewed as delinquent or disruptive by the parent generation. The film acknowledges the teen spectator and teen film genre by showcasing a dynamic interchange between the power and creativity of youthful music and its potential to disrupt the everyday rhythms of life. However, musical expression as a facet of youthful rebellion is not the primary theme of *Krush Groove*, and this aspect of the film is dropped once we leave the teen world of high school behind. History tells a different story, as I have already suggested. There is no overt link between musical performance and violence in the film, but screenings of this particular hip hop musical have been associated with more instances of actual conflict among patrons than any other of the same era.[88]

The rigidly defined generational spaces of 1980s mainstream teen cinema, it seems, are somewhat incompatible with the inclusiveness of hip hop culture. In the scene from *Wild Style* discussed in a previous chapter, the "Stoop Rap" of Double Trouble, a group of teens interact with a young child in a positive and productive way, sharing a cultural experience. When young children are dealt with at all in conventional white teen cinema, they are usually antagonistic towards their older siblings, and their abilities, feelings, and desires are incompatible with teen culture. For instance, teenaged Samantha's (Molly Ringwald) younger brother in *Sixteen Candles* clearly despises his sister and ridicules her whenever possible, and *Better Off Dead*'s teen star Lane (John Cusack) is hopelessly inept in comparison to the technical achievements of his younger brother Badger. While Lane has to rely on his girlfriend to fix his broken down Camaro, Badger creates a working space rocket and handheld laser. The point is taken to the extreme as Lane quips that his little brother shouldn't be playing with lasers. In response, Badger shoots the powerful gun at Lane as he attempts to enter his room, leaving a "blast hole" just a few inches from his older brother.

Valley Girl provides one the most compelling accounts of younger children's incompatibility with teen culture. In this film, children are absent from the teen world of girl talk, mall spending sprees, and house parties, except for one striking scene in which Peggy, popular "Val Girl" Suzie's younger sister, intrudes upon a pajama party lip-synch number. As the girls energetically dance and sing along to a vinyl record playing

Bonnie Hayes and the Wild Combo's "Girls Like Me," the camera pans to feature each girl's face in close-up—a technique suggestive of the camera movement used to film chorus girls in classical-era Hollywood Busby Berkeley musical numbers. The camera reframes, offering a medium long shot, which reveals the barely clad bodies of the teen dancers and also young Peggy, who has surreptitiously joined the party. Her entrance into the frame, however, causes the record to skip, which promptly brings the song and dance number to an abrupt close. After this gaffe, the teens immediately eject Peggy from the party with a terse "spaz get lost." The chorus line-inspired musical number is never resumed but a shot of the record being re-cued allows for the teen antics to recommence. Peggy not only interrupts the girls' fun, but also disturbs the playful illusion of a seamless musical number for the film spectator. We *know* that the teens are lip-synching and yet the disruption of this ostensibly cohesive relationship between diegetic music and a visual correlate of singing mouths and dancing bodies is still registered as a mild shock by the viewer. Thus, the sense of rupture caused by Peggy's presence is cleverly wedded to the narrative of the film, but more importantly, to the spectator's desire for a unified aural and visual experience.

Although these examples represent the predominant status of the relationship between teens and younger children in the majority of popular white-oriented teen productions of the time, some cinematic portrayals of this relationship envisioned more constructive interactions. For instance, *The Outsiders* (1983), Francis Ford Coppola's dramatic portrayal of youthful delinquency and class tensions set during the 1960s, *Night of the Comet* (1984), an apocalyptic sci-fi thriller featuring two valley girls as surviving heroines, and *The Legend of Billie Jean* (1984), a commercial flop from TriStar Pictures about sibling fugitives who battle teen thugs and nefarious adult forces in their bid to recover the money to repair a vandalized scooter, all featured positive relations between siblings and/or teens and younger children. Even so, the fact remains that the bulk of teen film oriented around racially homogenous mall culture and school classrooms overwhelmingly isolated teens from younger children and the parent generation.

In contrast to the peripheral status of children in most mainstream teen cinema in the early 1980s, hip hop musicals, and hip hop culture in general, emphasized youth in a variety of ways and was not just centered on teen exploits. For instance, the cover of *We Can Do This*, a compilation record featuring DJ Red Alert, a popular hip hop DJ from KISS-FM 98.7, depicts a young child poised over the studio microphone while Red Alert spins a record. We also hear a child's voice on the recording, announcing the station's call numbers. Grandmaster Flash's rap "Adventures of Grandmaster Flash on the Wheels of Steel" features young children asking the DJ to tell them the story of his life. Noteworthy here is also the sentiment of *Wild Style*'s title track, "Wild Style Subway Rap," performed by Chris Stein of Blondie and Grandmaster Caz. The uplifting words encourage listeners to utilize their own unique talents to fulfill personal dreams as well as turn their efforts towards communal improvement to "make our homes rate an A+." Further, hip hop is specifically noted as a particularly potent expression of individuality and creativity in the lines "use the beat in your heart and ink to be great." The rap then makes an explicit plea to children and young teenagers:

> Word, that's what it's all about, I'm gonna do my thing and won't let nothing else hold me back, strive to be number one always. That's the same thing I told my little brother, he said he wanted to drop out of school, and I had to tell him, you gotta push ... push.

Early hip hop, unlike most contemporary rap culture, encompassed the entire community, including children.

Wild Style, *Rappin'*, *Beat Street*, and the *Breakin'* series all feature neighborhood children as dancers or rappers. The older youth in these films teach younger children how to dance and perform. Additionally, when sibling relations in such musicals are more developed they also reveal a complexity and maturity far beyond the capacity of most contemporary conventional teen cinema. *Beat Street*'s narrative is, in large part, concerned with the relationship between Kenny and younger brother Lee, who is permitted to engage in Kenny's social scene in a limited but fulfilling way. Similarly, *Rappin'* offers a depiction of sibling relations in which John Rappinhood not only befriends his younger brother, but also goes to extreme measures to protect him and keep him out of jail following his theft of a car stereo. Thus, they envision a productive response to an actual historical crisis in the family structure that specifically affected inner-city communities. African American families in the 1980s were far more likely than white families to be comprised of a single income household with an absent father. In 1982, "19 percent of all families had female heads of household and one in five children lived with the mother only, compared to roughly half these proportions in 1970" and in the African American community "30 percent of families in 1970 and 46 percent in 1982 had female heads of household."[89] The preponderance of positive interactions between children and teens and other members of the community in the true hip hop musical (and some surface hip hop musicals) reveals the extent to which these films incorporated this historical familial crisis into their narrative. Most interactions between teens and children in hip hop musical film is orchestrated around music and dance culture, echoing the vital link between collective performance and social cohesion within urban communities of color.

Significantly, there is no prominent positive father figure within the inner city community in any of these films. When the hip hop musical does reveal a glimpse of family life it is never comprised of a stable nuclear family unit. John Rappinhood seemingly has no parents, only a grandmother in his home, while Lee and Kenny in *Beat Street* have only their mother. Similarly, we see no parents at all in *Wild Style*. In *Breakin'* and *Breakin' 2*, the stars of the films, Ozone and Turbo, live together in an inner-city Los Angeles community. Turbo is a teenager, while Ozone is a young adult. There is no mention of their family and the older roommate appears to take care of his young charge. This relation forms an alternate family structure in place of the traditional family unit.

The lack of fathers in these films should certainly be read against the actual disintegration of the family structure in poor inner-city neighborhoods as a result of increased poverty, the consequences of illegal drugs flooding black and Latino neighborhoods, and the disproportionate amount of black males in the U.S. prison system at this time. But the breakdown of the family unit was also a feature of white-centered teen slashers of this era. Remarkably, many slasher films function as a critique of "white flight" to the suburbs, and more generally of the social order represented by white male authority.[90] Although I have argued that the hip hop musical sets itself against the white-centered mainstream "teenpic" at this time, they both yearn for a suitable patriarchal figure, but in different ways.

The critiques launched by teen slashers always show the family (or what's left of it) as an uncaring, inadequate, and even malevolent force in teenagers' lives. When the killer emerges out of the darkness, parents are never around to protect their children. In *Nightmare on Elm Street*, parental actions are even the direct cause of child killer Freddy Krueger's supernatural savage attacks. A group of neighborhood parents seek retribution for the murder of neighborhood children by burning Krueger alive.

After this event he returns as a supernatural force of evil and proceeds to torture and murder the children of Elm Street through their dreams. Likewise, in *Friday the 13th* (1980) parental neglect indirectly unleashes the relentless teen killer Jason upon generations of hapless young campers. Mrs. Voorhees (Betsy Palmer) returns to Camp Crystal Lake many years after her son drowned while attending summer camp in the area. In the final moments of the film, she is unmasked as the killer. The mother's desire to kill, it is revealed, is initiated by her own feelings of guilt at having relinquished her son's care to others—irresponsible teen camp counselors who were making out instead of supervising, causing the child to drown.

In the hip hop musical, parental figures and adult members of the community are typically portrayed in a far more sympathetic light. The fragmented family units depicted in these films are usually comprised of caring, hard-working individuals who struggle to provide the best care possible for their young charges. Alternate structures of family and community in the hip hop musical allow people to come together in meaningful, if unconventional ways to combat the threats imposed on their neighborhoods by external and often uncontrollable forces. This is in stark contrast to the teen slasher, in which alternate forms of familial relations between victimized teenagers and older survivors of the killer's wrath are forged in order to combat the horrors caused directly or indirectly by neglectful members of the fragmented nuclear family and the dissolution of the suburban dream.

In closing, I would like to return to the violent events surrounding the release of *Krush Groove* and the general reception of the film. Many reports of strife surrounding this film stemmed from the inability of patrons to actually enter the theater due to overbooking.[91] Black (and presumably youthful) audiences turned up at cinemas in large numbers because they were no doubt excited by the prospect of seeing engaging and successful African American characters on screen.[92] Critical assessments of *Krush Groove* were varied. The *Washington Post* compared the film unfavorably to Prince's *Purple Rain* and referred to it as a kind of "'Purple Drizzle,' partly because of the story, which is scattershot; mostly because of the music, which isn't music at all, but rap, that tired fad of worn-out rock critics."[93] A reporter from the *Boston Globe* snidely remarked that

> *Krush Groove* isn't a movie—it's a video that turns the theatre into a jukebox. The crowd at the first show at the Pi Alley yesterday sang along with the music, so it was practically impossible to hear the dialogue. The simple story

involves several rap groups who make it big. The direction is flat, the acting is mediocre, and the production values are weak.⁹⁴

The article attacked the production qualities of the film, but the writer seems to be more irritated by the audience's enthusiastic reaction. *Krush Groove* received a lukewarm two-and-a-half stars from the *Chicago Tribune*'s music critic who lamented that musical films rarely capture the exhilaration of live performance. "Rap is no exception," she noted. "There are plenty of big names involved in *Krush Groove*, but the music alone isn't able to carry the film, and the plot certainly can't."⁹⁵ The black press offered mixed reviews of *Krush Groove*. In a particularly disparaging review, *New York Amsterdam News* reporter Charles Rogers refers to rap-oriented films in general as "the black junk films of the 1980s" and writes that "only hard-core, dyed-in-the-wool rappers will say that *Krush Groove*, the latest hip hop flick with a 'message,' adds up to more than 90 minutes plus of bad acting, a loud soundtrack, and ridiculous situations."⁹⁶ In contrast, an article from the *Baltimore Afro-American* praised the acting ability of the film's emerging star Blair Underwood, as well as the entire cast. This article also notes that *Krush Groove* "benefits from exceptional direction as well as tight scripting, fine acting, and polished performances."⁹⁷

Obviously, the large numbers of teens hoping to attend the film were not expecting to witness a great achievement in the cinematic arts. It was a cheaply made but energetic production that appealed to young people of color because there was a significant dearth of black characters in mainstream teen film and Hollywood cinema in general during the 1980s.⁹⁸ *Afro-American* movie critic Frederick I. Douglass specifically pointed to this issue in his review of the low budget Cannon film *Missing in Action* (1984), of which he notes there were "no blacks with speaking roles" and "not even any black prisoners of war to be rescued."⁹⁹ He goes on to remark that

> Hollywood has become totally oblivious of black audiences and the roles for black actors have dried up like that old raisin in the sun.... At least during the days of the so-called Blaxploitation films, young blacks could see and cheer for one or two black heroes.¹⁰⁰

Perhaps the violence and anger associated with *Krush Groove* patrons was not as inexplicable as most reports suggest. As we have seen, screenings at multiplex theaters brought racially and culturally distinct teen cultures in

Fig. 3.5. Photograph of Ida Peters, entertainment editor of the *Afro-American*, dancing with Michael Chambers, star of *Breakin'* and *Breakin' 2*, from the *Afro-American*, May 12, 1984. Photographer: Vanessa Johnson; courtesy of the *Afro-American*.

contact with each other during a contentious moment when both the suburb and urban environment were being redefined. The disparities between racially discrete urban/suburban communities found expression in teen film at this moment and in a world where malls and Molly Ringwald were the predominant symbols of American youth on screen, the large numbers left out of this equation embraced *Krush Groove* as an opportunity to witness a positive affirmation of their creative community. Indeed, Douglass concluded his review of *Missing in Action* by calling on the African American public to use their spending dollars in order to "begin influencing Hollywood to put us back on the silver screen."[101] This call seems to have been answered as young black patrons arrived at multiplexes across the country en masse to purchase tickets for *Krush Groove* only to be turned away due to overbooking.

Noting the absence of positive black youth on screen at the time, an article from the *Baltimore/Washington Afro-American* portrayed the young dance star of *Breakin'*, Michael "Boogaloo Shrimp" Chambers, as an antidote for the perceived excesses and lewd performance style of the few black superstars of the era, Michael Jackson, Eddie Murphy, and Richard Pryor. After criticizing these performers and finding fault with the production quality of *Breakin'*, the author goes on to note that "unlike most portrayals of black male teenagers, Chambers comes off as an intelligent, clean-living, and clean-motivated teenager."[102] The young actor seems to have had a particularly close relationship with the *Afro-American* and is seen with Ida Peters, the publication's entertainment editor, in two photographs from the newspaper's entertainment section—the first shows Chambers with Adolfo "Shabba Doo" Quinones and Lucinda Dickey, the two other stars of the *Breakin'* films, presenting Peters with a promotional poster for *Breakin' 2*, and the second features Chambers and Peters dancing together. This second photograph (fig. 3.5) appears in an article entitled "Shrimp Taught Me to Backslide" and is presented from the personal perspective of Peters. Underneath the photo a caption informs readers that Chambers "told Vanessa Johnson (photographer for the *Afro-American*) she reminded him of his aunt and Ida Peters, 'his grandmother.'"[103] This article again emphasized Chambers's "clean" persona by showcasing his "intergenerational" appeal through visual and textual material.

A year after the newspaper's coverage of Chambers it pronounced Blair Underwood, the "music man" of *Krush Groove*, to be a "New Star on the Horizon."[104] This article also emphasized the "clean" aspects of Underwood's persona, as author Valerie Smith-Madden reported that "Blair credits a strong family coupled with Christian conviction in helping him achieve and appreciate his impending stardom."[105] Although this "clean" image of the hip hop film star was about to dissolve into the tragic gangster figure of "New Black Realism" in the following years, it is very evident that the black press saw in these musicals an opportunity for the advancement of young performers of color (despite the films' other qualities). As an entry into American teen cinema that defied the racial homogeneity of preceding years, the hip hop musical exposed the deeply troubled racialized contours of geographical boundaries in the American psyche. It also delivered an antidote to the relentlessly consumer driven narrative of mainstream teen cinema because it provided a hopeful platform from which to imagine a confident young persona to represent communities of color in the entertainment industry.

Flashdance

Breaking, Ballet, and the Representation of Race and Gender

Introduction: Breakdancing in Print

The exceptionally popular urban phenomenon of breakdancing made its presence strongly felt in a variety of representational spaces, from medical journals to television pilots and advertising. For instance, in 1984 *The New York State Journal of Medicine* featured an article entitled "Hazards of Break Dancing," and the *Journal of the American Medical Association* ran a report called "Breaks and Other Bad News for Breakers" in 1985.[1] These commentaries, among other articles, were generally concerned with the dance style's inherent physical dangers, and describe case studies of specific injuries due to breakdancing—subdural hematomas and "Break-Dancing Neck."[2] The *Archives of Ophthalmology* even ran a piece entitled "Ocular Trauma From Break Dancing."[3] A brief editorial in *Parade Magazine* lingered over a report of "acute scrotal pain" and "testicular torsion," which allegedly plagued two adolescents following a vigorous breakdancing session.[4] In sum there were sixty-nine individual cases of injuries due to breakdancing reported between 1984 and 1987.[5] While many articles relate the possible injuries and side effects of breakdancing, there is very little written about the negative effects of other kinds of youth dance in the early 1980s. One exception to this, though, is a published medical investigation into the perils associated with heavy metal "head banging." The authors of "Head Bangers Whiplash" assert that

> vigorous dance styles of the youth culture have been reported to result in painful injuries. The current trend in dancing includes "head banging," which involves rhythmic repetitious movements and extreme flexion, extension, and rotation of the head and cervical spine. If the dancer has

shoulder-length or longer hair, the head banging requires an extra whip of the hair to keep it flowing and rotating. Dance-related severe pain in the cervical area may result from head banging.[6]

Interestingly enough, this article about heavy metal fans also linked its conclusions to previous studies of breakdance injuries by noting that

> breaking pains and arthralgias have been described among urban adolescents in relation to another type of dancing: break dancing. With that group, cervical spine injuries have even resulted in paraplegia and in muscle and ligament damage, as well as in vertebral fracture.[7]

Although heavy metal and "headbangers" were a very visible (and mainstream) youth culture contemporaneous with hip hop and breakdancing, there is surprisingly little documentation elsewhere of the "head bangers whiplash" condition cited in this report. The medical community, however, seemed to obsessively document any and every possible injury that could be connected with breaking. On the one hand, this speaks to a mainstream fascination with breakdance culture that was certainly evident in diverse representational outlets. On the other hand, there is a disproportionate amount of concern over the supposed dangers associated with this dance style, almost to the point of pathologizing it.[8]

More conventional representational spaces for breakdance culture included television, magazines, newspapers, public events, parties, and contests as performers from American urban centers popped, locked, and spun across the country and even across the globe. In 1984, Michael Holman hosted *Graffiti Rock*, an innovative television pilot that modeled itself on *American Bandstand* and other youth dance shows. The pilot aired on local New York station WPIX/Channel 11. It was oriented around hip hop culture, and featured rappers Run-D.M.C. and breakdance group, the New York City Breakers. Public venues also began to host large-scale breakdance events. For instance, 6,000 people gathered at Boston City Hall Plaza to watch a performance by the New York City Breakers in June 1984, while the Swatch watch company sponsored a breaking competition in August of the same year, which was taped for national broadcast.[9] Several soft drink companies, including Mountain Dew and Pepsi, also featured breakdancers in their television commercials during this time.[10] As early as 1983, the New York City Breakers entertained at a large corporate party for the brokerage firm Merrill Lynch, Pierce, Fenner, & Smith.[11] By 1984, American breaking crews toured Europe and Asia, performing at carnivals, high profile fundraisers, and even in a show for Queen Elizabeth II.[12]

The majority of breakdancing crews and solo performers who experienced brief commercial success in the 1980s, such as *Beat Street*'s Robert Taylor, the New York City Breakers, and the Rock Steady Crew, were predominantly young men, and the dance form itself is considered a masculine mode of expression. Women, however, also played an important, yet underexamined role in the cultural phenomenon of breakdance. It is all but forgotten that breakdance offered a lexicon for women (and girls) to challenge and confront potentially overbearing or threatening expressions of youthful masculinity. In fact, it is precisely the association of the form with male vigor, athleticism, and sublimated violence that allowed women to appropriate the dance in a critical manner. An examination of print material and films from the early 1980s will reveal the complex ways young women engaged with this particular performance style in order to express their own identity, and explore a variety of strategic dialogues that challenged the codes of masculinity in dance.

This chapter begins with a survey of instructional manuals devoted to breaking because they help contextualize the use of breakdance in mainstream cinema in relation to gendered spaces of performance. Further, this discussion will also draw on other sources of print media to explain diverse attitudes towards breakdance and gender outside of cinematic representations. A close examination of the plethora of printed material pertaining to this dance trend will show that breaking was significantly concerned with delineations of masculine and feminine behavior, and that it was often linked to both covert and overt displays of sexual power.

Finally, I address the brief overlap between ballet and breakdance in the early 1980s, an artistic conjunction also explored in *Flashdance*. This cultural intersection materialized as a thematic feature of hip hop on-screen, and also made an impact on the world of professional dance. As this nexus is traced through print, I argue that dance producers and promoters attempted to cull breakdance "from the street" and introduce it into the academy in order to "re-masculinize" public perceptions of the male ballet star. When the conventional spaces of dance culture endeavored to absorb breakdance, producers and promoters tried to alter the dance form in order to make it fit European expectations of performance. The resulting hybrid productions attempted to narrativize and structure breakdance while expunging its improvisational aspects, so that it would be acceptable for consumption by mainstream audiences.

This revisionist history of breakdance uses the methods of feminist historians to tease out important issues pertaining to gender that have previously remained buried in the archival record.[13] Obscure and less well-known publications are cited, and with this work the opinions of women and young girls contemporary with early breakdance culture are illuminated. When turning to cinema, attention is focused on how female characters interact with breakdance culture on screen. When breakdancing made its debut in feature films women were rarely featured as breakdancers, although a handful of examples (including *Flashdance, Breakin'*, and *Breakin' 2*) portray female dancers whose sexual power and performance skills are directly linked to their interactions with urban street dance. Moreover, their bodies become threshold spaces upon which black and Latino performance culture engages with mainstream academic dance practice. Early instances of hip hop on film may have failed to produce any female breakers that were substantial characters; however, many of these productions reveal gender to be a startlingly important category of analysis in relation to understanding the link between mainstream performance and dance that is associated with urban communities of color.

At least ten breakdance manuals were published between 1984 and 1985. These usually included extensive photographic examples of dance moves, a brief history of the evolution of breakdance, as well as information on appropriate dress and footwear, music choices, and cautionary advice regarding safety while breaking. Some manuals, such as *Break Dancing: Step-By-Step Instructions* (1984), provide a link between printed visual material and the first cycle of hip hop cinema.[14] Many of the photographs of breaking used in the book are actually taken from *Breakin'* and *Beat Street*. These cinematic images are woven into the visual representation provided by the crew of dancers photographed for the manual. Martha Cooper, who was a photographer on the set of *Wild Style*, is also listed as a consultant for the manual. She is just one of the surprising number of women that are cited as either dancers or consultants for this book. This parallels the manual's imagery as well, which seems to resist a dominant male identity for the breakdancer.

Breakdance: Electric Boogie, Egyptian, Moonwalk . . . Do it, another early breakdance manual, is coauthored by a woman, Bonnie Nadell, and features Susan Jeremy as one of the book's main dancers.[15] We read in the introduction that Jeremy is an important figure in the current breaking scene, and she is featured in several of the manual's explanatory photographs. Jeremy was also an extra in *Beat Street*, and the text of the book suggests that learning to breakdance was a strategic move for this performer who initially began her stage career as a comedian. Although *Breakdance* features women in several photos, and implies that Jeremy is a rising dance star, the book infers that gender does play a role in the type of breakdance one may perform. Indeed, Jeremy is only featured in the electric boogie section of the book, illustrating the proper execution of mime techniques used in this type of performance. Electric boogie is a set of dance moves originally distinct from breaking. It includes a combination of mime, locking, and the jerky elements of The Robot.[16] Michael Holman writes of an early dance crew which is credited with inventing this dance that

> instead of throwing their bodies in and out of control like locking, or in total hydraulic control like The Robot, they passed energy through their bodies popping and snapping elbows, wrists, necks, hips, and just about all the body joints along the way. Electric boogaloo was more like mime in the sense that it pantomimed a live wire of electrical current, but it still needed the control of The Robot to give it style.[17]

All of the more athletic breaking moves are demonstrated through photographs of male dancers, while images of Jeremy are used to explain the techniques of electric boogie (or electric boogaloo, as it was originally named). Interestingly, the manual *Breakdancing: Mr Fresh and the Supreme Rockers Show You How to Do It!* describes the clothing style for female breakers as "simple and sleek—no high fashion designer look for them, no long parkas, or knit suits. Just Levi's and Lee jeans—tight—and black short jackets."[18] On the previous page however, the reader is informed that "breakers need loose clothing so they can move when they do their Floor Rock, Spins, and Windmills."[19] Female breakers are described as wearing form-fitting clothing rather than the loose fit required of the demanding dance form. Paradoxically, however, in its introductory pages the book acknowledges that women are full participants in the scene as it describes the work of Rosanne Hoare, a professional jazz dancer who took up breakdancing and came to lead her own female breaking crew.[20] The differences ascribed to men's and women's clothing suggest that women do not need the freedom of movement required by men to participate in breakdancing. This is explained by the gendering of breakdance moves that generally relegated women to the confines of the less physically strenuous electric boogie. It is tempting to naturalize this gender division in terms of the sheer upper body strength needed to perform most of the floor work in breakdancing in comparison to the less physically challenging electric boogie. However, the differences between these two styles of dance might also represent another set of gendered categories. Holman writes that electric boogie imitates the movements of nature "like a lightning bolt or a rippling river, whereas breaking is more out of control and anti-nature or anti-gravitational like a flying saucer."[21] This seemingly new and innovative dance culture, at least in the manuals, adopts archaic gender distinctions that place women within the realm of the natural, and associate men with technology and anti-nature. Yet women do assume positions of control across the representational spaces of breakdance culture. From the authorship of breakdance-oriented books to powerful positions *vis-à-vis* men within the dance world, women were clearly important to this phenomenon even though it is generally assumed that breakdance was a male-centered mode of expression that often rigorously excluded female practitioners.

Richard Majors and Janet Mancini Billson, the authors of *Cool Pose: The Dilemmas of Black Manhood in America*, include breakdance in their list of activities that fall under the representational strategy of what they call "cool pose." According to the authors, "cool pose" is a ritualized form of masculinity full of both negative and positive characteristics that uniquely shapes and defines a significant amount of African American male experience.[22] They write that "cool pose" largely arises "out of the legacy of slavery."[23] Majors and Billson go on to argue that

> because black males in the United States have been subjected to systemic discrimination and unusually harsh conditions, we suspect cool behaviors have emerged with more frequency and intensity among low income black males than in other groups.[24]

Majors and Billson's description of "cool pose" is interesting because it links the strategies of 1980s hip hop culture with the coping mechanisms of black male Americans since the beginnings of slavery. African American men have historically needed to invent a kind of mask or behavioral tactic that negated the damaging psychic effects of slavery and post-slavery forms of racial discrimination. Likewise, hip hop culture attempts to overcome the material impoverishment of inner-city life (which can be hazardous both to one's emotional and physical well-being), and also functions to bring "a dynamic vitality into the black male's everyday encounters, transforming the mundane into the sublime and making the routine spectacular."[25] Majors and Billson are right to point out that personal style as a marker of identity has played a large role in the African American male psyche, and breakdance seems to have fulfilled this function very clearly, judging from the archival record. While Majors and Billson focus only on "cool pose" in terms of negative consequences for black women, I would like to explore the representation of breakdance in relation to gender and race in a more nuanced manner.

Women of color have also used the avenue of "cool pose" to parody or usurp male power and identity through the stylings of hip hop culture. Furthermore, the first wave of hip hop musical cinema has given us female characters who appropriate the spaces of black and Latino male power through artistic performance in the narrative of the film. This is in marked contrast to the slew of peripheral female characters who dominate "New Black Realism" of the later 1980s and early '90s.[26] In fact, many examples from this earlier cycle of films feature female characters who are not dependent upon men for their survival in the urban environment. In *Wild Style*, for instance, Rose heads a graffiti crew independent of Lee, her estranged boyfriend who is also a graffiti writer. She fulfills the traditional film musical dual role of love interest and performance partner for the male lead, yet she also transcends the conventions usually ascribed to this character. Rose organizes The Union, her own crew, and she also refuses to be objectified by male characters who decline to take her work seriously. This is exemplified during a scene in which her estranged love interest first discovers her at work with her own "writers." Prior to this moment in the film, other young men have referred to Rose as her lover's "female," a derogatory term, describing her as nothing more than an owned piece of property. The scene opens with Raymond and a group of other young men approaching The Union who are busy working on a legal wall mural. Rose is filmed from behind as she issues forth creative leadership of the artists under her tutelage while they paint. She humiliates Raymond by ignoring his verbal efforts to gain her attention; Rose is obviously no longer his "female." She controls the creative vision of her crew (we see her holding a sketched plan of the mural), and also manages the technical expertise of the artwork; we clearly hear her command "don't get drips now" to the all-male team of writers. The film then cuts to an image of Raymond illegally tagging a wall with his *nom de plume* Zoro. An obvious contrast is made between legal collaborative artistic work (The Union) and a romantic vision of clandestine art practice that involves becoming an outlaw. At the end of the film, Rose also articulates a conceptually superior view of the art form that she and her would-be romantic and artistic partner share, and it is her input that allows Raymond to complete his final graffiti "masterpiece."

When female characters come from outside of the impoverished urban community in films such as *Beat Street* and the *Breakin'* series, they also assume a powerful role in shaping the artistic stylings of male performers. However, these women are often white and/or representative of high culture. It is worth pointing out that the black press did take notice of racial difference in the casting of the two female leads of *Breakin'* and *Beat Street*. Abiola Sinclair, a writer for the *New York Amsterdam News*, compares the two films:

> *Beat Street* has an added plus: the love interest is between two black youths. Although she was very charming and engaging and didn't have a stuck-up bone in her body, the girl in *Breakin'* was white. It seems black girls never get to see themselves cast in a complementary light on the silver screen.[27]

Sinclair is astutely aware of the fact that the early 1980s marked a particularly striking nadir in the representation of black actors in American film. By contrast, the hip hop musical featured African American actors and other performers of color at this crucial time, and it often presented positive roles for women of color such as Rose in *Wild Style* and Rae Dawn Chong's character, Tracey, in *Beat Street*. *Krush Groove* also featured a realistic romantic relationship between musician Shelia E. and Russell Walker (Blair Underwood).

Many scholars have noted that the physically demanding aspects and competitive structure of breakdance prohibited women from participating. Describing hip hop dance in terms of a male centered ritual, dance scholar Katrina Hazzard-Donald writes that

> hip hop dance is clearly masculine in style, with postures assertive in their own right as well as in relation to a female partner. In its early stages, hip hop rejected the partnering ritual between men and women; at a party or dance, hip hop dance was performed between men or by a lone man. . . . Even in its early stages hip hop dancing aggressively asserted male dominance.[28]

Hazzard-Donald uses an ethnographic approach to the subject, and the argument is largely derived from her personal experience of social dance situations. It is persuasive to hear Hazzard-Donald state that at about 1973 or 1974 I attended a dance given by African American students at Cornell University. I took the initiative and asked a young man to dance; on refusing my invitation, he explained that he couldn't dance with women, that the way he danced was unsuitable for dancing with women. He proceeded to give me a demonstration of how this was so, running through several dance steps that I had seen performed by Fred "Rerun" Berry and the Lockers. Correctly performed, the dance did not allow for female partnering; it was a purely male expression and rarely performed by females.[29]

What Hazzard-Donald describes is one particular person's explanation of why breakdance was not conducive to partner dancing but this does not necessarily indicate that it habitually excluded women. Although much of hip hop dance and breakdancing does assert an aggressive male stance and posturing, there are many textual, cinematic, and photographic examples that complicate the notion that breakdancing insisted on a radical exclusion of women. In fact, it can be shown that female performers often found ways of reinventing these masculine spaces for their own creative uses. These appropriations frequently parodied and critiqued black masculinity, and often facilitated the empowerment of young girls and women. Women breakers, like their male counterparts, also danced non-partnered steps in group formations (when breaking is shown in ballet magazines, however, female breakers are usually paired with men).

The *News Tribune* (Woodbridge, N.J.) reported that an all-female breakdance crew, The Female Break Force, performed at an open competition in Woodbridge in February of 1984.[30] Seventeen-year-old Candace Tims, a member of the group, states that "the guys would break against each other instead of fighting. We were rejected by the guys so we decided to do it on our own."[31] In 1984, the *Christian Science Monitor* printed an article entitled "When my Daughter Moonwalks." It laments the loss of partner dancing in relation to breakdancing, yet recounts a mother's pride as she watches her daughter breakdance with confidence at a social gathering.[32] A successful breakdancing crew from Queens, the Dynamic Rockers, also had two female members. This group won a competition at the Ritz in New York City in September of 1983, in which the women in the group performed.[33]

In a 1984 article from the *New York Daily News*, Clarissa Lopez (aka Lady Rock), a South Bronx resident and member of the all-girl breakdance team the Lady Rockers, writes that she is a "very good breakdancer" who started breakdancing to overcome her shyness.[34] Above the text is a photograph of her crew donning mock poses of aggressive black masculinity. The five young girls camp it up in the newsprint image, obviously aware of the significance of violating gender norms and taboos in relation to dance performance. Ironic and playful, three of the five girls cross their arms over their body while flashing a rather knowing and self-aware smile at the spectator. Clearly, they are conscious that their corporeal adoption of "cool pose" represents a powerful comment on the gendered aspects of breaking, but the playfulness of the image also bears out a serious side. If "cool pose" is literally the refusal of black men to submit to their status as second class citizens, prescribed to them by white-centered American society, these girls are asserting an aggressive identity in defiance of white authority over blacks and other persons of color, *and* against black and white patriarchal oppression. Interestingly, Majors and Billson find that the strategy of "cool pose" adopted by African American men functions negatively in the lives of black women because

> cool behaviors may prevent couples from establishing strong, committed, and authentic relationships. The games and masks, the highly stylized expression of self that makes the cool male attractive, are the very same artifices that inhibit intimacy and genuine companionship.[35]

The authors also assert that some black women may use the strategies of "cool behaviors" to "counter the attitudes and actions of cool black males."[36] Rather than focusing on this practice by black women as a highly conscious strategy in which "cool pose" is adopted for ironic and critical purposes, Majors and Billson primarily attribute this behavior to simplistic dating rituals of "playing hard to get."[37] My reading of visual examples from the 1980s involving breakdance suggests otherwise. The *New York Daily News* photograph of the Lady Rockers is an excellent example. It is an ambivalent image of youthful femininity, as the girls seem both awkwardly and obviously posed, as well as confident and sardonic in their adoption of male posturing.

In 1984, *Dance Magazine* also published two images containing female breakers in an article entitled "Breaking Away 80's Style."[38] The first features Rosanne Hoare, performing a locking kick over the body of a male dancer bent into a bridge position. Clearly dominating the male dancer, she provides the energy and momentum in this image, while her partner appears static. Hoare's dominance is further reinforced by the text of the article, which states that she is a professionally trained jazz dancer who is manager and choreographer of the Brooklyn breakdance crew The Furious Rockers,[39] and also a house choreographer at the legendary Roxy venue, which the *New York Times* pronounced "a hot and crowded pantheon of hip hop music and dance" in October of 1983.[40] Another full-page image in this article features a male/female pairing which shows one of the few breakdance partner moves, the two-man spin. However, in this rendition the woman lifts the man into the air to propel him in a circular motion. Violating all norms of the jazz and ballet lift, where the man elevates the woman into the air, breakdance pictorial representation seems to allow for a forbidden, inverted articulation of gendered movement and space.

At roughly the same time, *Ballet News* ran a feature article that seemed troubled by the gendered aspects of breakdance. The text frames the dance form as a wholly masculine performance ceremony that offers young men "praise and admiration from the girls" for achievements in breakdancing.[41] In other words, breakdance is described primarily as a mating ritual whereby young men show off their skill and strength in order to interest potential female romantic partners. In describing a dance performance following a girls volleyball tournament at Jamaica High School in Queens, however, the writer notes that "a young lady leaps up, clumsily mimics electric boogie, then engages in a mock-serious dance dialogue" with one of the male dancers.[42] This quote suggests an uncertainty about the limits of breakdancing in terms of a gendered mode of expression and communication. The young lady's "clumsy mimic" may be a result of lack of skill, but the passage also suggests a knowing and challenging relationship to the masculinity on display—a reorienting of the typical function of uprock.

Uprock describes the combative and confrontational aspects of breaking, which are derived from the movements, gestures, and style of martial arts.[43] However, uprock often involved a mimed non-violent insult, such as implying that the challenging crew or dancer smells bad. It could also take the form of parodying a particular move performed by a dancer that was perceived as weak or unoriginal by a competitor. If the female dancer described in the article is ineptly and awkwardly mimicking the moves of the previous breaker, it seems to me that it is likely that she is using uprock to challenge and parody her would-be male suitor. She may be unable to perform as well as her male counterpart, yet it seems more likely that her reaction is in fact a mocking of the intense display of masculine bravado often found in breakdance. Like the image of the Lady Rockers who lampoon the overt displays of masculinity at the heart of breaking through their own unique version of "cool pose," this article from *Ballet News* also implies that women can indeed critique the aggressive and bombastic assertions of masculinity in hip hop culture through the lexicon of breakdance.

Both of these examples suggest a very strong case for the ambivalence of performance in relation to textual and visual accounts of the female breaker, and women's relationship more generally to breakdance. In fact, breaking offered a much more fluid and flexible idiom of expression than the rigidly gender-defined practice described by Hazzard-Donald. Because the dance form was associated with such overdetermined gender roles, this is what made it available to women as a space of critique, and a place where one could challenge the strictly defined codes of masculine and feminine behavior associated with hip hop culture in general. Moreover, women dancers contributed to the development of the dance style even before it became co-opted by the media storm of the '80s. Holman notes that

> Toni Basil, who was famous for shows like "Shindig" and "Hullaballoo," discovered Don Campbell and his Lockers and helped bring them to international fame. She was an incredible dancer herself and soon learned to lock. She became a member of The Lockers, helped develop their dance act, and got them on TV shows like *Saturday Night Live* and commercials such as Schlitz Malt Liquor Beer (the one with the bull). I remember seeing her and Don Campbell dance live at a nightclub called Crenshaw Flats in Los Angeles. I was blown away. She was actually better than he was![44]

While Toni Basil, a talented choreographer and singer who went on to receive nominations for both Emmy and Grammy Awards, is rarely mentioned in the context of the development of breakdance, Adolfo "Shabba Doo" Quinones of the Lockers is often cited as an important early influence along with James Brown and Michael Jackson.[45] Women not only choreographed breakdance groups but also taught breakdancing and were pupils of this newly emerging art form. Kimberly McKeever-Kaye provided breakdance lessons at the McKeever Dance Centre, which was located in the predominantly white, affluent bedroom community of New York City, Greenwich, Connecticut.[46] *Newsweek* also claims that young white suburban girls were learning to break in "Dewitt, Mich. (population 3,596)" even before the slew of breakdancing films was released in 1984.[47] The authors note that "Russell Brown teaches the moves to a class of 11-and 12-year-olds. His pupils break the demographic rules—they are all white and mostly girls."[48] Of course, young white suburban teens and housewives learning to breakdance in group classes largely decontextualizes the art form and renders the explosive political power of the female breaker moot. These accounts are generally celebratory and cursory, and they remove breaking from its initial context of inner-city America. The appeal of breakdance in this set of circumstances can more easily be explained by the popularity of group exercise/dance classes in the 1980s rather than a critical appropriation of representations of masculinity.[49]

Gwendolyn Pough discusses the use of "sass" as a rhetorical strategy to triumph over demeaning or degrading situations that devalue black female identity.[50] She notes that scholars have traced this performance strategy back to early slave narratives written by women, while she uses the concept to explain the work and image of female rap artists. "Sass" involves the physical projection of a self-conscious sense of worth in the face of forces that threaten to erase or elide black female subjectivity. It denotes a highly self-aware display of embodiment, an act that is wedded to intellectual assertiveness. Of course, as many black feminist scholars have argued, African American women are often doubly marginalized as both women and people of color, and by both white society in general, and black men in their own communities. Because an inordinate amount of negative appraisals and stereotypes already plague black men, communities of color expect black women to remain tacit on the misogynistic and sexist elements of African American culture. Kimberlé Crenshaw writes that

> although patriarchy clearly operates within the black community, presenting yet another source of domination to which black women are vulnerable, the racial context in which black women find themselves makes the creation of a political consciousness that is oppositional to black men difficult.[51]

Pough also notes that African American women have habitually been disempowered and marginalized in recent political and social black power engagements such as the Black Panthers and the Black Arts Movement of the same era.[52] "Sass," therefore, is unlike "cool pose" because it must attend to two distinct but related avenues of political and social marginalization, both within and outside of one's own race. Several examples discussed above could usefully be understood as examples of "sass" because they cannot be separated from their connection to communities of color. The "sassy" strategies used by these women to assert their own worth and identity in the context of hip hop culture have been complex (even if they have not been read that way by scholars) from the very beginning because they have had to take on this "double burden" of negotiating the sexism of their own communities as well as the racism and sexism of North American culture in general. It is not surprising that male critics and journalists of hip hop have often failed to see the complexity and subtleties of women's roles in, and contributions to, the hip hop community, especially when their strategies involve a confrontation of the hyper-masculine aspects of the culture.[53]

Gender and Breakdance in Cinema: Women's Bodies, Race, and the Spaces of Performance Culture

The relationship between women and breakdancing was an important point of signification in early mainstream hip hop musicals. Cinematic representations of breakdancing by women tended to utilize female actors who were either white or racially ambiguous. As we have seen, in *Breakin'* a white female jazz dancer who learns to breakdance resolves the conflicting spaces of the film narrative—the street and the dance academy. *Flashdance*, the smash hit of 1983, while foregoing the actual inclusion of a female breaker, relies on the gendered codes of breakdance to describe and explain the sexual transformation of heroine Alex (Jennifer Beals) and her eventual movement from the street and working-class bar into the Pittsburgh Conservatory of Dance. The film locates the star in a predominantly white working-class social milieu. Beals, however, is actually of biracial heritage, with an African American father and white mother. In both cases, female dancers are able to meld breakdance with institutional dance. Their bodily gestures transform the spaces of high culture by bringing "street dance" to the academy. With these actions, the supposed boundaries between both dance forms, which of course point to larger social issues such as the unequal distribution of wealth between racial groups, are made irrelevant by exhilarating displays of dance virtuosity during the film's final show sequences.

Flashdance repeats a very familiar trope of the backstage musical genre. A kid from the wrong side of the tracks wants to break into "legitimate" theater/dance/showbiz. She lacks proper training but makes up for it in perseverance and tenacity while charming her way into the arms of the "perfect man." The trajectory and culmination of a successful romance

178   Breaking, Ballet, and the Representation of Race and Gender

Fig. 4.1. Alex (Jennifer Beals) flashdancing at Mawby's in *Flashdance* (1983). Courtesy of Photofest.

parallels the performer's ascent to stardom or some other career achievement.[54] Alex, the female lead of *Flashdance*, works hard, toiling as a welder by day and dreaming of a place in a prestigious dance conservatory while performing erotic dances or flashdances in Mawby's, a seedy working-class bar, at night. The narrative also follows the path taken by her good friend and fellow Mawby's employee Jeannie Szabo (Sunny Johnson II), a waitress who dreams of transcending her blue-collar roots through the world of professional figure skating. Various other female flashdancers appear in the film, but none of the women except for Alex actually succeeds in fulfilling her dreams. Only Alex moves beyond her initial position as a flashdancer, or glorified stripper, through a successful audition for an upper-class dance conservatory.

In fact, Jeannie becomes a "bad" example when she fails to succeed during her big break on the skating rink. She falls during her routine and is carried off the ice as Laura Branigan's song "Gloria" continues to pulsate over the speakers, and Alex looks on in sympathy for her friend. Following this failure, Jeannie ends up dancing at a nude strip bar (this type of "bad" dancing is contrasted in the film to Alex's theatrical and artistic flashdancing at Mawby's, in which clothes are not entirely removed) while Alex performs triumphantly at her dance audition and finds romance as well. A rather harsh lesson is observed: if you blow your big break you could wind up a has-been dancing the "cooch" on a beer soaked stage.

The structure of the film is episodic and it maintains a choppy or abrupt rhythm as the narrative is repeatedly fractured by extended flashdance sequences at Mawby's bar. Rapid editing matches the upbeat and fast paced rock and pop tunes of the soundtrack. This has led many observers to note that *Flashdance* was nothing but one long calculated music video devised to cash in on this new market by specifically catering to a teen audience (the projected audience for television music video programming), despite the restricted rating that it received.[55] Serge Denisoff and George Plasketes have argued that, although industry lore suggests otherwise, the creators of *Flashdance* never intended for the film to be marketed through MTV. They note that while Paramount credited MTV with the enormous success of *Flashdance*, at no time was the film conceived of in terms of music video segments. It was actually constructed in a modular fashion so as to make different sequences mobile within the film during editing.[56] Regardless of the timeline of events related to the music video releases from *Flashdance*, it is certain that reviewers and critics at this moment were keenly aware of the potential relationship between the rotation of music videos on television and the aesthetic choices of filmmakers. In fact, Vincent Canby writes of *Body Rock* that it "looks not like a theatrical film but like a series of music videos that have been spliced together to make a feature length presentation."[57]

Although many reviewers and academics mention that a group of breakdancers, the Rock Steady Crew, momentarily perform in *Flashdance*, little critical attention has been given to their appearance in this film. The dance segment has primarily been viewed as a watershed moment for hip hop culture because large segments of the theater-going public were exposed to the energy and creativity of breakdancing for the first time. Peter Rosenwald suggested that the film made breakdancing "accessible to millions," while Catherine Foster, writing for the *Christian Science Monitor*, noted that "*Flashdance* catapulted this street art into a worldwide phenomenon."[58] An article from the *Washington Post* erroneously stated that "breakdancing first secured major national notice when, in the hit movie *Flashdance*, the heroine performed a spectacular breakdance routine to successfully audition for ballet school."[59] In fact, the heroine embarks upon a fairly standard jazz dance routine, although she does indeed incorporate a move stolen from breakdance—the backspin—during the final moments of her performance. While Rock Steady's appearance in the film was the first large-scale cinematic exposure of breakdancing to mainstream audiences, Nelson George notes that another facet of hip hop culture, rap, was demonstrating its crossover appeal through its ability to place on the popular music charts as early as 1983. Rap artists did not, however, see regular rotation on MTV until at least two years later.[60] One of the primary reasons for including a breakdance segment in *Flashdance* may have been just an attempt to appeal to youth audiences, but I argue here that upon closer examination of this film the Rock Steady Crew, and street dance in general, fulfill a specific narrative function, one that far exceeds a calculated anticipation of hip hop's dramatic ascent in mainstream media and cultural activities just one year later.[61]

The Rock Steady Crew were a racially and ethnically mixed breakdance group, and this is not surprising given the fact that both African American and Latino dancers (in particular Puerto Rican youth) were responsible for the major innovations of its formal and stylistic properties.[62] In addition, there were some white dancers in the crew, such as Mr. Freeze, who helped transform and refine the art form. Even through breakdancing can claim multiple racial origins, in *Flashdance* its presentation is closely affiliated with African American identity. Firstly, the film is set in Pittsburgh, and the town's steel industry is evoked in order to construct a poignant rendering of working class life. If breakdance signified racial "Otherness" for the general public, in *Flashdance* it can most effectively be read in relation to African American urban identity since it was black Americans, rather than Latino immigrants who played a significant role in shaping the city's steel industry. Secondly, although the Rock Steady Crew are a pan-racial group as I note above, when they dance in the street in the film, we see an almost exclusively black audience, further linking this performance to an African American communal context.[63] This is all the more striking given the relative scarcity of black characters elsewhere in this film.

The urban terrain of *Flashdance*, made up of the gritty steel mills and working-class bars of Pittsburgh, was historically a space of racial contestation shaped by the struggle for industrial employment between Polish immigrants and Southern blacks. In their article "Migration, Kinship, and Urban Adjustment: Blacks and Poles in Pittsburgh, 1900–30," John Bodnar, Michael Weber, and Roger Simon argue that the circumstances of black migration to Pittsburgh were marked by a particular kind of racism that valued Polish immigrants as steel workers over black Americans arriving from the South during the first two decades of the twentieth century.[64] They also note, "By 1910 blacks remained scattered throughout the occupational spectrum and had still not permeated the steel industry."[65] Bodnar, Weber, and Simon's analysis rejects the theory of "ethnic succession" as the primary reason for lower rates of black industrial employment in Pittsburgh. They argue that very specific forms of racist and therefore exclusionary social structures in the city's workplace prevented blacks from entering this industry, thereby impeding the establishment of the type of work kinship networks that were available to Poles and other ethnic groups at this time. The development of the U.S. steel industry is bound up with a history of racial conflict well into the twentieth century. Blacks could be used as scab labor by large steel companies because they were habitually denied membership in several major unions. Even after African Americans were admitted into trade unions, their needs have been continually overlooked by these organizations.[66] The steel companies strategically used the racism prevalent in the industry to divide the labor force, and prevent workers from organizing.[67] As late as the 1960s and '70s, African Americans were still fighting against banishment to the dirtiest and most dangerous jobs, and a reluctance on the part of the industry to train black workers for more highly skilled positions.[68]

If the social spaces of *Flashdance* are predominantly white working-class locales linked to the steel industry, this specific history of racial conflict emerges as a central issue of the film.[69] Following from this point, I argue that the continual negation and sublimation of racial identity within the cinematic text of *Flashdance* is a predominant theme that structures the film but eventually comes to the surface in a multitude of ways. These issues are driven home by several overlooked aspects of the film: the conspicuous punctuation of the narrative by a stream of Polish jokes told by Ritchie on the stage of Mawby's bar; the repressed biracial heritage of Jennifer Beals, achieved by locating her character in an all-white social context; the continual presentation of black-identified urban dance moves; and the employment of a Puerto Rican breaker as body double in the final performance routine.

Additionally, the only significant conversation between a white and black character in the film serves to emphatically underscore the perceived difference between racially distinct modes of social behavior. A workout sequence set to Joan Jett's "I Love Rock 'n' Roll" provides the acoustic backdrop to this series of shots that divides the bodies of Mawby's working girls into fragmented glistening limbs and other corporeal parts as they lift weights. Alex and Tina Tech, another white dancer, discuss whether or not a potential love interest of Tina's is "going to call." Heels (Durga McBroom), the one black character in the scene, becomes so infuriated with her white friends' passive "wait and see" attitude that she finally unleashes an abrupt and acrimonious racialized admonishment in which she suggests, "Look, just call the man . . . just say hey baby, what's happening . . . the way you're going on with this thing, your whole fuckin' life's gonna be over before you make up your mind. Just get up and call the dude." Tina replies with a timid, "Yeah, you really think so?" Heels then blasts her with, "God, I'm glad I ain't no honky."

Although most critical appraisals of this film argue that it is only concerned with heteronormativity and the policing of gender boundaries, a closer look at the narrative structure reveals another predominant concern just below the surface. Ella Shohat and Robert Stam have described the classical-era musical genre as a corpus that habitually mitigates "awareness of America's multicultural formation." Yet they also note that upon close examination these films reveal the presence of "submerged ethnicities" within the margins of the cinematic frame.[70] Shohat and Stam go on to argue that

> highlighting the exclusionary nature of the musical's communality illuminates the dialectics of presence/absence of marginalized communities even in exclusively white-cast films which almost despite themselves reveal the suppressed others through music and dance.[71]

Although *Flashdance* is not entirely devoid of people of color, my analysis will reveal that the identity of Alex, the film's star, is wholly predicated on a play between the revelation and suppression of a "submerged" black presence within the film. Here I also take a lead from Carol Clover, who argues that *Singin' in the Rain* (1952), "America's favorite object lesson on giving credit where credit is due," is "driven by a nervousness . . . about stolen talent *unrestored*."[72] Clover makes reference to the choreography used by Gene Kelly and Donald O'Connor in the film as examples of the "theft" and unacknowledged use of black talent by the entertainment industry. Dance is the representation and manifestation of this anxiety in *Singin' in the Rain*, but Clover also refers to voice-doubling and other uncredited uses of black talent by white performers more generally. Thus, she argues that the film exhibits a repressed anxiety that can be observed on two levels. On the one hand, *Singin' in the Rain* repeatedly interrupts the white narrative space of the film with Kelly and O'Connor's routines, which appropriate black dance moves. On the other, the all-white narrative surface of the film is explicitly ruptured with specific references to black performance, for instance when Cosmo (O'Connor) suggests that the new "talkie" be named *The Dueling Mammy*.[73]

In a similar manner, while the Rock Steady Crew only appears once in *Flashdance*, the presence of black- and Latino-identified urban street dance interrupts the very fabric of the film, suggesting that its predominantly white social spaces are constructed in relation to a historical interchange—the appropriation of African American dance and musical performance by white actors—that must continually be repressed. Rock Steady's number is far from being only a fleeting attempt to cash in on the rising popularity of breakdance. In fact, performance traditions primarily derived from communities of color significantly impinge upon the narrative development of the film, especially in relation to *Flashdance*'s characterization of feminine sexuality and dance ability.

Appearing only briefly in one sequence, members of the Rock Steady Crew are showcased in a musical interlude as Alex, with friend Jeannie, wind their way through the gritty streets of Pittsburgh. Upon leaving their all-girl workout session, the friends are initially confronted by a lone male breakdancer in the street performing the moonwalk, The Robot, and other mime-inspired gestures. Throughout this scene, we also see other members of the Rock Steady Crew dancing alone, or in pairs, accompanied by a "ghetto blaster" to the bottom left of the frame. The breakdancers occupy a central position in the spatial composition of the sequence, yet the scene is very short and the dancers never reappear in the film. Although Alex is the lead character in a film about dance, in this scene she merely participates as part of the breakdancing circle, cheering on the street dancers who wow the crowd with backspins and other slick moves. Throughout the performance, the camera is stationary but successive cuts suggest time ellipses as each edit brings more audience members into the frame, until the image is teeming with a sizable enthusiastic gathering of onlookers.

As noted earlier, the Rock Steady Crew's presence in the film points to larger questions about race, performance, and gender in the postclassical musical, even though their routine is usually discussed in relation to the savvy marketing strategies that surrounded the launch of *Flashdance*. Shortly after the film's release, young MTV fans were introduced to the star of *Flashdance*, and snippets of the thin narrative, through the relatively new music video format. Youth audiences were courted with extended dance numbers in a darkened club, sweaty workout sequences, and plenty of sexual energy in Irene Cara's successful video to accompany her soundtrack contribution "What a Feeling." The insertion of black-identified youth culture into a key music and dance sequence in the film might simply be counted as one more attempt to cash in on the youth market—in this case, with the growing awareness that young suburban kids were becoming increasingly interested in forms of urban African American music and dance.[74] However, viewing black music and dance performance in *Flashdance* in relation to the entire history of race and performance in the American film musical, as well as in the context of the 1980s and the opening up of new youth-oriented marketing strategies, allows another picture to emerge.

This picture reveals how the conservative politics of race, gender, and class in *Flashdance* actually rely upon much older representational cinematic strategies to articulate a seemingly new set of relations. *Flashdance* is, at its heart, a fairy tale musical, whereby class differences are magically erased through romantic coupling. Alex, the working-class welder and aspiring dancer, ends up forming a relationship with a very wealthy factory owner, her boss Nick. All that Alex needs to lift her out of her blue-collar existence is to be rescued by an affluent, and much older, male suitor. For women who do not marry up, such as Jeannie, the picture is pretty bleak, and class divisions remain rigid. Class empowerment and mobility do not require any direct political or collective action in *Flashdance*, but rather are reduced to the personal and the sentimental. If we originally see Alex as part of a female working-class dance collective at Mawby's, the final moments of the film make a point of emphasizing her individual achievements (in both love and career). Her female friends are left behind as we witness a solo dance performance, and finally, a portrait of Alex and her wealthy lover when *Flashdance* closes.

Furthermore, women are continually objectified and even literally reduced to the sum of their corporeal components in the film, as the editing repeatedly focuses on specific body parts during various dance and workout sequences. While this editing style was necessary in large part to hide the fact that Beals did not in fact perform the dancing herself, the 1980s have, in general, been recognized as a moment when a traditionalist backlash against feminism took root in American culture.[75] The overt sexism of *Flashdance* is certainly symptomatic of a new conservative attitude towards women and their social and political empowerment. More generally, it also reflects a new concern in Hollywood cinema of the 1980s with

Fig. 4.2. *Flashdance* (1983) trades the community for the couple, Nick (Michael Nouri) and Alex (Jennifer Beals). Courtesy of Photofest.

success stories that separate the individual from his or her social context.[76] It is made very clear in *Flashdance* that Alex must become detached from the concerns of her lower-middle-class community in order to achieve romantic and professional success. Unlike in the hip hop musical, which generally closes with the image of a unified community, *Flashdance*'s final moment, as noted, includes only Alex and her romantic partner in an embrace. Her ascent towards artistic, career, and romantic fulfillment must be at the cost of communal cohesion. In contrast, the hip hop musical allows for the star performer to achieve both personal and public success *and* stay attached to his or her local environment.

Black-identified street dance in *Flashdance* largely articulates the relation between sexuality and success in the dance world for Alex. In fact, black communal street dance is linked to a delineation of her aggressive sexuality, one that facilitates Alex's ability to snare a man and, as I later argue, perform her dance routines successfully. Thus, breakdancing, which is usually a collective ritual attached to local social and political action, is disconnected from communal empowerment. Instead, it is linked with the personal journey of one woman's desire to transcend class barriers.

It also comes as no surprise that the Rock Steady Crew's dance sequence directly follows the workout scene. The preceding weightlifting scene showcases the sculpted bodies of the female stars in order to emphasize their sexual attractiveness and availability. It could be understood as merely another instance of the female body on display for the male viewer. Yet the verbal exchange between Heels and Tina Tech insists that the viewer experience and understand black and white female sexuality in a dramatically different way whereby blackness is coded as aggressive and whiteness as passive. The film sets up a crudely oppositional relationship between black and white sexuality in the workout sequence in order to allow for the appropriation, merging, and transformation of raced-identified sexual characteristics in the film, which largely happens through dance.

The Duality of Black Sexuality in American Cinema: Threatening "Others" and Vicarious Pleasures

A predominant perception of black dance throughout the twentieth century has been the assumption that it is rooted in a powerful, uncontrolled, and therefore dangerous expressive sexuality. It is no doubt the case, as many writers have suggested, that much of the "moral outrage" against the hip gyrations of Elvis Presley was explicitly concerned with the very "blackness" of his performance.[77] Likewise, most of the admonitions put forth by both the black and white press against the "primitive" performance style of African American dancer and songstress Josephine Baker during the 1920s conflated her sexuality and race to the effect of marking her out as "a signifier of sexuality and desirability, and at the same time, because of her blackness, a signifier of danger and negativity."[78] Hollywood has endlessly utilized aspects of this racial trope, making it palatable for mainstream consumption by associating it with white screen stars. Marlene Dietrich's "Hot Voodoo" performance in *Blond Venus* (1932) is exemplary. In this early sound film, the "femme fatale" emerges from a gorilla suit, Hollywood's primary symbol of the "dark continent" and aberrant sexuality. These themes were even more explicitly pursued in the 1933 film *King Kong*.[79] Robert Stam and Ella Shohat note that this representational strategy, which links racial "Otherness" with the animalistic and overtly sexual, has also been repeatedly used by dominant discourses to signify blackness (and other peoples under Western domination) as brutish and inhuman and therefore representative of a regressive and atavistic rung on the evolutionary ladder.[80]

Although speaking specifically about the representation of jazz in film, Krin Gabbard argues that the history of black musical performance in American cinema is, in part, the covert representation of a sexuality that is denied overt expression in the bulk of mainstream culture.[81] He also suggests that films which locate white men in close proximity to some aspect of black music and dance, either through placing African American performers close to white entertainers or having the white musician/dancer appear in blackface, often attempt to imbue him with aspects of black sexuality and virility that have hitherto been unavailable to the white star throughout the narrative of the film. For instance, Gabbard notes that

> blacking up allowed a certain freedom of sexual expression for Jolson in the first *Jazz Singer*, just as it did in *Swing Time* (1936) when Lucky (Fred Astaire) kisses Penny (Ginger Rogers) for the first time just as he is about to apply burnt cork for his performance of "Bojangles of Harlem."[82]

The author later remarks, "Many of the white jazz biopics are somewhat more explicit about the impact of black sexuality on the white hero. Rather than allusions through blackface, many of the films bring on real black musicians to transfer the sexual power to the white protagonist."[83] He refers to the Bix Beiderbecke biography, *Young Man With a Horn* (1950), *The Glenn Miller Story* (1954), and *The Benny Goodman Story* (1956), among others. These observations draw on the historical relation between black and white male sexuality in the United States, described by Eric Lott in his aforementioned important work, *Love and Theft: Blackface Minstrelsy and the American Working Class*. This book focuses on black and white relations through performance culture in the nineteenth century, during the rise of the minstrelsy tradition. A central tenet of Lott's work suggests that recent European immigrants to the United States attempted to sever associations with their symbolic fatherland, and the values of European masculinity, through an adoption of what they assumed to be an authentic African American mode of performance—blackface minstrelsy. These ethnic groups, such as the Irish and Italians, were interested in rejecting the aura of effeteness and upper-class snobbery that was associated with European masculinity. Lott suggests that donning blackface allowed them to erect a new form of distinctly American masculinity that was grounded in a profound sense of libidinal energy, working-class strength, and popular culture. For these immigrant groups, such potentially liberating forces could be symbolized by the perceived raw power of the black body as it was endlessly reinvented through various modes of blackface.[84] Following from this, the alleged potency of black male sexuality in comparison to its white counterpart has often been theorized as an "ur," or base, instinctual desire that underwrites the representation of interactions between black and white performers in American popular culture to the present day. Of early nineteenth century American minstrels, Lott writes that "in a real sense the minstrel man *was* the penis, that organ returning in a variety of contexts, at times ludicrous, at others rather less so."[85] By donning blackface, white men were permitted to act on the phallic and sexual desires that had to be repressed in everyday life.[86]

Gabbard also suggests that the symbolic power of black sexuality was in fact the issuing force for the libido of the white performer in many American films about jazz artists. He suggests that phallic instruments associated with black jazz artists within classical Hollywood film, such as the trumpet and the clarinet, often represent the symbolic equivalent of sexual virility necessary for the white hero to succeed with his romantic endeavors.[87] Michael Rogin has made a similar argument in relation to *The Jazz Singer*. He remarks that the Jewish hero of the film, Jakie Rabinowitz, can only transcend his ethnic origins and truly become American by wearing the somatic markings of blackness.[88] This masking of identity offers him success in the entertainment world directly through his performance in blackface, while indirectly imbuing Jakie with the charismatic appeal of a star performer who can win the affections of a beautiful white woman.

While the attributes of black sexuality have functioned as a representational mode in a very unique and potentially empowering way relative to white American masculinity, they have signified an entirely different set of relations *vis-à-vis* white women, particularly in the American cinema. Numerous scholars have noted that the racist stereotype of the brutal black buck was specifically engineered as a holdover from Southern lynch mob mentality whereby violence against black men was justified through the belief that all black men symbolized a threat to the virginity of white womanhood.[89] Of course, this relation was solidified most famously and viciously in D. W. Griffith's film *The Birth of a Nation*.[90]

Historians of American film have traced two dominant axes along which black sexuality is signified in popular film. This representational schema oscillates between threat (when black performers are close to white women) and transference or investment through proximity (when black performers are close to white men). The relation seems to be heightened by, and very often symbolized through, music and dance performance in the cinema. *Flashdance*, however, complicates this theory of American sexual identity and race because Alex is a woman who, in some respects, takes on the typical role of the white male in relation to black male sexuality and performance culture.

Clearly, the group of breakdancers encountered in the street by the two young women is not a threat to the tough but tender Alex. In fact, *she watches them*, completely turning the tables on the film's incessant objectification of female bodies. This is in line with the complex and ultimately ambiguous delineation of femininity in the film, whereby women must be strong and sexually aggressive but also must know when to acquiesce to the advances and demands of the "right man"—one who will guarantee financial stability and class transcendence.

Alex is imbued with several strikingly male attributes and qualities. She is articulated as sexually aggressive, since we see her suggestively massaging her boss's groin with her foot while out for dinner at a posh restaurant. When his ex-wife approaches the couple in the same scene, the most memorable line from the encounter is Alex's smug remark that she "fucked his brains out." Her sexual power is also reinforced by her aggressive flashdance routines at Mawby's Bar, which I later discuss in detail. Further, she is physically strong enough to perform a man's job: welding in the gritty mills of the Pittsburgh steel industry. In fact, the opening sequence of the film deliberately plays with the gender ambiguity of Alex's character as the camera tracks a lone figure through the Pittsburgh streets into the bowels of the city's steel mills. When the frontal view of this character is finally revealed, Alex lifts her welder's mask to expose unexpectedly the face of a beautiful young girl to the viewer.

Even if Alex is delineated as tenacious and persistent regarding her desire to dance, and sexually confident even when pursued by a wealthy older man, the narrative of *Flashdance* ultimately insists upon forcing women back into submissive roles, dependent upon norms defined by class and gender. Chris Jordan argues that the film appears to support a fluid class structure and flexible gender roles on the surface, but it actually "suggests that a woman's best means of gaining power is by captivating a man with her body" and that "Alex's characterization is calculated to play on female adolescents' physical insecurities."[91] Jordan's argument does accurately portray the problem of the film in terms of gender and the constant

Fig. 4.3. Marine Jahan on the cover of *Fitness Trade Journal*, Summer 1985.

objectification of Alex, aptly noting how the actress playing the lead, Jennifer Beals, is part of a composite ideal woman. She provides the beautiful face for the dramatic sequences and close-ups, while most of the dance scenes utilize Marine Jahan, a different actress and dancer with a "perfect body." The final scene also uses a professional gymnast, Sharon Shapiro.

The fact that Beals did not do her own dancing in the film was disclosed through multiple media sources, including the *New York Times* and the television show *Entertainment Tonight*, at the time of *Flashdance*'s release.[92] Jahan's corporeal "ghost" in the film proved especially intriguing to viewers and the dancer was named body of the year by *Mademoiselle* magazine.[93] She also landed jobs advertising for Macy's and 9 West shoes.[94] Jahan promoted this footwear by dancing different numbers in successive pairs of shoes at department stores around the country to the thrill of supportive fans.[95] After this stint with fashion advertising, she endorsed and starred in a successful dance exercise video program called "Freedanse," which, in its opening sequence, utilized the skimpy costumes,

Fig. 4.4. Richard Colon (Crazy Legs) performs with his crew, Rock Steady, at Lincoln Center in 1981. Photographer: Charlie Ahearn; courtesy of Charlie Ahearn.

dramatic leaps, and pulsating rock music of *Flashdance*. The performer also appeared on the cover of *Fitness Trade Journal* in the summer of 1985, still riding the crest of the film's success as the caption beside her image read "From *Flashdance* to Fitness." (fig. 4.3) Jahan's emergence as a "hidden talent" obscured from viewers in the film was surely an appealing parallel to *Flashdance*'s narrative. Her subsequent "discovery" and success could no doubt be touted as a "real-life" version of the film's events.

The surprising celebrity status of Jahan upon the revelation of her role in the film is, without a doubt, tied to *Flashdance*'s articulation of female identity as fractured, multifaceted, and unstable in terms of both narrative elements and cinematic strategies of representation (close cropping of female body parts, use of strobe lighting in dance sequences to further suggest the fragmentation of space and bodies). Jahan even remarked that during her audition for the lead role in the film "they didn't ask me to read, they didn't ask me to dance. They took a Polaroid, said, 'Great legs,' and that was it."[96] Jordan is absolutely right to point out that the film produces an impossible amalgamation of female physical perfection, yet she makes nothing of the fact that within the predominantly white world of the film, the image of female perfection is actually a composite of black, white, and Latino beauty. As noted earlier, Beals is part African American, and one of her body doubles in the final dance scene was none other than the most famous performer of Rock Steady Crew, Richard Colon (Crazy Legs), a Puerto Rican male dancer!

Within the diegesis of the film, though, Alex is clearly articulated as a white character. She lives in a primarily white social milieu, and has a romance with her white boss. Despite the fact that we see her friend Jeannie's Polish working-class mother and father, Alex's parents are never glimpsed. Given her ambiguous appearance—honey complexion and dark wavy hair, which the camera repeatedly lingers over—the absence of a specific racialized familial context in which to locate Alex seems all the more striking. The character who fulfills the function of a surrogate parental figure is Hannah, an elderly white former ballerina who mentors Alex's desire to become a professional dancer. Interestingly, film critic Roger Ebert has even mistakenly assumed that Alex and Jeannie are sisters, which ultimately provides a (false) familial, racial, and ethnic context in which to locate *Flashdance*'s heroine.[97]

Flashdance is constrained by the demands of the fairy tale musical, which insists upon the eventual return of patriarchal dominance (signified by Alex's ultimate capitulation to her boss's amorous advances) and the formation of a romantic couple. Alex, however, is able to take on the role traditionally defined by white men in relation to the proximity of black performance as an instance of creative contamination, both sexually and in relation to dance/music performance in the film. By insisting on reading *Flashdance* within the history of the American musical rather than outside of it, as Jordan partially does, I suggest that race plays a large role in the characterization of Alex's dance ability and sexuality. I argue here that the most important aspects of Alex's character, her dance talent and sexual power, are in fact predicated upon their proximity to black and Latino performance culture, a relation that culminates in the flashdance sequences.

For instance, the breakdancers do not function on the same level as the other men in the film who constantly objectify Alex, because the male gaze is defined as almost exclusively white. Chris Jordan notes that all the men in *Flashdance* objectify Alex and her circle of friends, indicating that this is the normative set of relations between men and women on screen. These street breakers, however, are not a threat to Alex because the film signals their relation as one of creative contamination and class alliance rather than sexual desire and intimidation. She stops to watch their street performance and subsequently dances her way across a city intersection.

Alex follows their example by playfully dancing in the street as though she has been "infected" by their creative energy after viewing the performance.

The insertion into the film of a racially mixed, all-male breakdancing crew, along with a nearly exclusively black street audience (except for Alex and Jeannie), serves several functions within the narrative. It underscores the "authenticity" and "naturalness" of Alex's talent by identifying her with the status of black street dance. American cinema has habitually emphasized the "naturalness" of black talent in relation to music and dance. This apparent compliment actually implies a deeply racist sentiment: that blacks are "genuine" and innate entertainers because all they do is "play" rather than work. Music and dance punctuates everyday life, transforming all work time into "play," a process that undoubtedly assuages anxieties about the ethos of coerced and underpaid black labor in American history, and one that relies on the misconception that dancing is in fact a "playful" pastime rather than a strenuous and difficult art to master.[98] The association between African Americans and spontaneous, "natural" dance talent is apparent in early cinematic examples in which black characters break into a dance number for no obvious reason. *The Watermelon Patch* (1905) and the 1927 version of *Uncle Tom's Cabin* both show dance as a "natural" part of African American life and movement entering into the rhythm of everyday encounters without any apparent motivation. Later Hollywood musicals that featured black entertainers, such as the Bill Robinson–Shirley Temple films *The Little Colonel*, *The Littlest Rebel*, and *Rebecca of Sunnybrook Farm* (1938), also perpetuate this racist trope. The breakdance scene underscores Alex's "street" credibility and innate ability by linking her talent with the dance style and posturing of urban black masculinity. Not only is Alex capable of spontaneous performance in the street but she also hones her abilities in the gritty warehouse space of her apartment rather than in the refined spaces of an expensive dance conservatory (however, this is the ultimate goal for the budding dance star). Although Alex "sells out" at the end of the film and leaves the "street" behind for a high-class dance school, we have been assured of the authenticity of her talent early on in the narrative through this scene, which connects her abilities to African American dance.

Alex's identification with the breakdancers also points to a main theme of the narrative—that Alex's dance talent is explicitly related to her untamed, natural, and raw sexuality. This link is very closely connected to Gabbard's reading of black and white relations in jazz biopics whereby a black musician's very presence can imbue a white performer with both sexual prowess and a newfound musical capability. Her proximity to black dance culture enhances her own performance abilities, which in turn are revealed as the source of her sexual energy and power. However, the historically determined relation between whites and blacks, and the representation of music and dance in American cinema, are significantly altered because Alex is a woman. Thus, the momentary pairing of Alex with a group of street performers plays on (but also transforms) the presumed assumptions about black and white performance traditions and sexual power.

If the Rock Steady Crew teaches her a few moves, this exchange also imbues Alex with the ability to enact an aggressive sexual persona in her nightclub routine and personal life. Such a relation is very clearly evoked in Alex's initial dance performance at Mawby's Bar, in which she makes extensive use of mime and other electric boogie moves in highly eroticized dance sequences. Through the subsequent street performance of the Rock Steady Crew, the film later suggests that Alex has lifted this set of moves from black-identified street dance culture. In fact, *Flashdance* explores the notion of sexual "contagion" through performance relations between blacks and whites in the classical period and reforms them in order to incorporate attitudes towards gender and performance in the 1980s that were informed by a revival of conservative thought in American culture.

There is a continuum in the film between the initial club performance and the street dance scene with the Rock Steady Crew that explains the film's use of black dance to articulate the gendered and classed subjectivity of the heroine. The first dance number introduces Alex in male clothing as she enters the stage in an oversized man's suit (similar to a zoot suit), performing breakdance style electric boogie moves. However, after she rips the man's suit from her body to reveal a skimpy red piece of lingerie her dance moves transform into a modern-style jazz dance, abruptly leaving all breakdance coding behind. The movements of this newly feminized version of Alex, who sports a red diaphanous "teddy," become much more erotic and geared toward sexual arousal. This number implies that Alex's transformation into a highly erotic and aggressive female persona requires a masquerade of masculinity, one that is borrowed from the street and from black youth culture. She not only adopts the street dance style of communities of color but she also dons a zoot suit, the uniform of black and Latino youth culture during the 1940s.[99]

Flashdance seems to suggest that the adoption of black and Latino performance style is at the very heart of Alex's ability to transform herself on stage. In this light, I do not find the film to be as simplistic in terms of gender coding as Jordan and other writers have made it out to be. Previous criticism argues that the intersection of class and gender inequities are the only significant forces affecting Alex's transformation, and that the film is only interested in showing that women must acquiesce to the feminine ideals of physical perfection and, ultimately, submissiveness if they are to achieve success. For Jordan, the concluding dance sequence is the final "sell out" and reinforcement of hierarchical boundaries because Alex wins a place at the prestigious dance academy, accepts help from Nick in securing the audition, and submits to his desires for her. In my reading, however, these final moments of the film are somewhat conflicted in terms of social, racial, and sexual hierarchies since the enduring image of Alex's triumph in an all-white, upper-class dance conservatory is, in fact, a Puerto Rican male body executing a backspin—the hallmark move of the breakdance tradition. Moreover, the use of multiple body doubles for Alex's dance routines is apparent to the spectator, at least upon repeated viewings.

In spite of the assumption that the film works to reorient sexual relations in a more conservative direction, *Flashdance* offers a very ambivalent image of female sexuality linked to its representation of black and Latino street dance.[100] Alex's sexual identity and dance ability (aspects of her character that are often collapsed in the film) both rely on their proximity to street dance, while at the same time specific breakdance moves are stolen and incorporated into both white upper-class dance conservatories and working-class cultural spaces such as Mawby's. The successful transformation from working-class locales into upper-class cultural spaces requires that Alex maintain a link to racially and ethnically "Other" realms of cultural expression (but not necessarily "Other" communities), symbolized by the inclusion of street dance moves in her audition for the Pittsburgh Dance Company. This is made explicit in the final performance audition scene. A stone-faced panel of judges warms to Alex only *after* she makes an error, boldly starts again, and uses the street moves we have seen earlier in the film. This suggests that her entry into the conservatory is dependent upon the incorporation of breakdance choreography into the routine rather than a mastery of conventional dance abilities. The history of doubling, uncredited talent, and submerged racial identity in *Flashdance* firmly locates it within the kind of anxious framework drawn by Clover in her discussion of *Singin' in the Rain*. Jahan's inexplicable meteoric rise to fame can thus be read as a symptom of such anxieties whereby the public seized upon her persona as a viable substitute for the "real" talent that has been continually appropriated and plundered by American musical film.

Breaking In(to) the Conservatory: The "Manly" Art of Dance

The link between the dance conservatory (and professional dance more generally) and breakdancing in the final scene of *Flashdance* is not one of mere fantasy. In truth, this relation was an actual space of cultural interaction in the early 1980s. For instance, breakdancers appeared on the cover of *Ballet News* in August of 1984, while several New York Broadway and Off-Broadway shows welcomed "street trained" breakdancers into their performance spaces. An article from *Dance Magazine* in the same year noted that the New York musical "*The Tap Dance Kid* features a brief break-dancing number performed by Alfonso Ribeiro" and "Rick Atwell's forthcoming Off-Broadway musical *Street Heat* will include breakers Atwell recruited off sidewalks throughout New York City."[101] Ribeiro, a twelve-year-old with no formal dance training, was nominated for an Outer Critics Circle Award.[102] He also captured the attention of Michael Jackson, who, after witnessing his performance in the show, invited him to his Los Angeles home.[103] Another dancer from *The Tap Dance Kid*, Jimmy Tate, appeared at a promotional event with breaking crew Rhythm Technicians to advertise the aforementioned Swatch Watch World Breakdance Championship.

In addition, the San Francisco Ballet showcased numerous breakdancers in its opening gala performance that year.[104] An article in the *Christian Science Monitor*, also appearing in 1984, asks of breakdancing: "Is this a flash in the pan or will it last?"[105] The piece goes on to state that some dancers are "studying jazz or modern dance to continue a dancing career if break dancing dies out."[106] At the outset of that year, the *New York Post* ran an article discussing an event during which two important ballerinas from the city—Malinda Roy of the New York City Ballet and Beatrice Rodrigues of Joffrey Ballet—met and danced with the Kid Fresh breakdance crew at Minskoff Rehearsal Hall in midtown Manhattan.[107] This space was associated with the most prestigious dance companies, as it was extensively used by shows scheduled to premiere on Broadway. Promoter Akiva Talmi apparently staged the event in order to bring attention to his attempts at fusing street dance, ballet, and theatrical production values, which resulted in the launching of a multi-city national tour entitled *Breakdance U.S.A.* This show was "a multimedia event with choreographed breakdancers

Fig. 4.5. Jimmy Tate with the Rhythm Technicians, Aug. 23, 1984. Photographer: Jim Hughes; courtesy of the *New York Daily News*.

that also included other aspects of the hip hop scene—rap, song, live DJs, and MCs."[108] *Breakdance U.S.A.* also featured special effects such as "laser beams, smoke pod explosions, strobes, and flames."[109] Numerous other examples of this type of cultural fusion appear in a variety of articles, visual imagery, cinema, and actual conservatory programs from the era. Ballet, a dance form that "denies the substantiality of flesh by defying the forces of gravity" and "makes the body ethereal,"[110] became closely linked with the new form of folk culture that changed "the gravity point of dance from top to bottom" and demanded that people "dance not just with their bodies, but *on* their bodies."[111]

I am intrigued by three aspects of the relationship between ballet and breakdancing here. Firstly, I am concerned with the way in which debates about gender and dance manifest themselves in both art forms (I have addressed gender and breaking above). Secondly, there are the various forms of co-optation that primarily white mainstream interests utilized in order to bring "the street" into the conservatory and recital halls. Thirdly, I address the way in which these two issues are so integral to the representation of breakdance in film in the early eighties.

Most printed text and images that featured female breakers usually noted that women primarily participated in electric boogie and locking and popping, not the close-to-the-ground breaking, which demanded very intense athletic ability and strength—the kind of dance where a performer truly dances *"on* their bodies." This kind of breaking—floor work such as head-spins, backspins, and windmills—was, with a few exceptions, the purview of men. Even though prominent choreographer and dancer Rosanne Hoare proudly asserts that she is "one of the first females . . . ever to do straight break work," very few women actually followed her lead.[112] Most likely, the intense upper body strength needed to perform the kind of floor work that this dance style requires made it more suitable for men.

Contemporaneous with the emergence of hip hop culture in the later 1970s, debates about gender and ballet began to surface in magazines and journals dedicated to study of institutionalized dance. The first book devoted entirely to the study of men in ballet, *Danseur: The Male in Ballet*, was published in 1977.[113] Cobbett Steinberg explored this topic in his article "Dancing Men," which appeared in the 1978/9 Winter issue of *Ballet Review*.[114] An interesting piece, entitled "Masculinity in Dance," which was partly a response to the above article, attempted to clarify just what was at stake in forcefully asserting the masculinity of dancing men. The author, Igor Youskevitch, noted that previous explorations of masculinity in ballet often drew attention to the supposed hallmarks of "manliness" in the lives of male ballet dancers outside of the dance world—for instance, an interest in sports. Youskevitch points out that this of course has nothing to do with the *presentation* of masculinity through dance. This quality, he suggests

> is based on personal "philosophy" and approach to *interpretation* which has nothing to do with being just strong and athletic. As a matter of fact, overmasculinity in dance produces as adverse an impression as complete lack of it. The image of a football player has no room on the ballet stage.[115]

Youskevitch argues that expressions of masculinity through dance can only be measured as an abstract quality captured in a performer's own unique ability. One of the most well-known attempts to link male dance with more conventional notions of masculine sport comes from the "greatest," or at least the most famous American dancing man on the big screen, Gene Kelly. Throughout his life, Kelly continually emphasized the athletic ability that dance required, forever attempting to negate the popular opinion that dance was primarily the forte of women and "effeminate" men.[116] Both Steinberg and Yousketvitch mention *Life* magazine articles from 1963 that covered the lives and interests of male ballet stars, heavily emphasizing sports and other "manly" interests. While concerns about the overall masculinity of male dancers punctuated popular media prior to the 1970s, it did not become a subject of academic debate until the middle of the decade.

Dance scholar Ramsay Burt notes that presenting masculinity through movement was a preoccupation of American mid-century modern dance. Choreographers such as Ted Shawn reinvented the male dancer with "a heavy-handed return to ideals of 'natural', essential, instinctive, and 'traditional' masculinity," as an antidote to the supposedly overtly feminine sphere of European-derived ballet.[117] These expressions of a supposedly natural American masculinity appropriated non-Western identities, which had been championed by mid-century modernism as examples of natural, raw, and unmediated masculinity.[118] The nineteenth century specter of minstrelsy, in which black identities were utilized to express forbidden, repressed, or frustrated white sexual desire through dance, returned to the American stage during the mid-twentieth century and again in the 1980s.

While ballet has traditionally been associated with female dancers, the male ballet star "eclipsed ballerinas in terms of salary, media attention, and drawing power at the box office" in the 1970s and '80s.[119] This revived interest in masculinity and ballet is undoubtedly linked to a rise in the popularity of male dancers at this time, an occurrence unprecedented for twentieth century ballet, save for the renown of Vaslav Nijinsky during the Edwardian period. An astute *Village Voice* article on the recent increase in numbers of male ballet dancers in the late '70s noted that "no art is recognized as an art until men do it."[120] Men were becoming superstars in one of the only artistic fields dominated by women for over a century, and the newfound "star" status of male ballet dancers such as Rudolf Nureyev, and later Mikhail Baryshnikov, seemed to surpass the level of artistic success and fame enjoyed primarily by women. The authors of *Danseur: The Male in Ballet*, Richard Philip and Mary Whitney, note that although Nijinsky reintroduced the star danseur in ballet at a time when "a stigma was attached to men who dared to make a career of ballet," this renewed interest in the male dancer did not continue.[121] However, the 1960s and '70s in particular witnessed "a tremendous resurgence of interest in the danseur, in his technique, acting, and roles."[122]

Male ballet dancers were ascending the ranks and becoming more plentiful at about the same time breakdance emerged. Therefore, the enthusiasm with which many ballet companies, choreographers, and producers embraced the male breakdancer must bear some relation to the legitimation of male ballet dancers as athletes, and the justification of their craft as a muscular and powerful "manly" art form. Philip and Whitney even refer to the danseur as "ballet's equivalent of the sports hero."[123] They go on to note that

> it has become evident that the work of the danseur, who must combine strength, precision, timing, and spatial awareness with grace, musicality, and stage presence, is directly comparable to that of the athlete. Much like athletes, the danseur requires years of training to perfect his form and a daily class routine to warm up his muscles and protect him against an injury that might suddenly end his career. And few sports require the stamina, versatility, and sheer physical daring demanded of the male dancer in ballet today.[124]

Given the emphasis on athleticism in the above quote, it is not surprising that some choreographers and dancers actually welcomed breakdance as a form that would reinvigorate and permanently change ballet. Associating male ballet with urban dance originating in communities of color—a practice related in numerous accounts to hyper-masculinity, competition, and occasionally violence—could be seen as a strategic ploy to bolster the mainstream appeal of the male ballet dancer for North American audiences. Talmi asserted that "the dance world is starving for a new movement to revitalize both the classical and the modern idiom, and within a few years, every important stage is going to have breakdancing performed on it."[125] At the same time that breakdance could be envisioned as ballet's new creative grounding force, descriptions of the emerging dance form often characterized it as raw, brutal, overtly and aggressively masculine, and an outlet to "release competitive energies."[126] These qualities are directly antithetical to the careful, precise, and predominantly feminine attributes usually associated with the European tradition of ballet.[127]

The desire of mainstream commercial interests to capitalize on this relation took up a particular form of active recruitment of young breakers into the academy. For instance, while dance promoter Talmi attempted a forty-city tour of the United States in order to bring street dance into Carnegie Hall,[128] the San Francisco Ballet created a community outreach program in the mid-1980s which embarked on a two-way exchange with the breakdancers who lived in a nearby ghetto neighborhood. Forty-six local teenagers performed a surprise finale during the company's opening night gala in July. Fourteen boys were given scholarships to the ballet school. At the same time they became the San Francisco Ballet Breakers.[129]

This large-scale outreach effort by the ballet conservatory and other established dance entities to black and Latino youth can be seen in a variety of ways. For instance, it might be understood as a racist and malevolent institutional effort to control and sanitize the "raw" and "unrefined" energy of African American and Latino men, thereby redirecting any potential social disorder associated with racial "Otherness" into creative but orchestrated scenarios. Alternately, this conjunction might also be understood as a philanthropic and truly positive source of creative interchange whereby unrefined talent is managed by apparently benevolent mainstream institutions in order to benefit those who would not otherwise have access to formal training. While Talmi seems interested in exploiting the "next big thing" associated with youth and popular culture, the San Francisco Ballet's outreach program appears to be an honest attempt to integrate an institution of high culture with its surrounding environment to the benefit of both.

In this same vein, eminent choreographer Julie Arenal endeavored to merge ballet with breakdance in her company's productions *On the Move* and *The City*. Both performances premiered in 1984 at the Spoleto Festival USA in South Carolina before moving onto the Festival of Two Worlds in Spoleto, Italy, and the New York Express Company Theatre.[130] While a press release detailing these two productions stresses the need to order the improvisational aspect of breaking, it also emphasizes the hard work and dedication that has led to the unique and original lexicon of breakdance:

> Choreographer Julie Arenal has taken this phenomenon and shaped it into a traditional performance mode, using the raw energy of her performers aged 14–20 who hail from all five boroughs of New York. Rather than merely presenting breakdancing in its original demonstrational context, Ms. Arenal is the first to structure this exciting dance into the fine arts idiom. Although essentially unstructured, breakdancing has a highly developed vocabulary. The performers "train" through intensive practice sessions, working with their friends to develop a routine which is then "performed" in the streets, ghettos, and discos. The dancers spend most of their free time developing

their individual specialties, which include "the moon walk," "the wave," and "breaking."[131]

This press release repeatedly stresses the way in which Arenal has shaped, transformed, and even distilled the raw idiom of breakdance. Nevertheless, the resulting productions appear to have retained some important aspect of breakdancing—for instance, the association of a breaker with one particular move or style of breaking. *On the Move* was apparently designed to "highlight each performer's uniqueness." *The City* was also an attempt to present the experiences and difficulties faced by urban youth through dance techniques. In this respect, the shows appear to have worked towards a positive articulation of hip hop culture in which the creativity and resourcefulness of inner-city residents was set against the larger social and economic difficulties that plagued the dancers' communities.

Arenal's shows sought to retain some element of breaking's improvisational and urban "essence" as they transformed the idiom for theatrical venues. While improvisation is usually an element of breakdance touted as integral to the art form, *Beat Street*'s choreographer, Julliard-trained Lester Wilson, intimated that this not the case:

> What these kids do is carefully thought through.... To choreograph this film, I had to study their movements closely, see how they could be captured by the camera.... The discipline involved was to have them go over specific movements again and again until I captured it on film most effectively.[132]

Clearly, Wilson's words were meant to validate his role in the production by emphasizing the hard work involved in creating breakdance routines that would transfer successfully to the big screen, but he also argues for the commercial viability of the dance form by suggesting that it lends itself to organized cinematic choreography. Furthermore, the choreographer placed breaking alongside established forms like modern dance and ballet, and predicted that this urban street dance would "continue to develop as an idiom" and "assimilate new kinds of movement."[133]

Professional breaking crews were starring in feature films and also making relatively large sums of money performing at public events, appearing in commercial advertisements, and winning contests during 1984 and 1985.[134] The initial promise of breaking was certainly connected to the possibility of earning a lot of money very quickly. However, after the initial dance craze had subsided, the breaker was the one figure within the hip hop structure who was actually left without a career track or the potential to continue earning from his craft (except on street corners and the odd hip hop retrospective event). The DJ and the rapper have dominated more recent hip hop culture, and have seen a windfall of financial success. Less lucrative and more marginally, some graffiti writers have continued to work in the art world with moderate success.[135] Rarely, however, has the breaker found a similar way to maintain a viable career after the breakdancing hype subsided.[136] Akiva's prediction seems to have been dead wrong. With few exceptions, breakdancers faded into the background to make way for the rapper and DJ.[137]

Utopian attempts to combine ballet and breakdance proposed an art form that promised not only racial crossings but those of gender and class as well. The current of producers interested in this hybrid form tapped into the allure of a handful of emerging male ballet stars while assuring audiences that male dancers, although performing a dance style associated with women in the later half of the twentieth century, were overtly masculine and ardently athletic. This assurance was borrowed from, and even underwritten by, the displays of African American and Latino male sexual power associated with breakdancing. As we have seen, this relation has been repeated in American forms of popular and avant-garde performance, from nineteenth-century minstrel troupes to twentieth-century modernist dance recitals. Interestingly, this hybrid form also offers a return to ballet's "lowbrow" past. Although associated with "high culture," ballet has often incorporated folk elements (for instance, in the Russian genre of Character Dance). During the nineteenth century in France, ballet was also associated with prostitution. Ballet companies culled young girls from the working and lower classes to train as ballerinas, and these dancers interacted with affluent patrons backstage in an atmosphere characterized by historian Richard Kendall as "a virtual market-place for transactions between wealthy *abonnés* and underpaid dancers."[138]

The imaginings of a hybrid dance style that combined ballet and breakdance were largely naïve and shortsighted. All of the power lay in the hands of the producers, managers, and promoters of shows and institutions that attempted to bring this dance union to fruition. These individuals (who were, with few exceptions, professionally trained) brought black and Latino street dance to the threshold of European culture, incorporating it within its vocabulary. The asymmetrical power relations in this relationship are glaringly obvious. In many examples, cultural expression emerging within communities of color is co-opted by larger mainstream artistic entities and put in the service of further developing a European-born idiom. In early 1984, Ken Sandler noted that

> promoter Talmi, the front-runner in moving breakdancing off the streets and onto the ballet stage, has already hired a leading young ballet choreographer—Mary Giannone—to turn breakdance routines into narrative ballets and he has developed a number of other breakdance presentation techniques.[139]

This article ends with a quote from Talmi, who continued to work with Russian ballet productions. He proclaims of breakdancing: "First in the streets, now in nightclubs, next in Carnegie Hall."[140] The piece suggests that breakdancing will only become a "legitimate" art form after filtration through a European lens. Breakdancing is articulated as raw and unformed, in need of both "taming" and narrativizing, in order to be fit for consumption by "a trendy, culture-oriented audience."[141] Arrogant assumptions voiced by Talmi and others very plainly exposed how the idiom of breakdance was at risk as mainstream commercial interests attempted to absorb and reconfigure this "authentic" cultural product. Firstly, Talmi's comments (and the general attitude of the above article) reveal a classist and ethnocentric view of performance success whereby the goal of a street-derived art form is containment within the confines of upper-class and largely white-owned institutions. Secondly, nearly all accounts of breakdance within academic and institutional spaces insist on the need for a structuring and narrativizing of the form. The resulting cultural collaborations usually attempted to force breakdancing into the mold of an already established European cultural tradition, purging the dance style of its improvisational elements. Much like the earliest critiques of jazz, mainstream critics, practitioners, and writers faulted breakdance for an apparent lack of composition and order.[142]

These same tensions between mainstream and more marginal cultural spaces surface in nearly all hip hop-oriented films from this decade. The perils of maneuvering in the entertainment industry for individuals from poverty-stricken inner-city communities were racialized and privatized in the hip hop musical of the 1980s. Paradoxically, films such as *Wild Style*, *Rappin'*, and *Beat Street* also insisted on connecting personal struggles to the needs and interests of the larger community. In contrast, *Flashdance* allows Alex to leave the mill, the street, and the dance club behind, and for the most part, no traces of any communal relations exist at the end of the film—just the image of a smiling, happy, and wealthy white couple. Collaborations between the dance academy and urban breakdancing culture resulted in actual creative interactions in which progressive and positive cultural interchange was attainable (though rarely achieved), but *Flashdance* suppresses this possibility by focusing only on the trajectory of its "white" heroine who emerges victorious from the dance conservatory in the narrative of the film. However, as I have stated earlier, the final image of Crazy Legs does act as a repressed reminder of the ways in which the film actually constructs the sexual identity and dance talent of Alex. Both aspects of her character are contingent upon her relationship to black and Latino-inspired urban street culture. The film uses different class-identified spaces of cultural performance—the dance academy, the street, and the working-class bar—to showcase its use of breakdance. These spaces link the evolution of the heroine (from low-class stripper to successful dancer) with the transformative powers of black performance historically associated with white male entertainers in nineteenth-century minstrelsy shows and Hollywood blackface.

Even though I have focused on masculinity and blackness in my account of the "actual" spaces of interactions between official dance institutions and breakdance, socioeconomic relations and the representation of women within the space of the dance academy do seem to be integral aspects of films featuring breakdance in the 1980s. Along with *Flashdance*, the *Breakin'* series provides an intricate and interesting textual map in which to chart this argument. Kelly, the white female lead of the two films, played by Lucinda Dickey, was cast because of her dance ability, as were male leads, Adolfo Quinones and Michael Chambers, two dancers from communities of color. It is not surprising therefore that the realism of the scenarios is largely hampered by poor acting skills (since the stars were not seasoned professional actors), while the films' main attractions are flamboyant dance choreography, colorful and ostentatious costume design, and emerging musical talent. This particular situation should not be surprising given that some of the very earliest exploitation films centered on music and aimed at a youth audience, such as America's first rock 'n' roll flicks, settled for a similar trade-off.[143] However, as Thomas Doherty has pointed out, the narratives of these earlier films still provided important social meanings for their juvenile audience, and presented youth culture as a unique experience that was separate from, and often at odds with, adult life. For this reason, he notes, they should be looked at critically in their historical context, regardless of the "quality" of acting, writing, and other usual judgment criteria. Following Doherty's lead, the same methodology should be undertaken in looking at the *Breakin'* films. Like *Flashdance*, these exploitation films were largely organized around the gendering and racialization of performance spaces. They spoke to particular historical connections, such as the unique relation between popular culture and race that emerged with the appearance of the first breakers on midtown Manhattan street corners. These films also addressed the gendering of hip hop culture as it interacted with spaces of "cultural authority" and conventional theatrical performance.

At the beginning of *Breakin'*, Kelly is associated with the rehearsal rooms of the dance academy, toiling for a sadistic and predatory instructor who teaches modern jazz dance. The space of institutional dance is articulated as somewhat threatening, presided over by white male authority. In *Flashdance*, too, the Pittsburgh Conservatory of Dance and Repertory is shown to be a frightening and unfriendly space as leering eyes gawk at Alex's unkempt and unprofessional appearance when she first attempts to obtain an audition at the nearly all-white academy.

However, while these two films articulate the spaces of the professional dance academy in a similar manner, they deal with racially "Other" sexual desire in very divergent ways. *Flashdance* repeatedly yet covertly acknowledges the power of black sexuality and dance performance. In this film, we are even privy to an unabashed, albeit racist and reductive, expression of black sexuality in the previously discussed workout scene. And, as I have been arguing throughout the chapter, African American sexuality is a central, yet continually repressed theme (with the exception of the workout scene), in *Flashdance*. *Breakin'* further nullifies black and Latino sexual desire within the narrative, especially in relation to the link between performance success and heterosexual coupling. Firstly, Kelly is introduced to "street dance" culture by an African American male dancer named Cupcake—an absurd "queen" stereotype who flits through the film in lavender tights—while Kelly infantilizes him with childish dialogue and nicknames. Secondly, even though Ozone is the "music man" of the film, he fails to secure any kind of romantic union with Kelly in either of the *Breakin'* features. He is jealous of her relationships with white men, and neither of the films ever suggest that Kelly is even cognizant of the nature of Ozone's amorous desires. Although he appears onstage with his desired other at the end of both films, successful performance does not equal successful romantic partnering in these works. As noted in previous chapters, the Hollywood show musical habitually constructs a narrative in which romantic coupling is linked with significant achievements in the world of professional music and dance. This equation is nearly always signified at the end of the film when the male and female leads are revealed together in a public performance scenario. In both *Breakin'* films, however, the "music man" must be content with performance success only. Nevertheless, in order to propel the narrative forward and satisfy some aspects of the genre, Ozone must express his attraction for Kelly. *Breakin' 2* also follows the pattern of a traditional show musical in that we witness a final production number at the end of the film, and see the lead couple onstage together. Up until this point, however, the film continually assures the viewer that Kelly does not reciprocate Ozone's feelings, thereby circumventing the connection between performance success and the formation of a romantic partnership.

Black sexual desire is either repressed or infantilized in these films, and Kelly, like Alex, can only find her way to real performance success through "street dance." Kelly must leave the almost all-white space of the academy and cross over into the world of urban dance in order to find her way back to a successful professional career and the stage. She does not discover a way to enact a sexualized dance persona through her dalliances with urban black masculinity in the same way that Alex does. The white female star of *Breakin'* merely finds a way to rebel against her conservative parents and uptight dance teacher. However, both women must encounter an alternative and unfettered performance mode linked to a masculine, racially "Other," and lower-class culture in order to stand out and become successful in the staid world of professional dance.

Ed Guerrero has convincingly argued that Hollywood cinema of this era attempted to negotiate and contain the threat of a rising tide of black political power through certain blockbuster formulas, including the interracial buddy film, science-fiction extravaganzas, and the Rocky series. He further notes that "black sexuality in the 1980s was either constructed as something entirely perverse or, more often, absent in mainstream cinema."[144] This chapter adds to his assessment by showing the ways in which black desire could be negotiated by conventional cinema in more subtle and complex ways. Neither entirely absent nor "perverse," the examples discussed in this chapter explore how the simultaneous exposure and repression of the sexualities and desires of people of color have always been part of the classic Hollywood musical genre. While films such as *Flashdance* and the *Breakin'* series repress the subjectivity and desire of racial "Others," the strongest expressions of dance ability and creativity (and therefore potent sexuality, according to the logic of the classical musical) nonetheless always emanate from black and Latino urban culture.

Breakdancing left its imprint on film culture of the 1980s while also impacting an astonishingly wide array of cultural ephemera, social spaces, and media. But it was not, as others have argued, simply an aggressive expression of black masculinity, a mating ritual, or an activity that had overwhelmingly negative consequences for women. Rather, representations of the dance style in myriad media reveal that it functioned in a number of ways that offered a potentially empowering performance space to women as well. The apparent hyper masculinity of the dance style was also employed to alter public perception of other mainstream performance cultures, such as ballet. Especially in the case of cinema, the practice of breakdancing became a threshold activity where bodies (female bodies, in particular) could transgress boundaries of race, class, and even gender.

Conclusion

The emergence of hip hop cinema in the early 1980s presented a unique marketing challenge for producers, exhibitors, and distributors. These films clearly belonged to the Hollywood musical genre, but they also introduced a startlingly new (and unavoidably political) lexicon of music, dance, and artistic expression focused on inner city communities. When *Breakin'*, *Body Rock*, *Beat Street*, and *Prison Dancer* (a low-budget hip hop-oriented film that was never completed) were introduced at Cannes in 1984, for instance, only the producers of *Breakin'*, according to *Variety*, promoted their film as a breakdancing flick, and were "willing to sell the pic as a genre film."[1] Stan Lathan, the director of *Beat Street*, noted of his production that "I hesitate to call it a break-dance movie, but for many reasons it is being billed as such."[2] Lathan goes on to remark that "it's a story about kids trying to meet the challenges of manhood, and to make something of themselves as artists."[3] With *Beat Street*, Lathan attempted to introduce breakdance as merely one aspect of a music-centered coming of age story. When *Wild Style* opened at Cannes the previous year, promotional print material for the screenings featured a breaker dancing on his head against a blank white background. The accompanying text informed spectators that "Charlie Ahearn's *Wild Style* is a 'hip hop' romance set to the maximum cool beat of Breaking, Rapping, and Scratch-DJing." With a breakdancer occupying the center of the image, the advertisement curiously avoided indicating the most significant subject matter that *Wild Style* offered to spectators: an inside look at the world of graffiti writers. The breakdancing aspects of early hip hop musicals were frequently emphasized over all other facets of the culture, yet some producers were quick to downplay any traces of hip hop and simply sell the film on the general appeal of the musical.[4] Articles such as the aforementioned *Variety* piece, and another article from the *Boston Globe* that covered the "Cannes Breakdancing Films" from the same year, focus almost entirely on the dance aspect of these films. Such an emphasis on breaking overall is certainly understandable given that the "breakdance picture" could be easily associated with other musicals like *Flashdance* and *Footloose* that had more than proven the commercial viability of youth-oriented dance films.

As anxiety over the marketability of hip hop quickly waned, breakers, DJs, rappers, and graffiti artists appeared on screen in an astonishing variety of genres. To date more than seventy-five hip hop-themed feature films have been made since the earliest musical incursions into the performance culture. Ranging from horror flicks (*Da Hip Hop Witch*, 2000), opera adaptations (*Carmen: A Hip Hopera*, 2001), and lauded documentaries (*Scratch*, 2001; *Rize*, 2005) to a renewed interest in youth dance culture on screen (*Save the Last Dance*, 2001; *You Got Served*, 2004), it is apparent that a straightforward definition of hip hop cinema is difficult to articulate. American hip hop-oriented films continue to offer unique and complex intersections between established cinematic genres and a perpetually mutating performance culture.

The hip hop musical that flourished between 1983 and 1985 was a unique cycle of films that responded to contemporary political, social, and economic pressures coalescing around discourses of race, poverty, suburban decline, and urban blight through the format of the Hollywood musical genre. When hip hop culture, and the new "music man," were inserted into the tradition of American musical cinema a familiar, yet paradoxically new, space of negotiation was fashioned. The resulting films renewed historical anxieties that inscribed the burden of social progress onto the bodies of performers of color, while at the same time conventional culture (including the African American press) debated the moral and artistic attributes of hip hop. Furthermore, singular films such as *Krush Groove* were forced to bear an inordinate burden of signification linked to concerns over the ostensible fragility of suburban communities fighting to distinguish themselves from contemporary urban peril. Schultz's film, in particular, became synonymous with exposing both localized and more general racialized tensions when reports of youth violence during theatrical screenings surfaced in numerous newspapers. Ensuing discussions in the mainstream press exposed deeply rooted historical fears of "black engulfment" in relation to contemporary spaces of public entertainment, geographical distinctions between suburb and city, and the nature of racially discrete teen cultures.

When looking at the early development of hip hop film in the context of mainstream teen cinema, it is clear that the former offered an appealing alternative to the limited pleasures offered by mall culture and private social rituals in suburban centered teen movies. Such an alternative viewpoint directly engaged with the historical crisis of the black urban family in the 1980s. It celebrated new forms of filial relations and public rituals emerging through hip hop culture. These alternate familial and communal relationships depicted on screen showed that youth performance culture was a unique and powerful tool that could combat the assault on families in actual communities of color as a result of declining public assistance, decaying housing stock, and drug related violence.

As hip hop reinvents itself in both progressive and conservative forms through cinema, it continues to appropriate generic conventions in exceptional and unexpected ways. The American comedy *Marci X* (2003) deliberately played with audience expectations of genre by casting Lisa Kudrow (of *Friends* fame) as a Jewish American princess alongside black comedian Damon Wayans in a plot in which the titular Marci (Kudrow) must helm a rap record label. In case potential filmgoers missed the humor in featuring the ex-*Friends* star in a hip hop-oriented narrative, the tag line accompanying *Marci X* read "Hip Hop Meets Shop Till You Drop." More recently, global hip hop cinema has been nurtured by the development of film festivals such as Hip Hop Odyssey and Black Soil International, among others, which are dedicated to examining the performance culture across different national contexts. This turn has resulted in refreshing and distinctive entries such as *Microphone* (2010), an Egyptian film centered on the underground music and art scene in Alexandria, and the low-budget Vietnamese production *Saigon Electric* (2011), which utilized the musical format to contrast traditional Asian ribbon dance with modern urban performance. The dynamic and protean nature of the first images and sounds of hip hop culture on film exemplified by the contrast between *Delivery Boys* and *Wild Style* continues to define contemporary cinema as hip hop becomes ensconced and even parodied in popular mainstream media while at the same time it finds new life in international cinemas.

Notes

INTRODUCTION

1. Jon Caramanica, "Hip-Hop Heirlooms," *Vogue*, Fall 2008, "Fashion Rocks" supplement.

2. See Sharon R. Sherman, "Bombing, Breakin', and Getting Down: The Folk and Popular Culture of Hip-Hop," *Western Folklore* 43 (Oct. 1984): 287–93, Cheryl L. Keyes, "Verbal Art Performance in Rap Music: The Conversation of the 80s," *Folklore Forum* 17, no. 1–2 (1984): 143–52, and Barbara Crossette, "A Three Day Celebration of Bronx Folk Culture," *New York Times*, May 15, 1981. The latter covers the Conference on Folk Culture in the Bronx, which took place in the spring of 1981 and included a session on breakdancing that ran at the same time as a program entitled "A Synagogue on Intervale Avenue: Aging with Dignity in the South Bronx." The breakdance portion of the event included dance on film and a live demonstration, as well as a presentation from Martha Cooper, the former press photographer whom the article states "discovered" breaking when "sent to cover what her editors and the police had called a 'riot.'" For coverage of the 2007 National Folk Festival in Richmond, Virginia, which celebrated the twenty-fifth anniversary of *Wild Style*, see Cynthia McMullen, "Hip Hop on Down: *Wild Style* Reunion to Feature Old-School Performers at Folk Fest," *Richmond Times Dispatch*, Sept. 2, 2007.

3. Murray Forman and Mark Anthony Neal, eds., *That's the Joint: The Hip-Hop Studies Reader* (New York: Routledge, 2004).

4. Gary Dauphin, "Hip hop at the Movies," in *The Vibe History of Hip Hop*, ed. Alan Light (New York: Three Rivers Press, 1999), 203.

5. Paula Massood, *Black City Cinema: African American Urban Experiences in Film* (Philadelphia: Temple University Press, 2003), 122–24. See also Murray Forman, *The 'Hood Comes First: Race, Space, and Place in Rap and Hip-Hop* (Middletown, Connecticut: Wesleyan University Press, 2002), 255–58.

6. Nelson George, *Hip Hop America* (New York: Penguin, 1998), 108.

7. David Toop, *Rap Attack 2: African Rap to Global Hip Hop* (London: Pluto Press, 1984), 164.

8. See Tricia Rose, *Black Noise: Rap Music and Black Culture in Contemporary America* (Hanover: Wesleyan University Press, 1994), 4, 33. Rose, in her otherwise thoughtful and engaging study of rap music and hip hop culture, implies that early mainstream hip hop cinema was somehow "threatening" to the well-being of rap music: "By 1987, rap music had survived several death knells, Hollywood mockery, and radio bans and continued to spawn new artists, such as Public Enemy, Eric B. & Rakim, and LL Cool J" (4). The author does not explicitly state what she means by "Hollywood mockery" but given the omission of these films from her book, and the fact that hip hop musicals ceased to be produced by 1985, I can only surmise that she is referring to the cycle of films that are the subject of this book.

9. See Mark Winokur, "Marginal Marginalia: the African American Voice in the Nouvelle Gangster Film," *Velvet Light Trap* 35 (Spring 1995): 19–32, Michael Eric Dyson, "Out of the Ghetto," *Sight and Sound* 2, no. 6 (Oct. 1992): 18–21, Grant Farred, "No Way Out of the Menaced Society: Loyalty Within the Boundedness of Race," *Camera Obscura* 12, no. 2 35 (May 1995): 6–23, and Steven Kendall, *New Jack Cinema: Hollywood's African American Filmmakers* (Millbrae, CA: J. L. Denser), 1994. The three articles link their corpus of films through black urban identity and/or the African American gangster figure of hip hop music and culture. The last entry, published by a non-academic press, labeled these later films about ghetto-centric culture by an alternate nomenclature "New Jack Cinema" and explored the experiences of African American directors and black filmmaking in general.

10. There does exist one other attempt to organize the first hip hop cinema productions into a book-length corpus. This work, a Ph.D. dissertation by Aaron Dickinson Sachs entitled *The Hip-Hopsploitation Film Cycle: Representing, Articulating, and Appropriating Hip-Hop Culture*, University of Iowa, 2009, does not recognize or assess the significance and influence of the Hollywood musical genre in its discussion of what the author calls "hip-hopsploitation" cinema. Instead, Sachs discusses these films within an exclusionary model of exploitation cinema in order to advance the thesis that hip hop culture was originally represented in film as multicultural and pan-racial, rather than distinctly African American, prior to the assent of "New Black Realism." I am in disagreement with parts of this work, but the author does endeavor to provide a compelling account of the relation between hip hop and media technology.

11. Melvin Burke Donalson, *Hip Hop in American Cinema* (New York: Peter Lang, 2007), 7–24. This book does contain an informative but very cursory introductory chapter on the hip hop musical. Unlike most academic assessments of early hip hop cinema, Donalson acknowledges the films' significant connections to the Hollywood musical genre.

12. Thomas Doherty, *Teenagers and Teenpics: The Juvenilization of American Movies in the 1950s* (Philadelphia: Temple University Press, 1988), 72.

13. See Carol Clover, "Dancin' in the Rain," in *Hollywood Musicals: The Film Reader*, ed. Steven Cohan (London: Routledge, 2002), 162.

14. Henry Louis Gates, Jr., *The Signifying Monkey: A Theory of African-American Literary Criticism* (New York: Oxford University Press), 90–92. Gates notes that another

print in this series, *Dreadful Riot on Negro Hill* (1827), contains one of the earliest written attempts to represent black vernacular speech in verse form.

15. Tessa Watt, *Cheap Print and Popular Piety, 1550–1640* (Cambridge: Cambridge University Press, 1993), 11–38. The broadsheet ballad or penny ballad emerged as an early modern European form of print, which was sung or spoken aloud and associated with communal ritual and performance.

16. David Roediger, *The Wages of Whiteness: Race and the Making of the American Working Class* (London: Verso, 1999), 101–107.

17. Katrina Hazzard-Gordon, *Jookin': The Rise of Social Dance Formations in African-American Culture* (Philadelphia: Temple University Press, 1990), 46.

18. Ibid., 31–32. Regarding slave festival days and dances, the author notes that "no matter how much these occasions were intended to encourage resignation, slaves were able to seize dances as opportunities to resist white domination. A considerable amount of insurrectionary activity took place during slave holidays and days off, and even in tightly controlled situations themes of resistance were evident in both rural and urban settings. . . . Numerous slave insurrections resulted in legislation aimed to prevent slaves from visiting other plantations; from using drums, horns, or any other instrument that might signal rebellion." See also Jacqui Malone, *Steppin' on the Blues: The Visible Rhythms of African American Dance* (Urbana: University of Illinois Press, 1996). Malone's account downplays the insurrectionary aspect of African American dance under slavery and instead focuses on the role dance and music played in linking geographically separated slave communities to each other through shared relations to African culture.

19. Eric Lott, *Love & Theft: Blackface Minstrelsy and the American Working Class* (New York: Oxford University Press, 1993). Lott argues that the practice of minstrelsy was largely based on "cross racial desire," however repressed, rather than just the derision of black cultural practices. See also Michael Rogin, *Blackface, White Noise: Jewish Immigrants in the Hollywood Melting Pot* (Berkeley: University of California Press, 1996). Rogin is far less accommodating than Lott in his view of blackface racial solidarity and hybridity. He highlights the performance tradition's asymmetrical power relations and the very real exclusion of African American performers from the stage as whites appropriated black theatrical personas.

20. Lott, 29.

21. Ibid., 17. The author even suggests that the minstrel show not only played a part in "the racial politics of its time" but also largely "*was* the racial politics of its time—from its northern emergence as an entr'acte in about 1830 to the various New York stage versions of *Uncle Tom's Cabin* in the mid-1850s." Emphasis in original text.

22. Ibid., 63–87.

23. Alexander Saxon, "Blackface Minstrelsy," in *Inside the Minstrel Mask: Readings in Nineteenth Century Blackface Minstrelsy*, eds. Annemarie Bean, James V. Hatch, and Brooks McNamara (Hanover: Wesleyan University Press, 1996), 67–85.

24. Lott, 143–52.

25. Constance Valis Hill, *Tap Dancing America: A Cultural History* (Oxford: Oxford University Press, 2010), 5.

26. Marshall Stearns and Jean Stearns, *Jazz Dance: The Story of American Vernacular Dance* (New York: Da Capo Press, 1994), 36–37.

27. Robert W. Snyder, *The Voice of the City: Vaudeville and Popular Culture in New York* (New York: Oxford University Press, 1989), 12–25.

28. Ibid., 121. This act was performed at Hyde and Behman's Theater.

29. Even as the screen produced violent and grotesque images of female Irish bodies, stars like Maggie Cline, "The Irish Queen," found success on the vaudeville stage.

30. Ed Guerrero, *Framing Blackness: The African American Image in Film* (Philadelphia: Temple University Press, 1993), 10. Guerrero argues that the "plantation genre" emerged with *Birth of a Nation* (1915) and persisted in Hollywood film up until the 1970s, when the genre underwent a "sharp reversal of perspective" in the wake of intensified struggles for black civil rights during the 1960s.

31. Robert Jackson, "The Celluloid War Before *The Birth*: Race and History in Early American Film," in *American Cinema and the Southern Imaginary*, eds. Deborah Barker and Kathryn McKee (Athens: University of Georgia Press, 2011), 29. Jackson notes that historical evidence suggests "such films were considered a discrete genre" and that while at least ten watermelon themed eating films survive from roughly the first decade of cinema, many more were likely produced.

32. Lubin Summary, reproduced on the American Film Institute website, www.afi.com.

33. American Mutoscope and Biograph Company Summary, reproduced on the American Film Institute website, www.afi.com.

34. Jacqueline N. Stewart, *Migrating to the Movies: Cinema and Black Urban Modernity* (Berkeley: University of California Press, 2005), 73. Stewart argues that black criminality was such a pervasive and highly codified stereotype in the first few decades of cinema that the appearance of a black actor (or white actor in blackface) with a chicken or a watermelon already assumed an act of criminality or theft, which had taken place off screen.

35. Allan H. Spear, "The Making of the Black Ghetto," in *The Urbanization of America: An Historical Anthology*, ed. Allen M. Wakstein (New York: Houghton Mifflin Company, 1970), 272–75. Spear notes that when the number of blacks increased in Chicago between 1890 and 1910, an emerging affluent African American class sought housing in previously all-white neighborhoods. As a result, "community groups" such as the "The Hyde Park Improvement Club" emerged in order to prevent African Americans from purchasing and renting in white middle- and upper-class neighborhoods. See also Henry Louis Taylor, Jr., and Song-Ho Ha, "A Unity of Opposites: The Black College-Educated Elite, Black Workers, and the Community Development Process," in *Historical Roots of the Urban Crisis: African Americans in the Industrial City, 1900–1950*, ed. Henry Louis Taylor, Jr., and Walter Hill (New York: Garland Publishing, 2000), 32. The above authors argue that as home ownership became a reality for more and more Americans,

neighborhoods were transformed into *"defended territories* and battlegrounds between blacks and whites in the 1910s and 1920s."

36. "Violent Riots Close Ford's," *Afro-American*, Apr. 12, 1941. This article recounts the violent events of a massive autoworkers strike at Ford's River Rouge Michigan plant in 1941, and reflects on the automobile industry's role in drawing black laborers to Northern cities. "Colored workers have been employed by Henry Ford since he first opened his shop to make the original Model A machine. And when he announced that he would pay wages of $5 a day for common labor in his plant in 1914, which had been moved to Highland Park, the influx from the rural and urban centers of the South converged on Detroit in force. From 1915 to 1919 there was a steady stream of newcomers flooding the city. Everyone was talking about Ford and the high wages he was paying. At the same time there was a shortage of houses, rents soared, and the Motor City was in the midst of its pre-depression day boom."

37. "The Negro in the North," *Chicago Defender*, Apr. 23, 1921.

38. Ibid.

39. Henry Louis Gates, Jr., and Gene Andrew Jarrett, *The New Negro: Readings on Race, Representation, and African American Culture, 1892–1938* (Princeton: Princeton University Press, 2007), 1–20.

40. Jane M. Gaines, *Fire and Desire: Mixed-Race Movies in the Silent Era* (Chicago: University of Chicago Press, 2001), 5. The author remarks that "the Harlem elite virtually ignored these popular films and wrote them off as having nothing to do with art." Further, she makes the important point that "race movies" were never understood at the time of their production to be "high culture" even though historians have retrospectively attempted to transform the status of "race movies" and elevate them to such a stature.

41. Lester A. Walton, "Screen Dialect," *New York Age*, Jan. 1, 1918. Thank you to Jay Hufford for making this research available to me.

42. Ibid.

43. *Afro-American*, "Reform Needed on Race Stage," Aug. 24, 1923.

44. Gates, Jr., 172–80.

45. Ivan H. Browning, "Across the Pond," *Chicago Defender*, Dec. 15, 1928.

46. *Chicago Defender*, Jul. 22, 1929.

47. *Chicago Defender*, May 13, 1922.

48. *Chicago Defender*, "Ethel Radiates," Apr. 29, 1923.

49. Mark Hellinger, untitled, *Chicago Defender*, Sept. 29, 1928.

50. Ibid.

51. Ibid.

52. Valis Hill, 13.

53. "New Bert Williams Book Appears," *Baltimore Afro-American*, Apr. 6, 1923.

54. John Frederick Matheus, "Some Aspects of the Negro Interpreted in Contemporary American and European Literature," in Gates and Jarrett, eds., 210.

55. Thomas Sancton, "The Race Riots," *New Republic*, Jul. 5, 1943. Reprinted in *Reporting Civil Rights, Part One: American Journalism 1941–1963* (New York: Library of

America, 2003), 37–48. See also Ralph Ellison, "Eyewitness Story of Riot: False Rumors Spurred Mob," *New York Post*, Aug. 2, 1943. Reprinted in *Reporting Civil Rights Part One: American Journalism 1941–1963*, 49–51.

56. "Violent Riots Close Ford's." Although black newspapers such as the *Afro-American* appeared sympathetic to black laborers and their desire to continue earning a decent wage at the Ford plant without being interrupted by the demands of white unions who had largely excluded them and ignored them, the NAACP urged African American workers to side with the strikers. Further, the *Afro-American* detailed the financial rewards provided to black laborers by Ford in an employment environment frequently hostile to black workers; Boeing Aircraft, for instance, had a closed contract with the American Federation of Laborers that excluded black workers in at least one of their plants.

57. A. Philip Randolph, "Why F. D. Won't End Defense Jim Crow," *Afro-American*, Apr. 12, 1941.

58. For a brief overview of the "Soundie" phenomenon, see Maurice Terenzio, Scott MacGillivray, and Ted Okuda, *The Soundies Distributing Corporation of America: A History and Filmography of Their "Jukebox" Musical Films of the 1940s* (Jefferson, NC: McFarland & Co., 1991).

59. Thomas Doherty, *Projections of War: Hollywood, American Culture, and World War II* (New York: Columbia University Press, 1993), 220–21.

60. Donald Bogle, *Toms, Coons, Mulattoes, Mammies, and Bucks: An Interpretive History of Blacks in American Films* (New York: Continuum, 1989), 121. See also Thomas Cripps, *Slow Fade to Black: The Negro in American Film, 1900–1942* (New York, Oxford University Press, 1977), 357.

61. *Stormy Weather* (1943), an all-black cast musical showcase staring Lena Horne and Bill Robinson, is an exceptional anomaly at this historical juncture. Produced by Fox, it featured a romantic storyline between two black characters as well as a steady run of top African American musicians and dancers, and acknowledged the role of black Americans in the U.S. military.

62. Sean Griffin, "The Gang's All Here: Generic Versus Racial Integrations in the 1940s Musical," *Cinema Journal* 42, no. 1 (2002): 21–45.

63. Amy Herzog, "Discordant Visions: The Peculiar Musical Images of the Soundies Jukebox Film," *American Music* 22, no. 1 (Spring 2004): 27–39.

64. Ibid., 30.

65. Snyder, 44.

66. Herzog, 30.

67. Hilary Herbold, "Never a Level Playing Field: Blacks and the G.I. Bill," *Journal of Blacks in Higher Education* no. 6 (Winter 1994–5), 104–8.

68. Bruce Lambert, "At 50, Levittown Contends With its Legacy of Bias," *New York Times*, Dec. 28, 1997. The original Long Island, NY, Levittown lease agreements (that included an option to purchase) in the late 1940s stipulated that only white tenants could move in.

69. Glenn Altschuler, *All Shook Up: How Rock 'N' Roll Changed America* (Oxford: Oxford University Press, 2003), 1–34.

70. "NAACP Blamed for 'Rock and Roll' Music in South," *Baltimore Afro-American*, Apr. 3, 1956.

71. Altschluer, 61. In 1957, Frankie Lymon did cause a scandal by reaching out to dance with a white girl at the end of Alan Freed's *Rock 'N' Roll Dance Party*, a move that led to the show's subsequent cancelation.

72. Ilana Nash, *American Sweethearts: Teenage Girls in Twentieth Century Popular Culture* (Bloomington: Indiana University Press, 2006), 53. Perceptive historians such as Nash have shown that despite the overriding "whiteness" of most youth-oriented popular narratives, products such as serialized teen literature—in Nash's example, Nancy Drew detective stories, which relegated "minorities and the working class" to the status of "villains or . . . incidental characters, usually menial laborers"—could be negotiated by young readers from communities of color in ambivalent yet often ultimately satisfying ways. See also Kelly Schrum, *Some Wore Bobby Sox: The Emergence of Teenage Girls' Culture 1920–1945* (New York: Palgrave, 2004). Schrum uses some high school yearbooks from African American schools in her research but she does not examine racial difference as a significant facet shaping one's experience of adolescence in the United States.

73. "Truman and the Poll Tax," *Afro-American*, Apr. 9, 1946. The author notes, "President Truman told a group of teen-agers in Chicago last Saturday that the repeal of the poll tax is a matter that should be left up to the Southern States." The article does not mobilize the word "teen-ager" in relation to consumer culture or delinquency but rather employs the term to denote a group of young people as a political entity.

74. Dr. Palmer's targeted teen consumers in a 1955 advertisement in the May 31 edition of the *Baltimore Afro-American* as it announced that "teen-age girls, and boys too, who are experiencing the pimples of youth should find Dr. FRED Palmer's of great help in ending the embarrassment of ugly pimply skin." While Dr. Palmer's generally counted teenage skin ailments as one of the many problems it could cure, teens were specifically addressed in their 1963 advertisement, ominously titled "Teen-age Torture" as it linked "complexion success" with "date success." The cure-all elixir Black and White ointment also listed "Teen-age Pimples" as one of the conditions, along with ringworm and eczema, that it could treat in a February 4, 1956, half-page ad in the *Afro-American*.

75. "Gray Gets Our Vote," *Washington Afro-American*, Jun. 22, 1954.

76. Amy Nathan Wright, "A Philosophy of Funk: The Politics and Pleasure of a Parliafunkadelicment Thang!" in *The Funk Era and Beyond: New Perspectives on Black Popular Culture*, ed. Tony Bolden (New York: Palgrave, 2008), 38. Wright argues that the song "What is Soul" attempted to transform mainstream sociologists' prevailing assessments of black urban working people as a pathological underclass, who were largely to blame for their impoverished material condition, by utilizing poetic and sometimes humorous language to articulate the African American urban experience. Clinton locates soul in "What is Soul" as the material impoverishment of "a ring around

your bathtub" and the desperation of "a joint rolled in toilet paper" but it is also "rusty ankles and ashy kneecaps"—a nuanced and evocative description of inner-city life that beautifully fused bodily sensations, corporeal conditions, and memory with the dilapidated urban environment.

77. David Theo Goldberg, *Racial Subjects: Writing on Race in America* (New York: Routledge, 1997), 64–66. Immigrant communities from Mexico, Argentina, Columbia, The Dominican Republic, Puerto Rico, and many other Spanish-speaking regions made their presence increasingly felt in the social, political and cultural life of the United States towards the end of the 1970s. The U.S. Census Bureau responded by creating a new and unprecedented category of self-identification on the 1980 census count—Hispanic—that unites all people who trace their origins from any Spanish-speaking region. This undoubtedly reifies and reduces the obvious differences between national communities, yet it also attests to the undisputable influence that this arguably coherent cultural and political force has exerted in the United States in the last half-century.

78. Madeline H. Kimmich, *America's Children: Who Cares? Growing Needs and Declining Assistance in the Reagan Era* (Washington, D.C.: The Urban Institute Press, 1985), 1. See also Carmen DeNavas-Walt, Bernadette D. Proctor, and Jessica C. Smith, *Income, Poverty, and Health Insurance Coverage in the United States: 2009*, U.S. Department of Commerce and Economics and Statistics Administration, U.S. Bureau of the Census (Washington, D.C.: U.S Government Printing Office, 2010): Report P60, no. 238. Table B-2, 62–67. During the first two years of President Reagan's tenure, the poverty rate for black children increased by more than 5 percent while the rate for Hispanic children was even higher at 6.3 percent. In this two-year period, the poverty rates for white children increased by 3.1 percent. This dramatic increase in poverty among American children occurred during a significant economic downturn and was not entirely the result of reductions to federal aid programs. However, comparing poverty rates among children between the four years prior to Reagan's election and those following his two terms in office are very telling. Between 1976 and 1980, poverty among white children increased by 2 percent, black children by 1.7 percent, and Hispanic children by 3 percent. Between 1980 and 1988, the years bracketing Reagan's presidency, poverty rates among white children actually fell by .8 percent, while the poverty rates for black and Hispanic children rose by 1.2 percent and 4.4 percent, respectively.

79. Kimmich, 3. The author notes that "restrictions on federal funding were usually imposed in two ways: as direct reductions in grant programs (often accompanying a shift from service-specific grants to a block grant), or as changes in eligibility criteria or service coverage in entitlement programs."

80. "NUL State of America Says: Blacks Are a Forgotten People," *Baltimore Afro-American*, Jan. 19, 1982. This article presents an overview of the National Urban League's series of reports for 1981, dealing with education, economics, and affirmative action.

81. Ibid.

82. Ronald Lawson and Reuben B. Johnson III, "Tenant Responses to the Urban Housing Crises, 1970–1984," in *The Tenant Movement in New York City, 1904–1984*, eds. Ronald Lawson and Mark Naison (New Brunswick, New Jersey: Rutgers University Press: 1986).

CHAPTER 1

1. Douglas Kellner, "Film, Politics, and Ideology: Reflections on Hollywood Film in the Age of Reagan," *Velvet Light Trap* 27 (Spring 1991): 9–24. I invoke the term "ideology" here in the same manner as Kellner, who argues that it is most useful to understand ideology in relation to "theories, ideas, texts, and representations that legitimate domination of women and people of color, and that serve the interests of the ruling gender and race as well as class powers." (10) He suggests that while ideologically oppressive currents may be present in many mainstream films, these same productions are often beset with contradictions, and display multiple ideological viewpoints that may contradict their apparently conservative or liberal narratives. I find his broadening of Marxist terms of analysis very useful in understanding film culture of the 1980s.

2. Charlie Ahearn, *Wild Style: The Sampler* (Brooklyn: Powerhouse Books, 2007), 116–17, 154–61.

3. Ibid., 50–51

4. Stanley Meisler, "U.N. Holds Meeting on S. Africa: Jackson, Belafonte Assail US Conference Boycott," *Los Angeles Times*, Jun. 17, 1986. During the United Nations conference, Belafonte directly accused President Reagan of racism and insensitivity to the plight of African children. Meisler writes that "Belafonte, the singer who has taken an active role in the movement for sanctions against South Africa, described President Reagan as 'morally bankrupt, with racist attitudes.' 'Ronald Reagan will weep at the grave of Nazi fascists,' Belafonte told reporters, recalling the President's visit to the West German military grave at Bitburg last year, 'but he has no compassion for the children killed in Soweto.'"

5. Abiola Sinclair, "*Beat Street*: Authentic Look at Bronx Breakers," *New York Amsterdam News*, Jun. 9, 1984. The author notes that "Belafonte says the film is dedicated to the people of the South Bronx 'without whom there would be nothing to make a film about.'"

6. Geoffrey Baker, "¡Hip Hop, Revolución! Nationalizing Rap in Cuba," *Ethnomusicology* 49, no. 3 (Fall 2005): 19–20.

7. Doherty, 1988, 7–9. Doherty notes, "Together, these three elements—controversial content, bare-bones budgets, and demographic targeting—remain characteristic of any exploitation movie."

8. Cannon Films was purchased by two Israeli businessmen, Menahem Golan and Yoram Globus, in the late 1970s. Under their leadership, the company has produced

a slew of low-budget martial arts films, including *Bloodsport* (1988) and the entire *American Ninja* series (1986–1993), teen sex comedies, as well as more serious "quality" films including John Cassavetes's *Love Streams* (1984) and *The Assault* (1986), which won the Oscar for Best Foreign Language Film. In 1990, Cannon once again ventured into the familiar territory of youth-oriented dance cinema with *Lambada*, a dance flick intended to capitalize on the brief Latin-inspired dance craze of the late 1980s. The film starred *Breakin'*s Adolfo Quinones and was directed by Joel Silberberg.

9. "Yearly Box Office: 1984 Domestic Grosses," Box Office Mojo, http://www.boxofficemojo.com/yearly/chart/?yr=1984&p=.htm

10. Ibid.

11. Robert Sklar, *Movie-Made America: A Cultural History of the American Movies*, rev. ed. (New York: Vintage Books, 1994), 341. Many of the highest earners from this decade were big budget Hollywood spectacles that appealed to young audiences. These films were often serialized science fiction or fantasy-oriented special effects extravaganzas. *Breakin'* certainly doesn't fit this mold but it undoubtedly appealed to young cinemagoers, a feature that nearly always guaranteed success at this moment of rapid multiplex expansion facilitated by the proliferation of mall construction across the country.

12. Gene Siskel, "Break Dancin'," *New York Daily News*, May 29, 1984.

13. Ibid.

14. Rick Altman, *The American Film Musical* (Bloomington: Indiana University Press, 1987), 12.

15. Ibid., 211–12.

16. Ibid., 200.

17. The only exception to this observation is *Delivery Boys*.

18. Altman, 208. Altman argues that the show musical's finale is the ultimate testament to the genre's conservative and "strikingly middle-class view of the process of producing and marketing a commodity."

19. Ibid., 209.

20. Ibid., 209.

21. Ibid., 140–41. The author notes that as the influence of the Viennese tradition came to bear its weight upon early American cinema, the open sexuality of operetta was usually sublimated within the textual operations of the film musical, partly because the American audience was less familiar with such overt displays of sexual desire.

22. Ibid., 140.

23. Matthew Tinkcom, *Working Like a Homosexual: Camp, Capital, Cinema* (Durham: Duke University Press, 2002), 35–71. While I agree with Tinkcom's reading, these codes were merely available to be read by particular spectators. In turn, such particular queer aesthetics were also just as likely to go unnoticed by most mainstream filmgoers, and the elaborate dream world of romantic play constructed in the films (enabled by their queer aesthetic) also made their conservative plot elements all the more attractive to the general viewing public.

24. Altman, 145.

25. Fredric Jameson, *The Cultural Turn: Selected Writings on the Postmodern, 1983–1998* (London: Verso, 1998), 5. Jameson argues that within the postmodern era, the use of older representational forms no longer contains a critical or ironic comment as one would find in parody. Instead, he suggests that postmodernism is distinguished by "pastiche." While "pastiche" also utilizes and revisits previous styles and genres, Jameson notes that it "is the imitation of a peculiar or unique style, the wearing of a stylistic mask, speech in a dead language: but it is a neutral practice of such mimicry, without parody's ulterior motive, without the satirical impulse. . . . Pastiche is blank parody." See also Jean Baudrillard, *Simulacra and Simulation* (Ann Arbor: University of Michigan Press, 1994).

26. Lawson and Reuben B. Johnson III, 268. According to Lawson and Johnson, the South Bronx was not under threat so much from gentrification as it was from "severe decay and abandonment."

27. Lee Dembart, "Carter Takes 'Sobering' Trip to South Bronx; Carter Finds Hope Amid Blight on 'Sobering' Trip to Bronx," *New York Times*, Oct. 6, 1977.

28. Ibid. See also Manny Fernandez, "In the Bronx, Blight Gave Way to Renewal," *New York Times*, Oct. 5, 2007.

29. Vernon E. Jordan, Jr., "Has Carter Forgotten Black Needs?; Carter and Black Needs," *Washington Post*, Aug. 14, 1977.

30. Ibid.

31. "Reagan, In South Bronx, Says Carter Broke Vow; Raises Voice Above Chants," *New York Times*, Aug. 6, 1980.

32. Gerald M. Boyd, "Jackson Spends Night in South Bronx," *New York Times*, Mar. 31, 1984.

33. "Don't Save the South Bronx," *Washington Post*, Feb. 17, 1979.

34. Lee Lescaze, "Bronx Renewal Project Declared Dead by Koch," *Washington Post*, Feb. 8, 1979. See also Marshal Berman, "Introduction," in *New York Calling: From Blackout to Bloomberg*, eds. Marshal Berman and Brian Berger (London: Reaktion Books, 2007), 14–15. Berman notes that New York City had been dealing with a rash of uncontrolled fires for many years before the devastation of the South Bronx made national headlines. He writes that "starting late in the '60s, they burst out mainly in poor minority neighborhoods all over town but also in ethnically and economically mixed neighborhoods like my own Upper West Side. For years, midnight fires ate up not only buildings but whole blocks, often block after block. Then we found out that even while large sections of the city were burning down, most massively in the South Bronx, their firehouses were being closed and the size of their crews was being reduced—on the grounds that they were losing population."

35. "Reagan, In South Bronx, Says Carter Broke Vow; Raises Voice Above Chants." The author writes, "Standing in front of a building on which 'Decay' had been painted in bright orange, and across the street from another bearing the words 'broken promises,' the Republican Presidential candidate said he had not 'seen anything that looked like this since London after the Blitz.'"

36. C. J. Sullivan, "There's Hope for the South Bronx," in Berman and Berger, 76.

37. Jeff Chang, *Can't Stop, Won't Stop: A History of the Hip Hop Generation* (New York: St. Martin's Press, 2005), 11.

38. Ibid., 10. The Robert Moses Cross-Bronx Expressway project was initiated in 1953.

39. Marshall Berman, *All That is Solid Melts into Air: The Experience of Modernity* (New York: Penguin Books, 1982), 292–93.

40. Ibid., 292. The Cross-Bronx Expressway construction displaced some 60,000 residents of the Bronx (mostly Jews and ethnic whites, but some blacks as well). See also C. J. Sullivan, 78. The author notes that white residents of the Bronx continued to flee the area in large numbers following the roadway's initial destruction of primarily Jewish and white neighborhoods. Between 1970 and 1980, the population of white residents in the Bronx fell from over 1 million to just 550,000. By 2002, nearly half of the Bronx was Latino, one quarter of its residents were black, and just 14 percent were white.

41. Lawson and Johnson III, 210–11. The authors write that "a Rand Corporation study found that housing abandonment had increased sharply in New York City during the second half of the decade, with an average of 38,000 units per year being abandoned as compared with 15,000 between 1960 and 1964. Moreover, while the inventory of 'sound' housing had grown by 2 percent between 1960 and 1967, 'dilapidated' housing climbed by 44 percent, and 'deteriorating' housing by 37 percent."

42. Ibid., 211.

43. Ibid., 209–10.

44. Ibid., 235–36.

45. Ibid.

46. Ibid., 240–42.

47. Ibid., 242.

48. Paula Massood, "Mapping the Hood: The Genealogy of City Space in *Boyz N the Hood* and *Menace II Society*," *Cinema Journal* 35, no. 2 (Winter 1996): 85.

49. Ibid., 88.

50. Claude McKay, *Home to Harlem* (Boston: Northeastern University Press, 1987), 10. First published 1928 by Harper and Brothers.

51. Set in the inner city and oriented around violent male narratives, most of these films rely heavily on "gangsta rap," with its references to identifiable urban locales reinforcing the authenticity and realism of the films. The soundtracks, thus, provide a second layer of legitimacy to the urban locations ostensibly utilized in the films. For a discussion of city space in "New Black Realism" and its relation to earlier forms of black culture, see Massood, 1996. The author suggests that a distinct emphasis on the naming and identification of "real" urban environments in "New Black Realism" functions to align this work with a tradition of black American literature, which had also brought the background space of the novel to the very forefront of the text as blacks began migrating to urban centers in the North.

52. Ida Peters, "Flicks: *Beat Street*," *Afro-American*, Jun. 16, 1984.

53. Ibid.

54. Ahearn, 118.

55. William Robbins, "Amid New Spirit, Pittsburgh Opens Center," *New York Times*, Feb. 13. 1981.

56. Laurence A. Glasco, ed., *The WPA History of the Negro in Pittsburgh* (Pittsburgh: University of Pittsburgh Press, 2004), 24. The authors write, "What is known as 'The Hill' was populated slowly. In 1815 only thirteen of the towns 5,000 persons lived on Grant's Hill, but a business directory in 1837 listed 413 people on all that land now referred to as the Hill. These were chiefly merchants and professionals who had built in the growing suburb."

57. Ibid., 25.

58. Ibid.

59. Ibid.

60. Joel A. Tarr, "Infrastructure and City-Building," in *City at the Point: Essays on the Social History of Pittsburgh*, ed. Samuel P. Hays (Pittsburgh: University of Pittsburgh Press, 1989), 250.

61. Interestingly, Lionel Ritchie also presented music and dance as a utopian panacea in his early contribution to music television programming, *All Night Long*. In this successful video, a street scene explodes into a raucous neighborhood party which features breaking, contemporary jazz dance, and representations of traditional African dance forms. Towards the end of the video, a police officer enters the scene, parting the crowd with his stern walk. However, he too succumbs to the infectious rhythm and instead of chastising the offending revelers the officer embarks on a dance routine in which he uses his nightstick as a baton.

62. Mikhail Bakhtin, *Rabelais and His World* (Bloomington: Indiana University Press), 10. As the "unofficial" medieval carnivals discussed by Bakhtin elevated fools to the rank of kings, these symbolic inversions signified the suspension of social hierarchy and order on a broad scale. *Rappin'* suggests that the inversions found in hip hop culture portend the same radical possibilities as Bakhtin's medieval carnival days. Bakhtin writes that "as opposed to the official feast, one might say that carnival celebrated temporary liberation from the prevailing truth and from the established order; it marked the suspension of all hierarchical rank, privileges, norms, and prohibitions."

63. Mike Hurewitz, "Jailhouse Rock for Break Dance Muggers," *New York Post*, Oct. 4, 1984.

64. Ibid.

65. Lawson and Johnson III, 209–71.

66. M. G. Marshall and P. Arestis, "Reaganomics and Supply-Side Economics: A British View," *Journal of Economic Issues* 23, no. 4 (Dec. 1989): 972. See also Robert R. Keller, "Supply-Side Economic Policies During the Coolidge-Mellon Era," *Journal of Economic Issues* 16, no. 3 (Sept. 1982): 773–90.

67. For a critique of Reagan-era economic policies, see Lawrence Chimerie, "What Really Happened in the 1980s," *Challenge* 39, no. 3 (May/Jun. 1996): 32. The author notes

that "despite the seven-year expansion in the middle of the decade, average economic growth during the decade as a whole actually lagged behind growth in each of the three preceding decades, including the stagflation years of the 1970s. Moreover . . . the long expansion to a great extent simply represented a catch-up following back-to-back recessions in 1980 and 1982."

68. I imply no value judgment here. Authenticity simply refers to the extent to which the film consulted and utilized the talent of actual hip hop practitioners.

69. Tim McKeough, "Vanilla Ice on His New Reality TV Series," *New York Times*, Sept. 15, 2010. In a fitting addendum to *Cool as Ice's* disconcerting engagement of race, performance, and geographical space, Vanilla Ice, following his brief rap career, has transformed himself into a real estate mogul and is the star of reality TV show *The Vanilla Ice Project*, which first aired on the DIY Network in 2009. The program, and attendant manual, are designed to help one "pimp out properties and get paid." In essence, the program is a lesson on flipping properties for profit, a practice associated with gentrification—a major force of transition in urban areas that has had, and continues to have, a detrimental effect on communities of color.

70. See Jane Feuer, *The Hollywood Musical*, 2nd ed. (Bloomington: Indiana University Press, 1993), 123–38. See also Dave Kehr, "Cant Stop the Musicals," *American Film* 9, no. 7 (May 1984): 33–37, J. P. Telotte, "The New Hollywood Musical: From Saturday Night Fever to Footloose," in *Genre and Contemporary Hollywood*, ed. Steven Neale (London: BFI, 2002), 48–61, and James Hay, "Dancing and Deconstructing the American Dream," *Quarterly Review of Film Studies* 10, no. 2 (Spring 1985): 97–117.

71. Feuer, 124.

72. Hay, 106–7.

73. Feuer, 123–38.

74. Ibid., 135.

75. Chris Jordan, "Gender and Class Mobility in *Saturday Night Fever* and *Flashdance*," *Journal of Popular Film and Television* 24, no. 3 (Fall 1996): 120. Chris Jordan remarks that the film's message of class mobility for women in American society is predicated upon a "commodified self-image, and patriarchal domination."

76. Telotte, 49. What is different about these later musicals, notes the author, is that they "are pointedly about the role of music and dance in our lives" and "obviously treat these expressive elements . . . with a rather detached attitude." He argues that within such films as *Saturday Night Fever*, *Purple Rain*, *Footloose*, and *Dirty Dancing* "the expressive is clearly demarcated from the main narrative, even while realistically arising from it."

77. John Mueller, "Fred Astaire and the Integrated Musical," *Cinema Journal* 24, no. 1 (Fall 1984): 28–30.

78. Richard Dyer, "Entertainment and Utopia," in *Hollywood Musicals: The Film Reader*, ed. Steven Cohan (London: Routledge, 2002), 20. "Two of the taken-for-granted descriptions of entertainment, as 'escape' and as 'wish-fulfillment,' point to its central thrust, namely utopianism. Entertainment offers the image of 'something better' to escape into, or something we want deeply that our day-to-day lives don't provide.

Alternatives, hopes, wishes—these are the stuff of utopia, the sense that things could be better, that something other than what is can be imagined and realized."

79. Telotte, 49.

80. Ibid., 50–51. Telotte writes of the postclassical musical that "instead of denying reality's rule with song and dance, they construct a realistic frame around those expressive elements, becoming in the process proscenium-oriented. These films masquerade variously as social commentary, biography and documentary, but they share a common perspective, one which offers a more sober approach to the expressive role of music in the movies and in our lives."

81. Ibid., 50–53. Telotte also notes of the postclassical musical film that "while they do admit that there is a 'place' for song and dance in our lives, by underscoring the limited potential of music, they also affirm that we can no longer withdraw from the real world to immerse ourselves in the expressive one."

82. David Gonzalez, "*Wild Style* at 25: A Film that Envisioned the Future of Hip Hop," *New York Times*, Nov. 12, 2008.

83. Ibid.

84. Kehr, 34.

85. Ibid., 35–36. The author writes that "the mandate of the musical has always been to enshrine the popular music of its era. It is pointless . . . to ask the musical to return to other eras and styles. Whether rock is musically superior to the Tin Pan Alley tunes of the thirties and forties is not the point."

86. Ibid., 36. "For even at its best, rock poses a range of problems to narrative adaptation . . . there are few halftones in the music, which means that virtually every number must be a climax."

87. Ibid.

88. Ibid.

89. Ibid., 37.

90. Richard Dyer, "The Colour of Entertainment," in *Musicals: Hollywood and Beyond*, eds. Bill Marshall and Robynn Stilwell (Exeter: Intellect Books, 2000), 28.

91. Arthur Knight, *Disintegrating the Musical: Black Performance and Musical Film* (Durham: Duke University Press, 2002), 133. The author writes of *Hearts in Dixie*, *Hallelujah!*, and *The Green Pastures* that "like the vast majority of the Hollywood black-cast musicals, these early films focus on the 'folk'—Southern, rural, and apparently timeless blacks going about what purports to be 'a slice of life.'" See also Massood, 2003, 16. Massood argues that the use of the antebellum South as timeless idyll in the earliest Hollywood black-cast musicals functioned to "reconfirm ideology that removed African Americans, and all peoples of African decent, from a 'civilized' world that was urban and therefore modern."

92. James Snead, *White Screens, Black Images: Hollywood From the Dark Side* (New York: Routledge, 1994), 48–56.

93. The classical-era jazz biopic, which will be discussed further in Chapter 4, is a notable exception to this assessment. These films, which include, for example, *The Glenn*

Miller Story (1954), and *The Benny Goodman Story* (1955), operate with completely different racial boundaries regarding performance, desire, and sexual power.

94. Jim Sullivan, "Breakin' Out of the Ghetto and Makin' it Big at the Box Office," *Boston Globe*, Jun. 17, 1984.

95. Ibid. Zito notes that his original script was significantly altered and scenes were cut. One sequence that was scrapped for the final film included Kelly, the film's white middle-class female protagonist, convincing her parents of breakdancing's worth by comparing it to jazz in general and the music of Charlie Parker in specific. In this scene, she was to have suggested that this earlier performance tradition "once considered disreputable—something done in the street," which is now at the center of musical culture, bears a similarity to the future trajectory of breakdance. In protest, Zito used the pseudonym Charles Parker for his writing credit on the film.

96. S. Craig Watkins, *Representing: Hip Hop Culture and the Production of Black Cinema* (Chicago: University of Chicago Press, 1998), 17–35.

97. Michel de Certeau, *The Practice of Everyday Life* (Berkeley: University of California Press, 1988), 121.

98. Ibid. The author writes that the map is a "totalizing stage on which elements of diverse origin are brought together to form the tableau of a 'state' of geographical knowledge."

99. Harlan Jacobson, "Charles Ahearn interviewed by Harlan Jacobson," *Film Comment* 19, no. 3 (May/Jun. 1983): 65.

100. Jim Welsh, "Beat Street," *Films in Review* 35 (Aug./Sept. 1984): 435.

101. Jeff Millar, "Krush Groove Energetic," *Houston Chronicle*, Oct. 26, 1985.

102. Ibid. Millar writes that the cast of *Krush Groove* is "extraordinarily kinetic."

103. de Certeau, 97.

CHAPTER 2

1. Vincent Canby, "*Wild Style*, Rapping and Painting Graffiti," *New York Times*, Mar. 18, 1983. See also Jay Scott, "Right to the Source of Rap D.J.s, B-Boys, 'Writers,'" *Toronto Globe and Mail*, Feb. 10, 1984. This reviewer writes of *Wild Style* that "there is no structure, or, rather, the structure that does exist is so antediluvian it should be ignored . . . graffiti artist George 'Lee' Quinones, Finds Himself and Gets the Girl. Simple. Dumb."

2. "Removing the 'Graffiti Disease,'" *Afro-American*, Aug. 26, 1972. See also Carolyn Fortier, "Let's Stop Killing Our Communities," *Chicago Defender*, Feb. 17, 1973, and Fortier, "Vandalism: Who are the Victims," *Chicago Defender*, Feb. 24, 1973.

3. Fortier, Feb. 24, 1973.

4. Ibid.

5. Ibid.

6. "From Subway to Fame," *Afro-American*, Mar. 24, 1984. See also "Hip Hop Glossery [sic]," *Afro-American*, Jun. 16, 1984. The list also defined "piece" as "a graffiti artist's 'masterpiece.'"

7. "Clean Block Drive Ends," *Afro-American*, Sept. 2, 1939.

8. Ibid.

9. "Clean Block Campaign Gets Underway Early," *Afro-American*, May 31, 1941. Underscoring the link between cleanliness and civic duty was paramount during the months leading up the United States' official entry into the Second World War: "Our president has declared that a state of emergency exists in the country. Every man, woman, and boy over 18 years of age will be needed in the defense industries. Many so-called minor activities must be left to the younger members of the family. Minor repairs must be made, the home must be kept clean, painting done, yards fixed up and made beautiful. Children must learn to keep healthy, to reduce fire hazards by seeing that no trash collects anywhere on the premises, and take a general interest in things about the home."

10. "AFRO's 50th Annual Clean Block Workshop and Luncheon," *Baltimore Afro-American*, Mar. 31, 1984.

11. Raymond adopts the *nom de plume* of early twentieth century literary character Zorro, created by author Johnson McCulley in 1919. However, Raymond alters the spelling of the pulp fiction hero from Zorro to Zoro, fashioning a name that is both original and a facsimile. The initial Zorro was a clandestine figure who, like Raymond, maintained a secret identity, cleverly outwitting authority figures. Zorro was a masked nocturnal hero who crusaded for justice on behalf of the poor and working-class while, during the day, he lived as Don Diego Vega, a Spanish nobleman.

12. Both graffiti artists and Abstract Expressionists also used commonly available cheap commercial paint products.

13. Jacobson, 65.

14. See, for example, *Dames* (1934) and *Gold Diggers of 1933* (1933).

15. Herbert Kohl and James Hinton, "Names, Graffiti, and Culture," in *Rappin' and Stylin' Out*, ed. Thomas Kochman (Urbana: University of Illinois Press, 1972), 119–120. This article was originally published in 1969 in the journal *Urban Review*. The authors write that "recently a teacher was assaulted in a Manhattan junior high school because he refused to address several of his pupils by the names they considered their own. He insisted that the boys answer to their 'legal' names: that is, the names listed in his roll book. They laughed, and when he waved the roll book at them, they grabbed it and tore it up.... To the three boys the names Thomas Jackson, John Robinson, and Robert Lee were slave names, names that came to their families that identified them as descendants of slaves.... The boys once accepted a world without hope where they were resigned to being inferior. Now they have been converted to a new and different version of things. With it, they have assumed new identities that must be named and displayed to the world."

16. "Taki 183 Spawns Pen Pals," *New York Times*, Jul. 21, 1971.

17. Ibid.

18. Norman Mailer, *The Faith of Graffiti* (New York: Praeger, 1974), unpaginated. Interestingly, Mailer describes the emergence of graffiti in the late 1960s and early '70s in New York in terms of an organic matter, or a biological eruption in which "a communion took place over the city in this plant growth of names until every institutional wall, fixed or moving . . . every standing billboard, every huckstering poster, and the halls of every high-rise low rent housing project which looked like a prison (and all did) were covered by a foliage of graffiti which grew seven or eight feet tall."

19. This theme is taken up in the documentary *Style Wars* as well as the film *Basquiat* (1996), which chronicles the rise to fame of graffiti artist Jean-Michel Basquiat in the early 1980s.

20. Jean Fisher, "Wild Style," *Artforum International* 22 (Apr. 1984): 84.

21. Sharon Sherman, 292. For a nuanced discussion of the relationship between "authentic" culture and commercial entities, see also Andrew Ross, *No Respect: Intellectuals and Popular Culture* (New York: Routledge, 1989), 70. Ross writes that "it is often assumed . . . that commercialized music = whitened music, that the black performance of uncommercialized and therefore undiluted black music constitutes the only truly genuine form of protest or resistance against the white culture industry and its controlling interests, and that black music which submits to that industry automatically loses its autonomous power. To subscribe to this equation is to imagine a very mechanical process indeed, whereby a music, which is authentically black, constitutes an initial raw material which is then appropriated and reduced in cultural force and meaning by contact with a white industry. Accordingly, music is never 'made,' and only ever exploited, in this process of industrialization."

22. Lesley Speed, "Moving On Up: Education in Black American Youth Films," *Journal of Popular Film and Television* 29, no. 2 (2001): 84–85.

23. Altman, 273.

24. Ibid., 273–75.

25. Feuer, 13–15. In speaking of the appeal inherent in the "amateur" performer within the film musical, Feuer writes that "amateur entertainers can't exploit us . . . because they *are* us."

26. Ibid., 3.

27. Ibid.

28. Ibid., 28. The author writes of this filming technique that "it's the intrusion of the internal audience between us and the performance which, paradoxically, gives the effect of a lived—and more significantly—a *shared* experience. . . . The subjectivity of the spectator stands in for that of the spectral audience, rendering the performance utterly theatrical. We are, as it were, lifted out of the audience we actually belong to (the cinema audience) and transported into another audience, one at once more alive and ghostly."

29. Altman, 274. In discussing films of the mid-twentieth century, such as *Meet Me in St. Louis, Oklahoma!* (1955), and *Carousel* (1956), Altman writes that "the

multi-generational family . . . becomes permanently fixed as a standard element of the folk musical."

30. Andy Bennett, *Popular Music and Youth Culture: Music, Identity, and Place* (New York: St. Martin's Press, 2000), 134–36.

31. Robert Palmer, "The Pop Life; The Audience for Rappers Broadens," *New York Times*, May, 23, 1984.

32. Bakhtin, 7. Diminishing the boundary between performer and spectator is a long-standing aspect of the democratization of performance culture. In his discussion of medieval popular festivities, Bakhtin famously noted that "carnival does not know footlights, in the sense that it does not acknowledge any distinction between actors and spectators. Footlights would destroy a carnival, as the absence of footlights would destroy a theatrical performance. Carnival is not a spectacle seen by the people; they live it, and everyone participates because its very idea embraces all the people."

33. Wendy James, "Reforming the Circle: Fragments of the Social History of a Vernacular African Dance Form," *Journal of African Cultural Studies* 13, no. 1 (Jun. 2000): 143. The circle formation has a long history within African dance culture. It has been a constant feature of ritualized social life within Africa and throughout African communities of the diaspora. James writes that "the circular form has a robust and lasting quality, sometimes with mythical echoes, which must be linked to the way in which it defines a special, inward space of its own, a centre [sic] to which participants orient themselves and through which they relate to each other."

34. Massood, 2003, 11–43.

35. In this context, I am using the term "integration" to denote musical numbers that do not take place in a theater, club, or other designated space of entertainment.

36. "Kurtis Blow: Rapping to the Top," *Baltimore Afro-American*, Oct. 11, 1980.

37. Ibid.

38. "Record Cut to Honor King," *Baltimore Afro-American*, Jan. 28, 1986. All proceeds from record sales were donated to the Martin Luther King Jr. Center for Non-Violent Social Change in Atlanta, Georgia.

39. Richard Harrington, "The *King Holiday* Rap," *Washington Post*, Dec. 11, 1985.

40. Altman, 275.

41. Susan Stewart, *Crimes of Writing: Problems in the Containment of Representation* (Oxford: Oxford University Press, 1991), 217.

42. Melvin D. Williams, *The Human Dilemma: A Decade Later in Belmar* (rev. of *On the Street Where I Lived*) (Fort Worth: Harcourt Brace Jovanovich College Publishers, 1992), 28. *On the Street Where I Lived* was originally published in 1981, based on research performed in the 1970s. The author uses the terms "genuine" and "spurious" in relation to the extent that different segments of the black population have internalized the values of white mainstream culture.

43. "Reagan, In South Bronx, Says Carter Broke Vow; Raises Voice Above Chants."

44. Kimmich, 18–19.

232 Notes

45. D. Lee Bawden and John L. Palmer, "Social Policy: Challenging the Welfare State," in *The Reagan Record: An Assessment of America's Changing Domestic Priorities*, eds. John L. Palmer and Isabel V. Sawhill (Cambridge Massachusetts: Ballinger Publishing Company, 1984), 201–208. During his time in office, Ronald Reagan instituted a reversal of civil rights protection for minorities and women. This included a reduction in government spending on programs such as the Equal Employment Opportunity Commission and the Office of Federal Contract Compliance Programs (the body that produced affirmative action guidelines regarding employment by government contractors). A direct result of these cuts was a reduction of legal action and disciplinary procedures brought against potential violations in the areas of employment, housing, and schooling.

46. Margaret C. Simms, *The Economic Well-Being of Minorities During the Reagan Years* (Washington, D.C.: The Urban Institute, Project Report, Oct. 1984), 9–10. For instance, the Food Stamp and Public Service Employment programs saw large reductions in federal funding.

47. Ibid., iv. Simms writes, "When Mr. Reagan ran for the presidency in 1980, he asked, 'Are you better off today than you were four years ago?' As others have noted, that question might appropriately be asked again—at the end of President Reagan's first term in office. This question is particularly appropriate for minority groups because they have been more reliant on government assistance and protection than have nonminorities. If the question is phrased—'Is the average minority family economically better off today than it was four years ago?'—the answer must be 'No.' While white families gained 4.1 percent in disposable income (income from all sources net taxes) after adjusting for inflation, black families had a decline in real disposable income of 2.1 percent and Hispanic families had an increase of only 1 percent."

48. Manning Marable, "The Plight of the Single Black Mother," *Afro-American*, Mar. 1, 1986. Along with Marable's insightful review of the television program, this issue also printed a letter from Robert J. Smith, MD, of Murfreesboro, Tennessee who was similarly outraged by "The Vanishing Family—Crisis in Black America" and its failure to address the channels of repression that have led to the precarious position of black males in relation to dominant culture. Smith suggests that black male students are discouraged at an early age, jobs are systematically withheld from African American men, and that the mainstream media contributes to a narrow and damaging view of black masculinity. Interestingly, Smith begins his critique with representational spaces rather than lived experience. He writes that "it begins with CBS and its counterparts, who rarely ever show the black male in a positive role. He is usually depicted as a comedian or buffoon designed to tickle the funny bone of White America. He is also depicted as hoodlum characters such as those in 'Miami Vice' and other programs of that nature."

49. Altman, 278–81.

50. Knight, 124–25. The author remarks that threatening forces in white-cast folk musicals tend to come from outside of the community so that such negative influences

can be clearly expelled and separated from the folk collective at the end of the film. Black-cast folk musicals, by contrast, tend to absorb violence and dissonance within the black folk community. "Such violence" in these films, writes Knight, is "always a part of the constitution of both the black individual and group."

51. Ellin Stein, "Wild Style," *American Film* 9, no. 2 (Nov. 1983): 50. Although Ahearn somewhat dismisses the relationship between *Wild Style* and *West Side Story*, many thematic and stylistic connections are very apparent, particularly in this musical number. In this article, Ahearn remarks, "I didn't want to make *West Side Story*, although I love that movie. This is more like *On the Town*, a populist musical."

52. Craig Castleman, *Getting Up: Subway Graffiti in New York* (Cambridge, Mass.: MIT Press, 1982): 90–95.

53. Ibid., 95–100. There were graffiti gangs prior to the Ex-Vandals but these organizations, such as the Vanguards and the Last Survivors, restricted membership to their home territory and often deliberately engaged in violent brawls with other gangs. The first writing-only gang, the Ex-Vandals, were a highly organized group who wore colors and sent out teams of writers to secure their safety in gang-controlled neighborhoods.

54. Toop, 57.

55. Ibid., 14–15. Toop also writes that "competition was at the heart of hip hop. Not only did it help displace violence and the refuge of destructive drugs like heroin, but it also fostered an attitude of creating from limited materials. Sneakers became high fashion; original music was created from turntables, a mixer and obscure (highly secret) records; entertainment was provided with the kind of showoff street rap that almost any kid was capable of turning on a rival." See also Catherine Foster, "New Dance Craze Blends Acrobatics, Mime, and Inventiveness," *Christian Science Monitor*, Oct. 14, 1983. The author writes that "break dancing may also be helping to stem gang violence. Last year, the leaders of the 4,000-member Zulu gang and of a 500-member rival gang made a peace treaty, vowing to 'dance it out, rather than fight it out,' Gypsy Lee says." Gypsy Lee was the manager of some of the breakdancing talent in New York City in the early 1980s.

56. Sally Banes, "Breaking Changing," *Village Voice*, Jun. 12, 1984, 82.

57. Cathleen McGuigan, Mark D. Uehling, Jennifer Smith, Sherry Keene-Osborn, Barbara Burgower, and Nadine Joseph, "'Breaking Out,' America Goes Dancing," *Newsweek*, Jul. 2, 1984, 48. The article also states that "in San Francisco, 16-year-old Jarvis La Casse, whose street name or 'tag' is 'Jay Rock,' says, 'If you told me a few years ago that I'd be dancing, I'd laugh. It's like a thing: gangs getting ready to fight, but instead we dance.'"

58. Ethan Bronner, "The Power of Rap," *Boston Globe*, Mar. 4, 1986.

59. Mandalit del Barco, "Hip Hop Hooray: Breaking into the Big Time," *¡Mira! Magazine of the South Bronx Columbia School of Journalism* (Spring 1984), http://www.npr.org/programs/morning/features/patc/breakdancing/article.html.

60. Ibid.

234   Notes

61. Early hip hop culture had a great deal invested in the promise that music and dance performance could diffuse violence. While this utopian premise was explored in the hip hop musical of the 1980s, "New Black Realism" later put rap music and violence together on screen. The utopian thrust of early hip hop culture was transformed into a much darker and more pessimistic formulation with the birth of "New Black Realism" and "gangsta rap." Where music and dance had once offered hope and prosperity to poor urban youth, the soundtrack to this new cinema overwhelmingly reinforced the negative and violent aspects of inner city life. Exemplary of this shift are the lyrics from *Menace II Society*'s "Niggaz Got No Heart" by Spice-1 and Ice Cube's "How To Survive In South Central," which is featured in *Boyz in the Hood*.

62. Timothy Shary, *Generation Multiplex: The Image of Youth in American Cinema, 1981–1996*, Ph.D. diss., University of Massachusetts, 1998, 199–208. In his comparison of dance-oriented films of the 1980s and 1990s, Shary notes that whereas white characters use dance as a form of contained rebellion against parents and other authority figures, young people of color are often connected to dance rituals as a means of survival and as a way to protect the welfare of the community.

63. The realistic spatial confines of the proscenium have been challenged in some musical films. For instance, Busby Berkeley extravaganzas from the 1930s, such as *Gold Diggers of 1933* and *Gold Diggers of 1935* (1935), defied the spatial boundaries of their ostensible venues. These numbers, which clearly begin in a confined theatrical setting, often extend outward into space to include apparently endless expanses of realistic urban topography, rapidly transforming fantasy settings, and an infinite multiplication of dancing girls whose proliferation eventually blatantly disregards the spatial limitations of the venue.

64. Don Rhodes and John Parris Springer, eds., *Docufictions: Essays on the Intersection of Documentary and Fictional Filmmaking* (Jefferson, NC: McFarland & Co., 2006), 14–17. The editors note that there is a long history of convergence between fictional and documentary forms, which has intensified in recent decades. They suggest that the general term "docudrama" be employed for all films that are based on a mingling of the two, and that are about some actual event, group of people, etc., who exist or did exist in the real world.

65. George Stoney, documentary filmmaker, personal communication and lectures, Sept. 2003–May 2004.

66. Stein, 49. The author notes that "Quinones plays Zoro, a shy and retiring graffiti artist: Sandra 'Pink' Fabara plays 'Lady Bug,' his leading lady. . . . Quinones really is a painter, as are Fabara (one of the very few women graffiti artists) and Andrew 'Zephyr' Witten, who plays Zoro's sidekick. Niva Kislac, who portrays a socialite collector of new art (and new artists) really *is* an art patron. Rapper Busy Bee, DJ Grand Master Flash, and the Rock Steady Crew appear as themselves. Fred Brathwaite . . . plays 'Phade,' a charming and articulate promoter who is the bridge between the raw talent of the ghetto and the money of the art establishment. Brathwaite is a graffiti artist whose work has appeared on canvas in European galleries as well as on New York subway cars. . . .

Patti Astor, who plays a ditsy platinum-blonde journalist reporting on the hip hop scene, is in real life a veteran of the New York underground-film scene and a co-owner of Fun Gallery in New York's East Village, where she exhibits the work of, among others, Fred Brathwaite."

67. Dauphin, 203–4. The author writes, "Of the b-boy movies, Stan Lathan's 1984 *Beat Street* is the most memorable. . . . Even though it was fronted by names from the margins of Hollywood like Rae Dawn Chong and Leon Grant, it made excellent use of New York's hip hop talent. Real-life crews like Rock Steady and New York City Breakers populated the frame, luminaries Flip Rock and Prince Ken Swift giving onscreen seminars on their art while Kool Moe Dee and Melle Mel rapped and a then-unknown named Doug E. Fresh made an uncredited cameo."

68. Ida Peters, *Afro-American*, Jun. 16, 1984.

69. Kevin Grubb, "'Hip-Hoppin' in the South Bronx: Lester Wilson's *Beat Street*," *Dance Magazine*, Apr. 1984, 76.

70. Ronald R. Hanna, "*Breakin'* 2 Stars . . . as Lively Off Screen as On," *Baltimore Afro-American*, Dec. 22, 1984.

71. Bill Barol and Jennifer Smith, "A Street Spinner's Big Break," *Newsweek*, Jul. 2, 1984, 50.

72. Robert Stam, *Reflexivity in Film and Literature From Don Quixote to Jean-Luc Godard* (New York: Columbia University Press, 1992), xiii. The author defines reflexivity as "the process by which texts, both literary and filmic, foreground their own production, their authorship, their intertextual influences, their reception, or their enunciation."

73. Jean Luc Godard, the most radical filmmaker associated with so-called French New Wave Cinema, used various strategies of demystification to remind the audience that film is a constructed object. These included interrupting the narrative with animated words (*Weekend*, 1967), audible whispers by the director announcing the fact that the film's main character is played by an actor with a different name (*Two or Three Things I Know About Her*, 1967), and the employment of non-naturalistic acting styles (*Les Carabiniers*, 1963).

74. Stam, 1992, 90.

75. Ibid., 94–95.

76. Mueller, 31–36. Mueller describes the ways in which the dance numbers of Fred Astaire, and partners Ginger Rogers and Cyd Charisse, express the sexual desire and tension that is otherwise left out of or only vaguely hinted at in the rest of the film narrative.

77. Ahearn, 155–56.

78. Ibid., 156.

79. Ibid. Zephyr states that "during that era, every writer worth his salt had a black book under his arm always—except when we'd circulate them amongst ourselves. When you had someone else's book in your possession, you'd try to draw the best piece possible, attempting to 'burn' all the other pieces in the book."

80. Jacobson, 64–66.

81. For a history of conceptual art, see Charles Harrison, *Conceptual Art and Painting: Further Essays on Art and Language* (Cambridge, Mass.: The MIT Press, 2001).

82. Castleman, 61–65.

83. Jacques Derrida, *Of Grammatology* (Baltimore: Johns Hopkins University Press, 1976), 282.

84. Ibid., 285.

85. Julian Stallabrass, *Gargantua: Manufactured Mass Culture* (London: Verso, 1996), 143.

86. Ibid., 144. Stallabrass goes to great lengths to insist upon the erasure of the performative aspect of graffiti as it is read by the public, yet he notes that "artists take considerable personal risks in dedicating their gifts to the public. Subway writers in New York and elsewhere risk not only electrocution and being hit by trains but also the violence of the police."

87. Ibid., 139.

88. Ibid., 147.

89. Karen Jaehne, "Charles Ahearn: *Wild Style*," *Film Quarterly* 37, no. 4 (Summer 1984): 4.

90. Jacobson, 66. Of the similarities between the visual style of *Wild Style* and the aesthetic strategies of hip hop, Ahearn remarks, "I think it's a kind of kinetic cubism; it relates to a certain kind of style of cubism—cutting up and rearranging—like the way the records are heard in the background. Often you hear the same fifteen seconds—sometimes even five seconds—sometimes even *two* seconds of record being repeated and remanipulated. Sometimes the needle would only go that far on the record for the entire night. 'Wild Style' refers to pieces that are disjointed and then re-put together and added with a great deal of style. When the breakdancer comes off a dance he ends up like this, like that. If you look at the (graffiti) letters, they're doing the exact same thing—it's like a pose—I always hear graffiti artists going, 'He makes those letters *dance*.' That's what it's like—he gives them animation, life. The letters have a kind of like life. Graffiti puts kind of a muscular, aerobic power into the style of the letters, and I think that's a big part of it." Clearly, Ahearn is linking his practice as a filmmaker with those of the larger hip hop community. This was the only hip hop musical to conceive of the structure of the film in relation to the aesthetic sensibilities of hip hop.

91. Stam, 1992, 90–94.

92. Altman, 16–27. In describing the relationship between the plot and performance numbers in the Hollywood musical in general, Altman argues that "the plot . . . has little importance to begin with; the oppositions developed in the seemingly gratuitous song-and-dance number, however, are instrumental in establishing the structure and meaning of the film." (27) Altman poses this argument predominantly in terms of problematic gender roles and identities. He suggests that the structure of the musical reconciles two mutually exclusive terms creating a "concordance of opposites" that revolves around the romantic partnering of the two leads. Thus, the major thematic

aims of the film are expressed in the musical numbers rather than in the chronological progression of narrative events.

93. Jaehne, 3. Ahearn states, "I neither glorified nor dramatized these people. I tried just to create a situation where they could perform."

94. Fisher, 85.

95. Quoted in Castleman, 12.

96. Some limited examples of the Hollywood musical do acknowledge social problems in their narrative while also transcending these social constraints through song and dance. This is particularly evident in a selection of film musicals from the 1930s, such as *Gold Diggers of 1933*, where we observe the poverty of Depression-era New York as well as the fantastic spectacle of song and dance in a series of Busby Berkeley production numbers. The Deanna Durbin film *100 Men and a Girl* (1937) also explicitly forms its narrative trajectory around the effects of the Depression on trained orchestral musicians. It emphasizes the disparity between a group of indigent boarding house musicians and the opulent world of the orchestra's wealthy sponsor. The predominant form of the classical Hollywood musical, however, usually veers as far as possible away from any kind of exposition on contemporary social ills.

97. Stein, 49–50. The author writes that "Ahearn readily admits . . . he soft-pedaled some negative aspects of life in the South Bronx. 'I veered away from the violence,' he says. Another all-pervasive feature of ghetto life missing from the movie is heroin, the neighborhood's most self-prescribed form of escape." See also Alfred W. McCoy, *The Politics of Heroin: CIA Complicity in the Global Drug Trade* (New York: Lawrence Hill Books, 1991), 436–92. Heroin and crack cocaine import into the U.S. increased dramatically during the 1980s, and the wide availability of these drugs wreaked the most havoc on poorer inner-city neighborhoods such as the South Bronx and South Central Los Angeles. The infamous covert CIA actions that allowed the production of opium sources for the manufacture of heroin in Pakistan are widely documented, as is the U.S. government's role in allowing the Nicaraguan Contras to smuggle cocaine into America in order to support them in their fight against the leftist Sandinista government. Although it is uncertain whether the CIA willingly targeted black and Latino communities for drug distribution, it is incontrovertible that the CIA was well aware that their actions abroad facilitated the production and distribution of illegal drugs that would undoubtedly devastate the poorer neighborhoods of the United States.

98. Ibid., 50.

CHAPTER 3

1. Timothy Shary, *Teen Movies: American Youth Onscreen* (London: Wallflower, 2005), 5–6.

2. Steve Neale, *Genre and Hollywood* (London: Routledge, 2000), 120.

3. Georganne Scheiner, *Signifying Female Adolescence: Film Representations and Fans, 1920–1950* (Westport, Conn: Praeger, 2000), 6–12. Scheiner refreshingly looks closely at the impact of gender on public perceptions of teenage delinquency in the first half of the twentieth century. She notes that concerns about promiscuity and other forms of "sexual delinquency" in young girls were focused on working-class and immigrant populations. Her thoughtful introductory chapter provides significant evidence that large-scale changes such as urbanization and shifting patterns of immigration informed early medical and sociological perceptions of the American adolescent.

4. G. Stanley Hall, *Adolescence: Its Psychology and its Relations to Physiology, Anthropology, Sociology, Sex, Crime, Religion and Education*. 2 vols. (New York: D. Appleton and Company, 1904).

5. Doherty, 1988, 145–86.

6. Ibid., 34–53.

7. Schrum, 30–68. The author notes that appeals to teen girls as fashion consumers appear in high school yearbook pages and clothing catalogues from the 1920s and 1930s. See also Nash 174. Nash cites the efforts of market researcher Eugene Gilbert, who conducted polls to monitor and report the changing likes, dislikes, desires, and opinions of teenage consumers. See also Eugene Gilbert, *Advertising and Marketing to Young People* (Pleasantville, NY: Printers' Ink Books, 1957).

8. Shary, 2005, 37–43. See also Nash 178. This trend towards more realistic and sober depictions of youth issues and sexuality, which emerged in the late 1950s with *Peyton Place* (1957), was significant, Ilana Nash argues, because it was the first time that such complicated and disturbing portrayals of teen life were given serious dramatic treatment in mainstream film culture.

9. Shary, *Generation Multiplex: The Image of Youth in Contemporary American Cinema* (Austin: University of Texas Press, 2002), 6.

10. Thomas O'Connor, "John Hughes: His Movies Speak to Teen-Agers; Interview," *New York Times*, Mar. 9, 1986. O'Connor writes, "Mr. Hughes, a tall, intense, chain-smoker who favors T-shirts, spattered jeans and hair worn shaggy-long in the back, said that he was 'Mister Serious' during his adolescence in the 1960s in the affluent North Shore suburbs of Chicago, where all his films have been set and where he still maintains a home."

11. Eric Avila, *Popular Culture in the Age of White Flight: Fear and Fantasy in Suburban Los Angeles* (Berkeley: University of California Press, 2004), 4–5.

12. Ibid., 4. In his introduction, "Chocolate Cities and Vanilla Suburbs: Race, Space, and the New "New Mass Culture," Avila notes of postwar America that "suburbanization, a mode of urbanization in which cities extend outward rather than upward to accommodate the spatial appetites of homeowners, retailers, and industrialists, reached a pinnacle in the years between 1945 and 1970." He goes on to write that "during the 1950s, for example, suburbs grew at a rate ten times faster than

that of central cities, while the nation's suburban population jumped from 35.1 to 75.6 million between 1950 and 1970."

13. John R. Logan and Mark Schneider, "Racial Segregation and Racial Change in American Suburbs, 1970–1980," *American Journal of Sociology* 89, no. 4 (Jan. 1984): 876.

14. Vernon Jordan, "Suburban Housing Discrimination Blues," *Afro-American*, Oct. 31, 1981.

15. Ibid. See also Robert W. Lake, *The New Suburbanites: Race and Housing in the Suburbs* (Rutgers: Center for Urban Policy Research, Rutgers University), 1981.

16. Logan and Schneider, 887.

17. Shary, 2002, 6.

18. Elayne Rapping, "Hollywood's Youth Cult Films," *Cineaste* 16, no. 2 (1987/88): 14. Rapping refers to "Ryan-built havens" in her article. Although she does not explain this term, it is most likely a reference to the large American corporation, Ryan Companies, which has been building malls throughout the United States for several decades. See also John Lewis, *The Road to Romance and Ruin: Teen Films and Youth Culture* (New York: Routledge, 1992). Lewis makes the case that consumption and commodification have always been the subject of youth films. He is rather negative in his appraisal of all youth films and teen culture, both mainstream and independent.

19. The corpus of films from the 1980s discussed in Rapping's article include *Porky's* (1981), *Fast Times at Ridgemont High* (1982), *Valley Girl* (1983), *Risky Business* (1983), *The Breakfast Club* (1985), *Ferris Bueller's Day Off* (1986), *River's Edge* (1986), *At Close Range* (1986), and *Some Kind of Wonderful* (1987).

20. Shary, 2002, 6–7.

21. Ibid., 11.

22. Some suburban teen films use the locale of the mall in a somewhat parodic way that may be understood as a critical comment on capitalist culture. This is especially apposite in relation to the phenomenon of the teen mall horror flick inaugurated by *Dawn of the Dead* (1978). These films, including *Chopping Mall* (1986) and a recent remake of *Dawn of the Dead* (2004), which feature flesh eating zombies and murdering robot-like security guards in mall settings, have been read as a critique of the values of standardization wrought by consumer capitalism.

23. David Riesman, *The Lonely Crowd: A Study of the Changing American Character* (New Haven: Yale University Press, 1971), 20. Sociologists, economists, anthropologists, and historians have suggested that significant shifts in American postwar social life and economic structures produced a new class of citizens, frequently referred to as a new or emerging middle class. Riesman writes that "many of the economic factors associated with the recent growth of the 'new' middle class are well known. . . . There is a decline in the numbers and in the proportion of the working population engaged in production and extraction—agriculture, heavy industry, heavy transport—and an increase in the numbers and the proportion engaged in white-collar work and the service trades."

24. Jerry Jacobs, *The Mall: An Attempted Escape From Everyday Life* (Prospect Heights, Illinois: Waveland Press, 1984), 2. The author writes that "the post–World War II boom period produced an abundance of automobiles, cheap gas, and a population of employed workers able and anxious to purchase them. This in conjunction with the expansion of suburban bedroom communities and an eager buying public, produced the beginnings of the 'flight to suburbia' by automobile. Following this mass exodus of people from the central city on their trek to suburbia went the reluctant merchants and department store owners formerly situated in the downtown areas. These located themselves along arterial roads forming the development of many a 'Miracle Mall' or 'Strip.'"

25. Jacobs, 1. This information originally printed in *Wall Street Journal*, Apr. 21, 1982.

26. Riesman, lxiv.

27. Marshall McLuhan, "American Advertising," in *Mass Culture: The Popular Arts in America*, eds. Bernard Rosenberg and David Manning White (New York: The Free Press, 1957), 435.

28. Paul F. Lazarsfeld and Robert K. Merton, "Mass Communication, Popular Taste and Organized Social Action," in Rosenberg and White, 464. The danger of Lazarsfeld and Merton's arguments is that they tend to demonize all mass culture save for certain aspects of "authentic" popular culture that may have originated in local and regional contexts. As such, they deny the complex exchange between the perceived creator of a cultural product and the ways in which a consumer may experience that product, tailoring it for his or her own particular enjoyment.

29. James J. Farrell, *One Nation Under Goods: Malls and the Seductions of American Shopping* (Washington: Smithsonian Books, 2003), 7.

30. Ibid., 19.

31. O'Connor.

32. Vincent Canby, "Film View; Putting Teenagers Under the Lens," *New York Times*, Mar. 16, 1986.

33. Ibid. Canby astutely notes that the cloying ending of *Pretty in Pink* "seems to deny whatever little the film had going on before—that is, its comically grotesque portrayal of wealth's spoiled playthings who treat the economically disadvantaged Andie so badly. Yet Mr. Hughes, I suspect, knows exactly what he's doing. He puts Andie into terrible situations and then denies that they are terrible. Andie lives in a broken home that is happy and sunny. Her father is a shiftless slob and a boozer, but he's always neat as a pin, never appears on screen drunk, has no hangovers and is cheerful in the morning. Blaine McDonough treats Andie badly but is a sweet guy anyway. Andie's loyal suitor, Duckie Dales (who's also economically disadvantaged), loves Andie dearly and deserves her, according to the tenets of such fiction. Yet when he hands her over to the affluent snobs, it's seen as an act of noble renunciation."

34. Laura Mulvey, "Visual Pleasure and Narrative Cinema," in *Film Theory and Criticism: Introductory Readings*, ed. Leo Braudy and Marshall Cohen (New York: Oxford University Press, 1999), 838. Mulvey's influential essay argues that mainstream

Hollywood cinema replicates and enforces the structure of the patriarchal social order through a gendered system of active male "looking" and passive female "specularization." While men are the cinematic characters that enable narrative progression, women on screen, according to the author, arrest narrative movement, in order to allow their bodies and faces to be visually consumed by the male characters in the film, and in the audience. Mulvey writes that "according to the principles of the ruling ideology and the psychical structures that back it up, the male figure cannot bear the burden of sexual objectification. Man is reluctant to gaze at his exhibitionist like. Hence the split between spectacle and narrative support the man's role as the active one of forwarding the story, making things happen."

35. Robin Wood, *Hollywood from Vietnam to Reagan* (New York: Columbia University Press, 1986), 216. Wood writes of '80s teen films generally that both virgin and experienced male characters are given the power and pleasure over female characters through a depiction of scopic mastery. He notes that "with both figures, the innocent and the experienced, the basic pattern is the same: male as hunter, female as hunted, male as looker, female as looked-at."

36. Timothy Shary, 2002, 194. Shary notes that "the protagonists in *Weird Science* do indeed gain self-worth through their crude experimentation, and their image as horny nerds is thereby transformed into that of confident, even arrogant young men—after all that Lisa has done for them, she remains a disposable commodity."

37. Wood, 219. The author writes of this film that "as the women cease to be objects of the male gaze, their autonomous desire is used to express . . . a critique of male presumption."

38. Dawn Michaelle Norfleet, "*Hip-hop Culture" in New York City: The Role of Verbal Music Performance in Defining a Community* (Ph.D. diss., Columbia University, 1997), 84.

39. Francis N. Njubi, "Rap, Race, and Representation," in *Images of Youth: Popular Culture as Educational Ideology*, eds. Michael A. Oliker and Walter P. Krolikowski (New York: Peter Lang, 2001), 167. The author writes that early hip hop music groups "promoted the music by hiring youths to stand on street corners and in parks with a cassette player blaring out the music. For years, the mode of dissemination was the cassette tape and the block parties."

40. W. Fitzhugh Brundage, "Working in the 'Kingdom of Culture': African Americans and American Popular Culture, 1890–1930," in *Beyond Blackface: African Americans and the Creation of American Popular Culture, 1890–1930*, ed. Brundage (Chapel Hill: University of North Carolina Press, 2011), 25.

41. Jean Baudrillard, *The System of Objects* (London: Verso, 1996), 194–95.

42. Ibid.

43. Anne Friedberg, *Window Shopping: Cinema and the Postmodern* (Berkeley: University of California Press, 1993), 113.

44. "Moribund Mall Makeover: Sherman Oaks Galleria by Gensler," *ArchNewsNow*, Oct. 9, 2002, www.archnewsnow.com.

45. Avila, 10. The author notes that "shopping malls, like theme parks, offered a more particularized notion of community that appealed to white suburban consumers." Avila goes on to quote Lizabeth Cohen who suggests that the shopping center "sought perhaps to contradictorily legitimize itself as a true community center and to define that community in exclusionary socioeconomic and racial terms."

46. Friedberg, 113.

47. Karl Marx, *Capital: A Critique of Political Economy* (New York: The Modern Library, 1906), 84–87. Marx writes that "the equalization of the most different kinds of labour [sic] can be the result only of an abstraction from their inequalities, or of reducing them to their common denominator, viz., expenditure of human labour power or human labour in the abstract.... The determination of the magnitude of value by labour-time is therefore a secret, hidden under the apparent fluctuations in the relative value of commodities."

48. Randall Robinson, *The Debt: What America Owes to Blacks* (New York: Dutton, 2000). Robinson explores and justifies current demands by African Americans for decades of unpaid labor enforced through slavery. For a comprehensive analysis of race based wage discrimination in the steel industry, see John Hinshaw, *Steel and Steelworkers: Race and Class Struggle in Twentieth-Century Pittsburgh* (Albany: State University of New York Press, 2002).

49. Rita Kempley, "'Wild Style': Populist Art," *Washington Post*, Jan. 27, 1984.

50. Richard Harrington, "The *Wild Style* Breaks into Town; Spins and Splits at the Big Throwdown," *Washington Post*, Jan. 27, 1984.

51. Stein, 50. "I want the film to involve the audience in a participatory way, like *The Rock Horror Picture Show* does.... My goal was to make a film that the community it documents would want to see."

52. Clifford May, "On L.I Fights Follow a Film on Rap Music," *New York Times*, Nov. 6, 1985.

53. Ibid.

54. Ibid.

55. Ibid.

56. Ibid.

57. Ibid. "Scott Lund, the teen-ager injured last weekend, said he thought 'it was clear-cut that it was a racial thing.' He said the movie-goers who attacked him and his girlfriend as they were entering the theatre to see *Nightmare on Elm Street* 'seemed defensive and challenging, like they were I think,' he said, 'they were trying to live out the fantasy way of life they saw in the film.'" In an unbelievably regressive turn, the article also turns to supposed "experts" to assess the psychological impact of rap music: "The words of rap tend to be boastful, though not particularly suggestive of either sex or violence. But listening to and identifying with such music, according to Thomas Pettigrew, a social psychologist at the University of California at Santa Cruz, can inspire 'a state of generalized arousal. It can whip people up.'"

58. "Sunrise Multiplex," *Cinema Treasures*, http://cinematreasures.org/theater/9227/.

59. Ibid. The thread indicates more than one reference to arcade games situated in the lobby of the theater.

60. Ibid.

61. Ethan Bronner, "'Rap' Movie Patrons Blamed for Hub Damage," *Boston Globe*, Nov. 10, 1985.

62. "Youth Gang Incidents Erupt in California and Nevada," *Christian Science Monitor*, Jan. 14, 1986.

63. Ibid.

64. Bill Brownstein, "Theatre Posts Guard for Opening of Krush Groove," *Montreal Gazette*, Jan. 10, 1986.

65. David J. Fox, "Not All *Godfather III* Violence is on the Screen: Movies: A Theater Patron is Killed as Gang Warfare Erupts in a Long Island Multiplex," *Los Angeles Times*, Dec. 27, 1990.

66. Ibid.

67. Sarah Lyall, "Cinema is Battleground of Geography and Psychology," *New York Times*, Mar. 29, 1991.

68. Ibid.

69. Ibid.

70. Ibid.

71. Ibid.

72. Ibid.

73. Ibid.

74. Ibid.

75. 1988 City Files, County and City Data Books, University of Virginia Library, www2.lib.virginia.edu/ccdb.

76. Larry Rother, "Restoring Hispanic Theater in Bronx," *New York Times*, Jan. 12, 1986.

77. Ibid.

78. Ibid.

79. Ibid.

80. Sam Howe Verhovek, "Salsa and Heartthrobs: A Palace of Hispanic Life Returns," *New York Times*, Sept. 28, 1987. Historically, the Teatro Puerto Rico was one of the only places where Spanish-speaking families from all boroughs of New York could come together to experience their culture before the theater's decline in the 1970s.

81. Rother.

82. Greg Wilson, "Espada Guilty in Grant Row," *New York Daily News*, Jul. 6, 2001. In 1995 Sandra Love, who helmed the non-profit organization Information Networking and Community Assistance, secured a grant for the theater to defray operating costs. Instead, she allegedly funneled the majority of funds to the Soundview Health Center and a large part of the remainder to Bronx senator Pedro Espada's political campaign.

83. Rapping, 16.

84. Sally C. Clarke, "Advance Report of Final Divorce Statistics, 1989 and 1990," *Monthly Vital Statistics Report* 43, no. 9 (Mar. 22, 1995). Supplement, Centers for Disease Control and Prevention/National Health Statistics. See table 1. http://www.cdc.gov/nchs/data/mvsr/supp/mv43_09s.pdf. Between 1950 and 1976, the divorce rate in the United States had doubled.

85. "Breaking . . . Fresh and Exciting!" *Baltimore/Washington Afro-American*, May 4, 1984.

86. Ibid.

87. Doherty, 1988, 63. See also R. Serge Denisoff, *Tarnished Gold: The Record Industry Revisited* (New Brunswick, NJ: Transaction Books, 1986), 14. In *Blackboard Jungle*, a group of teenage students demolish a high school teacher's jazz record collection while the film's title track plays over the images of delinquent destruction.

88. Peter Keer, "7 Youths Injured in Concert Fights," *New York Times*, Dec. 28, 1985. Screenings of the film have not only been linked with violence but an associated music concert entitled The Krush Groove Christmas Party, in New York City, which featured performers from the film, was also followed with numerous violent incidents, including a shooting.

89. Kimmich, 9.

90. Pat Gill, "The Monstrous Years: Teens, Slasher Films, and the Family," *Journal of Film and Video* 54, no. 4 (Winter 2002): 29. Of the slasher, Gill writes that "these films offer a sustained conservative critique of family life, mourning the middle class dream while mocking it. Parents refuse to commit to their children: their disinclination, work, pleasures, or addictions prevent them from taking their parental responsibilities seriously. None of the parents, even the most well-meaning and kind, ever succeeds in making the connections necessary to create a functioning family."

91. Bronner, Nov. 10, 1985. The author writes of a *Krush Groove* screening in Boston that "more than 1,000 youths left the Sack Pi Alley Cinema on Washington Street at about 10 p.m." He goes on to note that "half had seen the earlier show of the feature film and half had been turned away from the later screening after their efforts to get in resulted in damage to the theatre and cancellation." See also "200 Teen-agers Fight Outside Theatre on L.I." The article reports that "last weekend, two people were hurt in nearby Valley Stream when about 1,000 customers waiting to see *Krush Groove* stormed the Sunrise Multiplex Cinemas after they were told the theatre was overbooked."

92. Stephen Holden, "A Young Company Guides Rap Music into the Mainstream," *New York Times*, Aug. 11, 1987. *Krush Groove* reportedly cost $3 million to produce and returned an impressive $15 million at the box office.

93. Paul Attanasio, "Crude *Krush Groove*," *Washington Post*, Nov. 1, 1985.

94. Michael Blowen, "*Krush Groove* More Like Krashing Bore," *Boston Globe*, Nov. 9, 1985.

95. Lynn Van Matre, "Good Rap, Bad Rap: Music Tops Plot in *Krush Groove*," *Chicago Tribune*, Oct. 25, 1985.

96. Charles Rogers, "Hip Hop Flick *Krush Groove* Doesn't Have the Juice," *New York Amsterdam News*, Nov. 16, 1985. See also Charles Rogers, "UTFO: From "Roxanne" to Riches?," *New York Amsterdam News*, Jul. 20, 1985. Charles Rogers's writings for the *Amersterdam News* display a paternalistic, if not hostile, attitude towards hip hop culture in general. He writes of the rap group UTFO that "interviewing UTFO, the Brooklyn based rappers of Roxanne, Roxanne" fame, it's difficult to get a word in edgewise much less a question." He goes on to state that "they're too busy slapping each other high-fives, trading inside jokes, and clowning around among themselves to simply answer questions from me." This authoritarian attitude sometimes found its way into publications that were generally sympathetic and supportive of hip hop culture. For instance, see Racine S. Winborne, "Teen Trend for the Eighties is 'Rap' and Scratch Music," *Baltimore Afro-American*, Dec. 6. 1983. The article infers that established jazz vocalist Jean Carne finds rapping to be a simplistic and juvenile musical form: "She equates rapping with artist [sic] who simply don't know how to sing." Some positive descriptions of the music are given by DJs, but overall the tone of the article is somewhat disapproving and the author describes current rap as "madcapped" and "repetitive."

97. Ronald Hanna, "Blair Underwood," *Baltimore Afro-American*, Nov. 9, 1985.

98. Guerrero, 113–14. The author writes that "in the beginning of the 1980s and under the political impulse of Reaganism, blacks on screen, in front of and behind the camera, found themselves confronted with the 'recuperation' of many of the subordinations and inequalities they had struggled so hard to eradicate during the years of the civil rights movement and the emergence of Black Power consciousness that followed it . . . Concurrently, the 1980s saw a steady reduction of films with black narratives and leading roles as black actors found themselves increasingly pushed into the margins or background of the cinematic frame."

99. Frederick I. Douglass, "*Missing in Action* is Missing in Acting," *Baltimore/Washington Afro-American*, Nov. 23, 1984.

100. Ibid.

101. Ibid.

102. "'Breaking' . . . Fresh and Exciting."

103. Ida Peters, "Shrimp Taught Me to Backslide," *Afro-American*, May 12, 1984.

104. Valerie Smith-Madden, "Blair Underwood . . . New Star on the Horizon," *Afro-American*, Jun. 29, 1985.

105. Ibid.

CHAPTER 4

1. AKC Leung, "Hazards of Break Dancing," *New York State Journal of Medicine* 84, no. 12 (Dec. 1984): 592. See also G. R. Hansen, "Breaks and Other Bad News For Breakers," *Journal of American Medical Association* 252, no. 14 (1985): 2047.

2. For instance, see S. L. McNeil and others, "Multiple Subdural Hematomas Associated with Breakdancing," *Annals of Emergency Medicine* 16, no. 1 (Jan. 1987): 114–16, D. Q. McBride, L. P. Lehman, and J. R. Mangiardi, "Break-Dancing Neck," *New England Journal of Medicine* 312, no. 3 (1985): 186, R. A. Norman and M. A. Grodin, "Injuries from Break Dancing," *American Family Physician* 30, no. 2 (1984): 109–12, and P. J. Goscienski and L. Luevanos, "Injury Caused by Break Dancing," *Journal of the American Medical Association* 252, vol. 24 (1984): 3367.

3. B. C. Joondeph, A. V. Spigelman, and J. S. Pulido, "Ocular Trauma From Break Dancing," *Archives of Ophthalmology* 104, no. 2 (Feb. 1986): 176–77.

4. Lloyd Shearer, "Break-Dancing," *Parade Magazine*, Mar. 13, 1985, 20.

5. Belinda Fu, "Injuries of Breakdancing," *Radiology* 140, no. 3 (Dec. 2000), www.radiology.ucsf.edu/learning_ctr/breakdance.shtml.

6. M. R. Kassiver and N. Manon, "Head Bangers Whiplash," *Clinical Journal of Pain* 9, no. 2, (Jun. 1993): 138.

7. Ibid., 139.

8. Barbara Browning, *Infectious Rhythm: Metaphors of Contagion and the Spread of African Culture* (New York: Routledge, 1998), 5–6. Browning notes that beginning with the European colonial period, Western culture has often associated African derived forms of music and dance with metaphors of infection and contagion. Black music and dance, she argues, have been cloaked in a pseudo-medical discourse in which this cultural "Other" threatens to literally invade corporeal boundaries and infect whites with simultaneously exhilarating and dangerous rhythms. In reference to African culture, Browning writes that "the metaphor of contagion, even when invoked by Europeans, often takes seemingly benign forms ('infectious rhythm' as a dispersal of joy), but it can also often lead to hostile, even violent, reactions to cultural expressions." The concept of the African beat as contagious and infectious, has, at particular historical moments, also been used to evoke metaphors of political contagion and "inflammation" as well. See "News Sent by Drums Keeps Africa Astir," *Baltimore Afro-American*, Apr. 13, 1923. (originally from the *Associated Press*): "Agitation in a form resembling bolshevism has appeared in East Africa and sentiment favorable to the nationalist movement started by Marcus Garvey is rampant in Liberia, while the troubles in West Africa recently required military suppression. . . . Much of this agitation is said to be due to inflammatory reports spread among the tribes by drum talk."

9. Hank Gallo, "Big Bucks Beckon the Best Breakdancer," *New York Daily News*, Aug. 23, 1984. See also Stephen Koepp, "Breaking Through to Big Profits," *Time*, Oct. 1, 1984, http://time.com/magazine/article/0,9171,954411,00.html.

10. Koepp.

11. Foster, 23–24.

12. del Barco. The author notes that "Crazy Legs, the 18-year-old president of Rock Steady, with six other members of the crew, have made four world tours so far, and are planning a fifth. . . . They're a sensation in France, Italy, Japan and England. . . . The

crew has also toured around the United States, breaking in the Jerry Lewis Muscular Dystrophy Telethon, and at the Kennedy Telethon last December in Brooklyn."

13. Joan Scott, *Gender and the Politics of History* (New York: Columbia University Press, 1988), 15–50. My approach is partly informed by the work of Scott. Rather than simply compiling a history of women in breakdance, I have attempted to analyze how gender is mobilized as "a primary way of signifying relationships of power" within the representation of breakdance culture (42). Although this chapter begins with an "unearthing" of women in the archival record (an important first step in producing a feminist history), it works toward highlighting the ways that gender informed mainstream representations of cultural and racial crossings within both cinema and print.

14. J. Sullivan and L. Calicott, *Break Dancing: Step-By-Step Instructions* (New York: Beekman House, 1984).

15. Bonnie Nadell and John Small, *Break Dance: Electric Boogie, Egyptian, Moonwalk . . . Do it* (Philadelphia: Running Press, 1985).

16. Michael Holman, "Locking and Poping (Electric Boogie)," http://www.hiphopnetwork.com/articles/bboyarticles/popinelectricboogie2.asp.

This article reprinted from Michael Holman, *Breaking and the New York City Breakers* (New York: Freundlich Books, 1984).

17. Ibid.

18. Mr. Fresh and the Supreme Rockers, *Breakdancing: Mr. Fresh and the Supreme Rockers Show You How to Do It!* (New York: Avon Books, 1984), 44.

19. Ibid., 43.

20. Ibid., 21–26.

21. Holman.

22. Richard Majors and Janet Mancini Billson, *Cool Pose: The Dilemmas of Black Manhood in America* (New York: Lexington Books, 1992), 4.

23. Ibid., xii.

24. Ibid., 4–5.

25. Ibid., 2.

26. Gwendolyn D. Pough, *Check it While I Wreck it: Black Womanhood, Hip-Hop Culture, and the Public Sphere* (Boston: Northwestern University Press, 2004), 128. Pough, in describing female characters in ghetto-centric narratives of the 1990s, writes that "the ghetto girl is denied a fullness of womanhood, and societal influences, such as systemic and intersecting oppressions and the implications of these for her life, are not taken into consideration. Therefore, representations of the money-hungry and sexually promiscuous black woman living in a poor urban area are given as unproblematized truths or humorous stereotyped caricatures."

27. Sinclair.

28. Katrina Hazzard-Donald, "Dance in Hop Hop Culture," in *Droppin' Science: Critical Essays on Rap Music and Hip Hop Culture*, ed. William Eric Perkins (Philadelphia: Temple University Press, 1996), 225.

29. Ibid.

30. "Dancers 'Break' from Tradition," *The News Tribune, Woodbridge (N.J.)*, Feb. 24, 1984.

31. Ibid.

32. Shirley L. Larsen, "When my Daughter Moonwalks," *Christian Science Monitor*, Sept. 11, 1984.

33. Sally Banes, "Unruly Dolls and Ritz Rockers," *Village Voice*, Oct. 18, 1983, 118. Banes writes that "the Dynamic Rockers won the top prize with choreography that also moved the spins and other floorwork of breaking into the air, as they worked in pairs, one dancer acting as support while a second spun on his head or shoulders. They teamed up in formations to step in perfect synchrony, red costumes glittering, or formed a pyramid for more dancers to vault in flying leaps, looking somehow like a combination of astronauts and circus acrobats. Two young women in the crew took their turns as well. The crowd went wild."

34. Clarissa Lopez, "Breakdancing with the Lady Rockers," *New York Daily News*, Sept. 23, 1984.

35. Majors and Billson, 41–45.

36. Ibid., 44.

37. Ibid., 44. The only acknowledgment of critical appropriations of "cool pose" by black women occurs in one vague sentence in which the authors assert that "black women use cool behaviors to help counter the effects of racism and social oppression too."

38. Peter Rosenwald, "Breaking Away 80's Style," *Dance Magazine*, Apr. 1984, 70-75.

39. Dan Cox, "Brooklyn's Furious Rockers: Break Dance Roots in a Breakneck Neighborhood," *Dance Magazine*, Apr. 1984, 79.

40. Michael Norman, "Frosty Freeze and Kid Smooth Break for Fame at Roxy Disco," *New York Times*, Oct. 18, 1983.

41. Joyce Mollov, "Getting the Breaks," *Ballet News* 6, no. 2 (Aug. 1984): 16.

42. Ibid., 19.

43. Mr. Fresh and the Supreme Rockers, 13. See also Nadell and Small, 62.

44. Holman.

45. Sherman, 287–88. The author cites a number of breakdance manuals, which indicate early breakdancing influences. James Brown's accompanying dance to "Get On the Good Foot" and Michael Jackson's Robot dance routine, developed in the mid-1970s when he was with the Jackson 5, are both mentioned in the article. See also Mollov, 18. Mollov notes that William Craft, the manager of Breakers Exchange International, also describes Brown as an early influence on breakdance. Basil only appeared in a few early performances, most notably on a segment of *Saturday Night Live* in 1975, but continued to influence the group by acting as their promoter and manager.

46. Margaret Pierpont, "Breaking in the Studio," *Dance Magazine*, Apr. 1984, 82. McKeever notes that her clientele includes women as well as men. She states that "it's important to do big movements, movements that follow momentum. We have housewives flinging their arms and saying, "We bad."

47. Cathleen McGuigan and others, 49.

48. Ibid.

49. On February 29, 1984, Manhattan Cable Channel C aired the program *Boogie Before Bedtime*, which featured a bellydance routine, aerobics, and a segment with the Rockwell Break Dancers.

50. Pough, 49.

51. Kimberlé Crenshaw, "Demarginalizing the Intersection of Race and Sex: A Black Feminist Critique of Antidiscrimination Doctrine, Feminist Theory and Antiracist Politics," in *Feminist Legal Theory I: Foundations and Outlooks*, ed. Frances E. Olsen (New York: New York University Press, 1995), 466.

52. Pough, 41–73. See also bell hooks, *Rock My Soul* (New York: Atria Books, 2003), 1–17. In reference to the words of Black Panther Eldridge Cleaver, hooks writes that "labeling black females 'race traitors' should have galvanized masses of black females and males to protest. Instead, there was widespread agreement on the part of black males and females who were socialized to accept patriarchal thinking without question that black male development would be furthered by the subordination of black women" (7). See also Michelle Wallace, *Black Macho and the Myth of the Superwoman* (London: Verso, 1990), 13. Wallace was one of the first African American feminist writers to publish a critique of the Black Power Movement of the 1960s. She writes in her opening chapter that "for perhaps the last fifty years there has been a growing distrust, even hatred, between black men and women. It has been nursed along not only by racism on the part of whites but also by an almost deliberate ignorance on the part of blacks about the sexual politics of their experience in this country. As the Civil Rights Movement progressed, little attention was devoted to an examination of the historical black male/female relationship, except for those aspects of it that reinforced the notion of the black man as the victim of 'matriarchal' tyranny. The result has been calamitous. The black woman has become a social and intellectual suicide; the black man, unintrospective and oppressive."

53. Pough, 8. The author calls attention to the sexism of writers like Nelson George who claims, in his book *Hip Hop America*, that no female artists have been important to the development of rap music. Pough notes that early female rap artists like MC Lyte and Salt-n-Pepa used aggressive lyrics and performance styles to directly challenge the overt masculinity of conventional rap music.

54. Altman, 233.

55. Roger Ebert, "Flashdance," *rogerebert.com*, http://rogerebert.suntimes.com/apps/pbcs.dll/article?AID=/19830419/REVIEWS/304190301/. Among his other criticisms, Ebert finds *Flashdance* to be "so loaded down with artificial screenplay contrivances and flashy production numbers that it's waterlogged."

56. R. Serge Denisoff and George Plasketes, "Synergy in 1980s Film and Music: Formula for Success or Industry Mythology?" *Film History* 4, no. 3 (1990): 258–59. The authors write that "*Flashdance* was not originally designed for video use.... The most telling historical fact is that Michael Sembello's 'Maniac' appeared on the MTV rotation as of 11 May, a month *after* the premiere of *Flashdance*."

57. Vincent Canby, "*Body Rock*, A Loud Splice of Life," *New York Times*, Sept. 28, 1984.

58. Rosenwald, 70. See also Foster, 23.

59. Ken Sandler, "Breakdancing! Spinning into the Big Time: From Street Thrills to Art Form," *Washington Post*, Dec. 30, 1983.

60. George, 81–100.

61. Banes, Jun. 12, 1984, 82. Banes, a writer who has always been critical of the commercialization of hip hop culture, wryly notes that "the front cover of *Vogue* this month sports a beautiful (white) model in a graffiti-decked hat. Perhaps the same inner-city elementary school teacher who four years ago told me breaking and graffiti were equally criminal will be moved to buy just such a hat, or designer Terry McCoy's graffiti shoes or chairs, or Willi Wear graffiti clothes. They must have seen *Flashdance*."

62. Mollov, 15. The author writes that "three styles make up breakdancing. 'Electric boogie,' contributed by black and Spanish-speaking California youths . . . The 'pop' which moves through the body in darting discontinuities that suggest the fleeting blips . . . of a computer monitor . . . The Latin contribution is the third domain of breakdancing, 'webbo,' or 'wavo,' a special footwork that adds another dimension."

63. I don't wish to conflate or reify Puerto Rican and African American urban performance and experience. However, in terms of representation, many early expressions of hip hop, especially within cinema, attempted to evoke an urban performance style that unproblematically envisioned a pan-ethnic and multiracial street culture. This is evident in *Wild Style*, where African Americans, Puerto Ricans, and whites all live in relative racial harmony, and are all participants in hip hop culture. *Beat Street*, *Delivery Boys*, and *Rappin'* also make a point of emphasizing the racial heterogeneity of the communities around which their stories revolve. This tendency is closely related to the utopian thrust of these films which is modeled in part on the structure of the folk musical, a form which privileges communal harmony and unity over discord and difference.

64. John Bodnar, Michael Weber, and Roger Simon, "*Migration*, Kinship, and Urban Adjustment: Blacks and Poles in Pittsburgh, 1900–30," in *The Making of Urban America*, ed. Raymond A. Mohl (Delaware: Scholarly Resources, 1988), 170–86.

65. Ibid., 176.

66. Hinshaw, 92–95. The author remarks that large labor unions in the steel industry habitually failed to favorably resolve grievance issues for black workers. He also produces evidence suggesting that blacks themselves failed to take a sustained interest in union meetings and organizing in general. However, this data must be seen in relation to the notorious racism of the unions, and their lack of efficacy in terms of fighting the unjust treatment of black workers by the companies.

67. Ibid., 42.

68. Hinshaw, 200–29.

69. Roediger, 20–21. Although I emphasize here the specific history of racial conflict that arose with the formation of social networks within Pittsburgh's steel

industry, this particular local account must be seen in relation to the formation of racialized working-class identity in the United States more generally. As Roediger has pointed out, wage labor performed by European immigrants or their decedents in the North was sharply distinguished from slave labor performed in the South, so much so that whiteness became synonymous with "worker" as opposed to both Southern slave labor and racially constructed notions of inherent black laziness. He notes that the terms "white" and "worker" became fused in the nineteenth century and that they "became paired during a time in which the United States, whose citizens were taught by their revolutionary victory and republican ideology to expect both political and economic independence, became a nation in which, by 1860, roughly half the nonslave labor force was dependent on wage labor and subject to new forms of capitalist labor discipline."

70. Ella Shohat and Robert Stam, *Unthinking Eurocentrism: Multiculturalism and the Media* (London: Routledge, 1994), 220–23.

71. Ibid., 23.

72. Clover, 157–59.

73. Ibid., 164.

74. Watkins, 188–95.

75. Elizabeth Traube, *Dreaming Identities: Class, Gender, and Generation in 1980s Hollywood Movies* (Boulder: Westview Press, 1992), 20. The strong feminist sentiment of the 1960s and '70s was increasingly under attack by political and social leaders aligned with New Right dogma during the 1980s. According to Elizabeth Traube, at this moment "Hollywood joined the New Right leaders in directing socially rooted discontents against independent, upwardly mobile women. Movies as well as political discourse attacked uncontrolled, ambitious women as the cause of a moral crisis that, given its definition, called for a strong, authoritarian patriarch."

76. Ibid., 67–96. In her insightful chapter, "Secrets of Success in Postmodern Society," the author notes that a new concern with the individual and with "the cult of personality" became central to the conservative, business-oriented rhetoric of the 1980s. She argues that this tendency can be traced in several films (for instance, *Ferris Bueller's Day Off* [1986] and *Nothing in Common* [1986]) from the middle of the decade.

77. Marshall Stearns and Jean Stearns, 3. The authors write that "Elvis Presley was not exactly doing the Twist, but as did the hula hoop craze, he helped light the fuse . . . his motions were a relatively tame version of the ancient Snake Hips of the Negro folk, popularized in Harlem by dancer Earl Tucker during the early twenties."

78. Charlene Register, "The Construction of an Image and the Deconstruction of a Star—Josephine Baker Racialized, Sexualized, and Politicized in the African-American Press, the Mainstream Press, and the FBI Files," *Popular Music and Society* 24, no. 1 (Spring, 2000): 45.

79. Snead, 1–27. Snead argues that the film used the giant ape monster Kong as a symbol of threatening and terrifying blackness, which brings destruction and chaos into civilization. According to the author, the film legitimated the specious and absurd fears

stirred by *The Birth of a Nation* a generation earlier: that all black men are obsessed with white women and pose a direct threat to them. (In *King Kong* an enormous ape desires a young white woman.) Of course, the flip side of this reading also points to white male fantasies of a powerful black male sexuality that is uncontrollable and voracious—an aggressively virile phallic fantasy to counter fears of white male sexual lack.

80. Stam and Shohat, 1994, 137–40.

81. Krin Gabbard, *Jammin' at the Margins: Jazz and the American Cinema* (Chicago: University of Chicago Press, 1996), 138–59.

82. Ibid., 54. Gabbard also argues that phallic instruments associated with black jazz artists within classical Hollywood film, such as the trumpet and the clarinet, frequently represent the symbolic equivalent of sexual virility necessary for the white hero to succeed with his romantic endeavors.

83. Ibid., 83.

84. Lott, 22–29. Lott notes that minstrelsy and the adoption of a "black mask" by white Americans is related to earlier forms of European street festivals, carnivals, and traditional entertainment figures such as clowns and harlequins. Even before the minstrelsy tradition was established, blackface was a common "mask" worn by American immigrants during public events, riots, and festivals. Therefore, blackface was linked to transgressive social and political action several years prior to the establishment of minstrelsy as a popular form of entertainment.

85. Ibid., 25–26.

86. Leslie Fiedler, *Love and Death in the American Novel* (Cleveland: The World Publishing Company, 1960). Some of the earliest writings on this historical relation in American culture can be found in the work of Leslie Fiedler. He argues that the foundation of American literature, texts such as *Moby-Dick; or, The Whale* (1851) and *The Adventures of Huckleberry Finn* (1884), are, at their core, stories of "innocent" love between men, which continually negotiate white desire for racial "Otherness." According to Fiedler, there is always a longing for "the dark skinned" other, and an obsessive fascination with his ability to abandon or live outside of the "civilized" ways of Western European culture in these works. For such familiar American heroes as Huck Finn, the dark-skinned friend—in this case, Jim—brings him closer to the instinctual, and a life outside of restrained European codes of polite behavior.

87. Gabbard, 54–56.

88. Rogin, 73–120.

89. Bogle, 10–17.

90. Ibid., 13–14. Of this film and the two "black buck" stereotypes found in this epic, Lynch and Gus, Donald Bogle writes that "the pure black bucks were always Griffith's really great archetypal figures. Bucks are always big, baaddddd niggers, oversexed and savage, violent and frenzied as they lust for white flesh . . . Griffith played on the myth of the Negro's high-powered sexuality, then articulated the great white fear that every black man longs for a white woman . . . Consequently, when Lillian Gish, the frailest, purest of all screen heroines, was attacked by the character

Lynch—when he put his big black arms around this pale blonde beauty—audiences literally panicked."

91. Chris Jordan, 121.

92. Kathryn Kalinak, "Flashdance: The Dead End Kid," *Jump Cut* no. 29 (Feb. 1984): 3–5.

93. "Hot Dancing Sensation," *National Fitness Trade Magazine*, Summer 1995, 5–8.

94. Ibid.

95. Ann Butler, "Renewing the Feeling: *Flashdance* Opening Doors for Marine Jahan," *Pittsburgh Post-Gazette*, Apr. 10, 1984. The article notes of Jahan that "for the second straight year she is appearing in department stores across the nation dancing to promote 9 West shoes.... At noon in Kauffmann's junior shoes department, she went on before an audience of several hundred on a small makeshift stage.... She did three brief numbers, featuring three different pairs of shoes—the first, a secretarial mime to Donna Summer's throbbing 'She Works Hard for the Money,' followed by an aerobic workout, and finally in black heels a flashdance to 'What a Feeling'.... The crowd seemed to be mostly women shoppers, although there were some businessmen and youths. Afterwards, several dozen waited in line for autographed photos."

96. Genevieve Buck, "Marine Jahan is the 'Other' Flashdancer," *Toledo Blade*, Jan. 3, 1984.

97. Ebert. Ebert writes of the film that "Jennifer Beals plays Alex, an 18-year-old who is a welder by day, and a go-go dancer by night, and dreams of being a ballet star, and falls in love with the Porsche-driving boss of the construction company. These are a lot of 'character details' even if she didn't also have a saintly old woman as a mentor, a big slobbering dog as a friend, a bicycle she rides all over Pittsburgh, a loft the size of a sweatshop, a sister who ice skates, a grumpy old pop, and the ability to take off her bra without removing her sweatshirt."

98. Dyer, 2000, 25. Dyer writes that "except in the few all-black musicals, black performers in MGM-style musicals nearly always play characters who are nothing but entertainers. They may be, and often are, slaves, servants, waiters, or prostitutes, but all they ever *do* in those roles is entertain."

99. Bruce Tyler, "Zoot-Suit Culture and the Black Press," *Journal of American and Comparative Cultures* 17, no. 2 (Jun. 1994): 21–33. The author notes that the zoot suit became a symbol of black youth power during the 1940s, signaling resistance to both racist white culture and oppressive black middle-class mores. This style of dress was also closely associated with Latino youth cultures of the same era. During these early wartime years, racial tensions on the West Coast led to the infamous "zoot suit riots" in which hundreds of Latino youth were harassed, beaten, and arrested by American servicemen (from both the army and navy) and the local police force.

100. Kalinak. The author suggests that the most disturbing aspect of *Flashdance* is its presentation of women performing exhilarating and physically liberating dance sequences, while nevertheless embedding these moments of emancipation within a limited and "disappointing fantasy framework."

101. Rosenwald, 74.

102. "The Tap Dance Kid Alfonso Ribeiro Boogies in the Footsteps of Idol Michael Jackson," *People*, Jul. 16, 1984, http://www.people.com/people/archive/article/0,,20197121,00.html.

103. Ibid.

104. McGuigan and others, 47.

105. Foster, 24.

106. Ibid.

107. Paul Tharp, "Breakdancers Get Ballerinas into the Whirl," *New York Post*, Jan. 17, 1984.

108. Mollov, 19.

109. Ibid.

110. Cobbett Steinberg, "Dancing Men," *Ballet Review* 7, no. 1 (1978–79): 63.

111. Akiva Talmi, quoted in Sandler, 1983.

112. Cox, 80.

113. Richard Philip and Mary Whitney, *Danseur: The Male in Ballet* (New York: McGraw-Hill, 1977).

114. Steinberg, 1978–9.

115. Igor Youskevitch, "Masculinity in Dance," *Ballet Review* (Fall 1981): 90–1.

116. Clover, 159. The author notes how Kelly was always at pains to emphasize the athleticism and overt masculinity of dance. Of *Singin' in the Rain*, she writes that "the three Kelly/O'Connor dances . . . are muscular, apparently impromptu, unrestrained, exuberant, largely tap-based routines in which the interest lies to a considerable extent in the athletic feats of the (male) body: how fast the feet, sinuous the twists, high the jumps." Clover argues that Kelly fully literalized his intentions when, during the television program, *Dancing: A Man's Game*, Kelly attempted to show how dance mimicked the moves of the most athletic and therefore masculine sports.

117. Ramsay Burt, *The Male Dancer: Bodies, Spectacle, Sexualities* (London: Routledge, 1995), 103. The author notes that proponents of American modern dance such as Ted Shawn did not universally reject male ballet dancers but believed that the entire production system had gradually emasculated the artistic form.

118. Ibid., 107. Burt writes that modern dance choreographer "Shawn's earliest solos such as *Savage Dance* and *Dagger Dance*, both of 1912, and *Dance Slav* (1913) were concerned with primitive or non-western warrior cultures, as were subsequent pieces like *Invocation to the Thunderbird* (1918), *Spear Dance Japonaise* (1919), and *Pyrrhic Warriors* (1918)." He goes on to note that "in these Shawn seems, like Edgar Rice Burroughs, to have been borrowing the outer appearances of primitive and non-western cultures in order to evoke a 'natural' masculinity with which these 'Others' were believed to be in touch."

119. Burt, 4.

120. Steinberg, 65.

121. Philip and Whitney, 12.

122. Ibid.

123. Ibid., 17.

124. Ibid.

125. Sandler, 1983.

126. Robert Lindsey, "Dancing in the Streets With a Dream," *New York Times*, Jan. 27, 1984.

127. Ramsay, 102. The author writes that "the American association of masculinity with toughness renders male dance problematic, dancing still being, in many people's minds, a feminine realm."

128. Rosenwald, 74.

129. Mollov, 19.

130. "Julie Arenals Choreographers Company Presents New York Express," 1984.

131. Ibid. The wave refers to a popular electric boogie dance move that resembles a current of electricity moving through the body. The movement usually begins in one hand, travels up the arm to the head, and back down through the other arm.

132. Grubb, 78

133. Ibid.

134. Koepp. The Swatch Watch break dance competition held in 1984 offered a total of $25,000 in prizes.

135. In the summer of 2006, the Brooklyn Museum presented a show entitled *Graffiti*, which featured large-scale works from some pioneering artists including Sandra Fabara (Lady Pink), Futura, and Tracy (Tracy 168). That same year another Brooklyn art space, the Danny Simmons Corridor Gallery, put together *Propaganda: The Dissemination of Ideas E*, a group show featuring both graffiti writers and documentarians. At the opening of 2008, the Lott Gallery in Manhattan's prestigious Chelsea gallery block featured graffiti artists in the show *Writer's Strike*.

136. *The Freshest Kids: A History of the B-Boy*, DVD, directed by Israel (QD3 Entertainment, 2002). In an interview segment from this powerful documentary, Richard (Crazy Legs) Colon, who was an influential breaker and member of the Rock Steady Crew, discusses the aftermath of the break dance media frenzy. The experience was devastating for Colon who went from the street to stardom, and back again in a few short years. He notes that "one minute we were in the limelight, everything was straight ... traveling all around the world ... walk up to a club, hey come on in ... a club you helped build as far as reputation you know ... and the next thing you know it's like go to the back of the line ... Boom ... how do you really nurture someone and prepare them for what can happen ... especially someone coming from the ghetto when all you see is like money ... from that to having loot in your pocket ... and to next thing ... just like having the rug pulled under you...I went through a ill identity crisis." Michael Holman, breakdance promoter and manager of the New York City Breakers, is also interviewed in the same segment. He notes that the breakdance media hype didn't survive because there simply wasn't enough product to sell to keep it commercially viable. When mainstream media discovered rapping, producers and record labels seized

the opportunity to further financially exploit hip hop culture through record sales and music video.

137. Some breakers still perform on New York street corners and subways for money, and a 1997 show at the Joffrey Ballet entitled *Kali Ma* included a breaker in the performance. *Kali Ma* tape obtained through personal communication with the Joffrey Ballet. See also Anna Kisselgoff, "Ballet Meets Break Dancing as the Feld Vision Evolves," *New York Times*, Mar. 7, 1997. A performance entitled "Yo Shakespeare" by New York's Ballet Tech used a combination of breaking and traditional ballet. However, it is suggested that all of the dancers were trained in the academy. No mention is made as to how breaking was actually learned by the troupe.

138. Richard Kendall, "Signs and Non-signs: Degas' Changing Strategies of Representation," in *Dealing With Degas: Representations of Women and the Politics of Vision*, eds. Richard Kendall and Griselda Pollock (London: Pandora Press, 1992), 192–93.

139. Ken Sandler, "Breakdancing Goes Legit," *New York Daily News*, Jan. 3, 1984.

140. Ibid.

141. Sandler, 1983.

142. K. N. F., "Jazz' Intoxicates Just Like Whiskey Says Physician: Music Said to Act as Drug to Release Stronger Animal Passions," *Afro-American*, Apr. 20, 1923. This article warned of the explicit danger of jazz, arguing that "the quick and staccato tempo of jazz music, with the plaintive and pleading notes of the violin and the clarinet calling and the imploring tones of the saxaphone [sic]: the rhythmic beating of the drums, all these send a continuous whirl of impressionable stimulations to the brain, producing thoughts and imaginations which overpower the will." The author goes on to argue that upon listening to jazz "reason and reflection are lost and the actions of the person are directed by the stronger animal passions." Although the article does not explicitly state that jazz is problematic because it lacks structure, this is directly implied because the author suggests that this type of music overwhelms human reason, a turn that would ultimately be signaled by the assent of passion and chaos over order and measured reflection. See also Anne Shaw Faulkner, "Does Jazz Put the Sin in Syncopation," *Ladies Home Journal*, Aug. 1921, 16, 34. Reprinted in *Keeping Time: Readings in Jazz History*, ed. Robert Walser (New York: Oxford University Press, 1999), 32–36.

143. Doherty, 1988, 65–82.

144. Guerrero, 127.

CONCLUSION

1. "Breakdancing Goes From Harlem Streets to the Croisette in Pics," *Variety*, May 9, 1984, 287. See also J. Sullivan, "Breakin' Out of the Ghetto and Makin' it Big at the Box Office," *Boston Globe*, Jun. 17, 1984. The author notes that Cannon Films, the production

company responsible for *Breakin'*, began filming with the intention this film would be the very first Hollywood breakdancing release.

2. Janet Maslin, "Capturing the Hip-Hop Culture," *New York Times*, Jun. 8, 1984.

3. Ibid.

4. *Variety*, 287. "Spokesmen for the films have been coy about heralding the breakdance aspects of their products too loudly. 'Yes, it has break dancing in it,' says Pamela Godfrey, international ad-pub veepee for Orion which produced *Beat Street*, 'but it's more of a musical.'"

Bibliography

1988 City Files. County and City Data Books, University of Virginia Library, www2.lib.virginia.edu/ccdb.
Ahearn, Charlie. *Wild Style: The Sampler.* Brooklyn: Powerhouse Books, 2007.
Altman, Rick. *The American Film Musical.* Bloomington: Indiana University Press, 1987.
Altschuler, Glenn C. *All Shook Up: How Rock 'N' Roll Changed America.* Oxford: Oxford University Press, 2003.
ArchNewsNow. "Moribund Mall Makeover: Sherman Oaks Galleria by Gensler." Oct. 9, 2002. http://www.archnewsnow.com.
Avila, Eric. *Popular Culture in the Age of White Flight: Fear and Fantasy in Suburban Los Angeles.* Berkeley: University of California Press, 2004.
Baker, Geoffrey. "¡Hip Hop, Revolución! Nationalizing Rap in Cuba." *Ethnomusicology* 49, no. 3 (Fall 2005): 368–402.
Bakhtin, Mikhail. *Rabelais and His World.* Bloomington: Indiana University Press, 1984. First published 1965 by Khudozhestvennia literatura.
Banes, Sally. "Unruly Dolls and Ritz Rockers." *Village Voice,* Oct. 18, 1983.
———. "Breaking Changing." *Village Voice,* Jun. 12, 1984.
Barol, Bill, and Jennifer Smith. "A Street Spinner's Big Break." *Newsweek,* Jul. 2, 1984.
Baudrillard, Jean. *Simulacra and Simulation.* Ann Arbor: University of Michigan Press, 1994. Originally published in French in 1981 by *Éditions Galilée.*
———. *The System of Objects.* London: Verso, 1996. Originally published in French in 1968 by *Éditions Gallimard.*
Bawden, D. Lee, and John L. Palmer. "Social Policy: Challenging the Welfare State." In *The Reagan Record: An Assessment of America's Changing Domestic Priorities,"* edited by John L. Palmer and Isabel V. Sawhill, 201–208. Cambridge Massachusetts: Ballinger Publishing Company, 1984.
Bennett, Andy. *Popular Music and Youth Culture: Music, Identity, and Place.* New York: St. Martin's Press, 2000.
Berman, Marshall. *All That is Solid Melts into Air: The Experience of Modernity.* New York: Penguin Books, 1982.
———. "Introduction." In *New York Calling: From Blackout to Bloomberg,* edited by Marshall Berman and Brian Berger, 9–38. London: Reaktion Books, 2007.

Bodnar, John, Michael Weber, and Roger Simon. "*Migration*, Kinship, and Urban Adjustment: Blacks and Poles in Pittsburgh, 1900–30." In *The Making of Urban America*, edited by Raymond A. Mohl, 170–86. Delaware: Scholarly Resources, 1988.

Bogle, Donald. *Toms, Coons, Mulattoes, Mammies, and Bucks: An Interpretive History of Blacks in American Films.* New York: Continuum, 1989.

Box Office Mojo. "Yearly Box Office: 1984 Domestic Grosses." http://www.boxofficemojo.com/yearly/chart/?yr=1984&p=.htm.

Browning, Barbara. *Infectious Rhythm: Metaphors of Contagion and the Spread of African Culture.* New York: Routledge, 1998.

Brundage, W. Fitzhugh. "Working in the 'Kingdom of Culture': African Americans and American Popular Culture, 1890–1930." In *Beyond Blackface: African Americans and the Creation of American Popular Culture, 1890–1930*, edited by Brundage, 1–42. Chapel Hill: University of North Carolina Press, 2011.

Burt, Ramsay. *The Male Dancer: Bodies, Spectacle, Sexualities.* London: Routledge, 1995.

Caramanica, Jon. "Hip-Hop Heirlooms." *Fashion Rocks. Vogue* supplement, Fall 2008, unpaginated.

Castleman, Craig. *Getting Up: Subway Graffiti in New York.* Cambridge, Mass.: MIT Press, 1982.

Chang, Jeff. *Can't Stop, Won't Stop: A History of the Hip Hop Generation.* New York: St. Martin's Press, 2005.

Chimerie, Lawrence. "What Really Happened in the 1980s." *Challenge* 39, no. 3 (May/Jun. 1996): 29–34.

Cinema Treasures. "Sunrise Multiplex." http://cinematreasures.org/theater/9227/.

Clarke, Sally C. "Advance Report of Final Divorce Statistics, 1989 and 1990." *Monthly Vital Statistics Report* 43, no. 9 (Mar. 22, 1995). Supplement, Centers for Disease Control and Prevention/National Health Statistics. http://www.cdc.gov/nchs/data/mvsr/supp/mv43_09s.pdf.

Clover, Carol. "Dancin' in the Rain." In *Hollywood Musicals: The Film Reader*, edited by Steven Cohan, 157–73. London: Routledge, 2002.

Cox, Dan. "Brooklyn's Furious Rockers: Break Dance Roots in a Breakneck Neighborhood." *Dance Magazine*, Apr. 1984.

Crenshaw, Kimberlé. "Demarginalizing the Intersection of Race and Sex: A Black Feminist Critique of Antidiscrimination Doctrine, Feminist Theory and Antiracist Politics." In *Feminist Legal Theory I: Foundations and Outlooks*, edited by Frances E. Olsen, 443–71. New York: New York University Press, 1995.

Cripps, Thomas. *Slow Fade to Black: The Negro in American Film, 1900–1942.* New York, Oxford University Press, 1977.

Dauphin, Gary. "Hip hop at the Movies." In *The Vibe History of Hip Hop*, edited by Alan Light, 201–207. New York: Three Rivers Press, 1999.

del Barco, Mandalit. "Hip Hop Hooray: Breaking into the Big Time." *¡Mira! Magazine of the South Bronx Columbia School of Journalism*, Spring 1984. http://www.npr.org/programs/morning/features/patc/breakdancing/article.html.

de Certeau, Michel. *The Practice of Everyday Life*. Berkeley: University of California Press, 1988.

DeNavas-Walt, Carmen, Bernadette D. Proctor, and Jessica C. Smith. *Income, Poverty, and Health Insurance Coverage in the United States: 2009*. U.S. Department of Commerce and Economics and Statistics Administration, U.S. Bureau of the Census. Washington, D.C.: U.S. Government Printing Office, 2010.

Denisoff, R. Serge. *Tarnished Gold: The Record Industry Revisited*. New Brunswick, NJ: Transaction Books, 1986.

———, and George Plasketes. "Synergy in 1980s Film and Music: Formula for Success or Industry Mythology?" *Film History* 4, no. 3 (1990): 257–76.

Derrida, Jacques. *Of Grammatology*. Baltimore: Johns Hopkins University Press, 1976.

Doherty, Thomas. *Teenagers and Teenpics: The Juvenilization of American Movies in the 1950s*. Boston: Unwin Hyman, 1988.

———. *Projections of War: Hollywood, American Culture, and World War II*. New York: Columbia University Press, 1993.

Donalson, Melvin Burke. *Hip Hop in American Cinema*. New York: Peter Lang, 2007.

Dyer, Richard. "The Colour of Entertainment." In *Musicals: Hollywood and Beyond*, edited by Bill Marshall and Robynn Stilwell, 23–30. Exeter: Intellect Books, 2000.

———. "Entertainment and Utopia." In *Hollywood Musicals: The Film Reader*, edited by Steven Cohan, 19–30. London: Routledge, 2002. Originally published in *Movie* 24 (Spring 1977): 2–13.

Dyson, Michael Eric. "Out of the Ghetto," *Sight and Sound* 2, no. 6 (Oct. 1992): 18–21.

Ebert, Roger. "Flashdance." rogerebert.com. http://rogerebert.suntimes.com/apps/pbcs.dll/article?AID=/19830419/REVIEWS/304190301/.

Farred, Grant. "No Way Out of the Menaced Society: Loyalty Within the Boundedness of Race." *Camera Obscura* 12 no. 35 (May 1995): 6–23.

Farrell, James J. *One Nation Under Goods: Malls and the Seductions of American Shopping*. Washington: Smithsonian, 2003.

Faulkner, Anne Shaw. "Does Jazz Put the Sin in Syncopation." *Ladies Home Journal*, Aug. 1921. Reprinted in *Keeping Time: Readings in Jazz History*, edited by Robert Walser, 32–36. New York: Oxford University Press, 1999.

Feuer, Jane. *The Hollywood Musical*. 2nd ed. Bloomington: Indiana University Press, 1993.

Fiedler, Leslie. *Love and Death in the American Novel*. Cleveland: The World Publishing Company, 1960.

Fisher, Jean. "Wild Style." *Artforum International* 22 (Apr. 1984): 84.

Forman, Murray. *The 'Hood Comes First: Race, Space, and Place in Rap and Hip Hop*. Middletown, Connecticut: Wesleyan University Press, 2002.

Forman, Murray and Mark Anthony Neal, eds. *That's the Joint: The Hip-Hop Studies Reader*. New York: Routledge, 2004.

Mr. Fresh and the Supreme Rockers. *Breakdancing: Mr. Fresh and the Supreme Rockers Show You How to Do It!* New York: Avon Books, 1984.

Friedberg, Anne. *Window Shopping: Cinema and the Postmodern*. Berkeley: University of California Press, 1993.

Fu, Belinda. "Injuries of Breakdancing." *Radiology* 140, no. 3 (Dec. 2000), www.radiology.ucsf.edu.

Gabbard, Krin. *Jammin' at the Margins: Jazz and the American Cinema*. Chicago: University of Chicago Press, 1996.

Gaines, Jane M. *Fire and Desire: Mixed-Race Movies in the Silent Era*. Chicago: University of Chicago Press, 2001.

Gates, Jr., Henry Louis. *The Signifying Monkey: A Theory of African-American Literary Criticism*. New York: Oxford University Press, 1988.

———, and Gene Andrew Jarrett. *The New Negro: Readings on Race, Representation, and African American Culture, 1892–1938*. Princeton: Princeton University Press, 2007.

George, Nelson. *Hip Hop America*. New York: Penguin, 1998.

Gilbert, Eugene. *Advertising and Marketing to Young People*. Pleasantville, NY: Printers' Ink Books, 1957.

Gill, Pat. "The Monstrous Years: Teens, Slasher Films, and the Family." *Journal of Film and Video* 54, no. 4 (Winter 2002): 16–30.

Glasco, Laurence A., ed. *The WPA History of the Negro in Pittsburgh*. Pittsburgh: University of Pittsburgh Press, 2004.

Goldberg, David Theo. *Racial Subjects: Writing on Race in America*. New York: Routledge, 1997.

Goscienski, P. J., and L. Luevanos. "Injury Caused by Break Dancing." *Journal of the American Medical Association* 252, no. 24 (1984): 3367.

Griffin, Sean. "The Gang's All Here: Generic Versus Racial Integration in the 1940s Musical." *Cinema Journal* 42, no. 1 (Fall 2002): 21–45.

Grubb, Kevin. "'Hip-Hoppin' in the South Bronx: Lester Wilson's *Beat Street*." *Dance Magazine*, Apr. 1984.

Guerrero, Ed. *Framing Blackness: The African American Image in Film*. Philadelphia: Temple University Press, 1993.

Hall, G. Stanley. *Adolescence: Its Psychology and its Relations to Physiology, Anthropology, Sociology, Sex, Crime, Religion and Education*. 2 vols. New York: D. Appleton and Company, 1904.

Hansen, G. R. "Breaks and Other Bad News For Breakers." *Journal of American Medical Association* 252, no. 14 (1985): 2047.

Harrison, Charles. *Conceptual Art and Painting: Further Essays on Art and Language*. Cambridge, Mass.: MIT Press, 2001.

Hay, James. "Dancing and Deconstructing the American Dream." *Quarterly Review of Film Studies* 10, no. 2 (Spring 1985): 97–117.

Hazzard-Donald, Katrina. "Dance in Hop Hop Culture." In *Droppin' Science: Critical Essays on Rap Music and Hip Hop Culture*, edited by William Eric Perkins, 220–34. Philadelphia: Temple University Press, 1996.

Hazzard-Gordon, Katrina. *Jookin' The Rise of Social Dance Formations in African-American Culture*. Philadelphia: Temple University Press, 1990.

Herbold, Hilary. "Never a Level Playing Field: Blacks and the G.I. Bill." *Journal of Blacks in Higher Education* 6 (Winter 1994–5): 104–108.
Herzog, Amy. "Discordant Visions: The Peculiar Musical Images of the Soundies Jukebox Film." *American Music* 22, no. 1 (Spring 2004), 27–39.
Hinshaw, John. *Steel and Steelworkers: Race and Class Struggle in Twentieth-Century Pittsburgh*. Albany: State University of New York Press, 2002.
Holman, Michael. "Locking and Poping (Electric Boogie)." http://www.hiphopnetwork .com/articles/bboyarticles/popinelectricboogie2.asp. This article is reprinted from Michael Holman, *Breaking and the New York City Breakers*. New York: Freundlich Books, 1984.
hooks, bell. *Rock My Soul*. New York: Atria Books, 2003.
Jackson, Robert. "The Celluloid War Before the Birth: Race and History in Early American Film." In *American Cinema and the Southern Imaginary*, edited by Deborah Barker and Kathryn McKee, 27–51. Athens: University of Georgia Press, 2011.
Jacobs, Jerry. *The Mall: An Attempted Escape From Everyday Life*. Prospect Heights, Illinois: Waveland Press, 1984.
Jacobson, Harlan. "Charles Ahearn interviewed by Harlan Jacobson." *Film Comment* 19, no. 3 (May/Jun. 1983): 64–66.
Jaehne, Karen. "Charles Ahearn: *Wild Style*." *Film Quarterly* 37, no. 4 (Summer 1984): 2–5.
James, Wendy. "Reforming the Circle: Fragments of the Social History of a Vernacular African Dance Form." *Journal of African Cultural Studies* 13, no. 1 (Jun. 2000): 140–52.
Jameson, Fredric. *The Cultural Turn: Selected Writings on the Postmodern, 1983–1998*. London: Verso, 1998.
Joondeph, B. C., A. V. Spigelman, and J. S. Pulido. "Ocular Trauma From Break Dancing." *Archives of Ophthalmology* 104, no. 2 (Feb. 1986): 176–77.
Jordan, Chris. "Gender and Class Mobility in *Saturday Night Fever* and *Flashdance*." *Journal of Popular Film and Television* 24, no. 3 (Fall 1996): 116–23.
"Julie Arenal's Choreographers Company Presents New York Express." 1984. Promotional material for Arenal's dance troupe New York Express and the productions *On the Move* and *The City*. Break Dance File, Lincoln Center for the Performing Arts Library, New York.
Kassiver, M. R., and N. Manon. "Head Bangers Whiplash." *Clinical Journal of Pain* 9, no. 2 (Jun. 1993): 138–41.
Kalinak, Kathryn. "Flashdance: The Dead End Kid." *Jump Cut* no. 29 (Feb. 1984): 3–5.
Kehr, Dave. "Can't Stop the Musicals." *American Film* 9, no. 7 (May 1984): 33–37.
Keller, Robert R. "Supply-Side Economic Policies During the Coolidge-Mellon Era." *Journal of Economic Issues* 16, no. 3 (Sept. 1982): 773–90.
Kellner, Douglas. "Film, Politics, and Ideology: Reflections on Hollywood Film in the Age of Reagan." *Velvet Light Trap* 27 (Spring 1991): 9–24.

Kendall, Richard. "Signs and Non-Signs: Degas' Changing Strategies of Representation." In *Dealing With Degas: Representations of Women and the Politics of Vision*, edited by Richard Kendall and Griselda Pollock, 186–201. London: Pandora Press, 1992.

Kendall, Steven. *New Jack Cinema: Hollywood's African American Filmmakers*. Millbrae, CA: J. L. Denser, 1994.

Keyes, Cheryl L. "Verbal Art Performance in Rap Music: The Conversation of the 80s." *Folklore Forum* 17, no. 1–2 (1984): 143–52.

Kimmich, Madelaine H. *America's Children Who Cares? Growing Needs and Declining Assistance in the Reagan Era*. Washington, D.C.: The Urban Institute Press, 1985.

Knight, Arthur. *Disintegrating the Musical: Black Performance and Musical Film*. Durham: Duke University Press, 2002.

Koepp, Stephen. "Breaking Through to Big Profits." *Time*, Oct. 1, 1984.

Kohl, Herbert, and James Hinton. "Names, Graffiti, and Culture." In *Rappin' and Stylin' Out*, edited by Thomas Kochman, 109–33. Urbana: University of Illinois Press, 1972.

Lake, Robert W. *The New Suburbanites: Race and Housing in the Suburbs*. Rutgers: Center for Urban Policy Research, Rutgers University, 1981.

Lawson, Ronald, and Reuben B. Johnson III. "Tenant Responses to the Urban Housing Crises, 1970–1984." In *The Tenant Movement in New York City, 1904–1984*, edited by Ronald Lawson and Mark Naison, 209–76. New Brunswick: Rutgers University Press, 1986.

Lazarsfeld, Paul F., and Robert K. Merton. "Mass Communication, Popular Taste and Organized Social Action." In *Mass Culture: The Popular Arts in America*, edited by Bernard Rosenberg and David Manning White, 457–73. New York: The Free Press, 1957.

Leung, AKC. "Hazards of Break Dancing." *New York State Journal of Medicine* 84, no. 12 (Dec. 1984): 592.

Lewis, John. *The Road to Romance and Ruin: Teen Films and Youth Culture*. New York: Routledge, 1992.

Logan, John R., and Mark Schneider. "Racial Segregation and Racial Change in American Suburbs, 1970–1980." *American Journal of Sociology* 89, no. 4 (Jan. 1984): 874–88.

Lott, Eric. *Love & Theft: Blackface Minstrelsy and the American Working Class*. New York: Oxford University Press, 1993.

Mailer, Norman. *The Faith of Graffiti*. New York: Praeger, 1974.

Majors, Richard, and Janet Mancini Billson. *Cool Pose: The Dilemmas of Black Manhood in America*. New York: Lexington Books, 1992.

Malone, Jacqui. *The Visible Rhythms of African American Dance: Steppin on the Blues*. Urbana: University of Illinois Press, 1996.

Marshall, M. G., and P. Arestis. "Reaganomics and Supply-Side Economics: A British View." *Journal of Economic Issues* 23, no. 4 (Dec. 1989): 965–75.

Marx, Karl. *Capital: A Critique of Political Economy.* New York: The Modern Library, 1906.
Massood, Paula. "Mapping the Hood: The Genealogy of City Space in *Boyz N the Hood* and *Menace II Society*." *Cinema Journal* 35, no. 2 (Winter 1996): 85–97.
——. *Black City Cinema: African American Urban Experiences in Film.* Philadelphia: Temple University Press, 2003.
Matheus, John Frederick. "Some Aspects of the Negro Interpreted in Contemporary American and European Literature." In Gates and Jarrett, 204–11. First published in 1934.
McBride, D. Q., L. P. Lehman, and J. R. Mangiardi. "Break-Dancing Neck." *New England Journal of Medicine* 312, no. 3 (1985): 186.
McCoy, Alfred W. *The Politics of Heroin: CIA Complicity in the Global Drug Trade.* New York: Lawrence Hill Books, 1991.
McGuigan, Cathleen, Mark D. Uehling, Jennifer Smith, Sherry Keene-Osborn, Barbara Burgower, and Nadine Joseph. "'Breaking Out,' America Goes Dancing." *Newsweek*, Jul. 2, 1984, 48.
McKay, Claude. *Home to Harlem.* Boston: Northeastern University Press, 1987. First published 1928 by Harper and Brothers.
McLuhan, Marshall. "American Advertising." In Rosenberg and White, 435–42. This article was originally published in *Horizon* 93–94 (Oct. 1947): 132–41.
McNeil, S. L., W. A. Spruill, R. L. Langley, J. R. Shuping, and J. R. Leonard 3rd. "Multiple Subdural Hematoas Associated with Breakdancing." *Annals of Emergency Medicine* 16, no. 1 (Jan. 1987): 114–16.
Mollov, Joyce. "Getting the Breaks." *Ballet News* 6, no. 2 (Aug. 1984): 14–19.
Mr. Fresh and the Supreme Rockers. *Breakdancing: Mr. Fresh and the Supreme Rockers Show You How To Do It!* New York: Avon Books, 1984.
Mueller, John. "Fred Astaire and the Integrated Musical." *Cinema Journal* 24, no. 1 (Fall 1984): 28–40.
Mulvey, Laura. "Visual Pleasure and Narrative Cinema." In *Film Theory and Criticism: Introductory Readings*, edited by Leo Braudy and Marshall Cohen, 833–44. New York: Oxford University Press, 1999. Originally published in *Screen* 16, no. 3 (Autumn 1975): 6–18.
Nadell, Bonnie and John Small. *Break Dance: Electric Boogie, Egyptian, Moonwalk . . . Do it.* Philadelphia: Running Press, 1985.
National Fitness Trade Magazine. "Hot Dancing Sensation." Summer 1995.
Nash, Ilana. *American Sweethearts: Teenage Girls in Twentieth Century Popular Culture.* Bloomington: Indiana University Press, 2006.
Neal, Steve. *Genre and Hollywood.* London: Routledge, 2000.
——, ed. *Genre and Contemporary Hollywood.* London: BFI, 2002.
Norfleet, Dawn Michaelle. *Hip-hop Culture" in New York City: The Role of Verbal Music Performance in Defining a Community.* Ph.D. diss., Columbia University, 1997.

Norman, R. A., and M. A. Grodin. "Injuries from Break Dancing." *American Family Physician* 30, no. 2 (1984): 109–112.
Njubi, Francis N. "Rap, Race, and Representation." In *Images of Youth: Popular Culture as Educational Ideology*, edited by Michael A. Oliker and Walter P. Krolikowski, 151–84. New York: Peter Lang, 2001.
People. "The Tap Dance Kid Alfonso Ribeiro Boogies in the Footsteps of Idol Michael Jackson." Jul. 16, 1984. http://www.people.com/people/archive/article/0,,20197121,00.html.
Philip, Richard, and Mary Whitney. *Danseur: The Male in Ballet*. New York: McGraw-Hill, 1977.
Pierpont, Margaret. "Breaking in the Studio." *Dance Magazine*, Apr. 1984, 82.
Pough, Gwendolyn D. *Check it While I Wreck it: Black Womanhood, Hip-Hop Culture, and the Public Sphere*. Boston: Northwestern University Press, 2004.
Rapping, Elayne. "Hollywood's Youth Cult Films." *Cineaste* 16, no. 2 (1987/88): 14.
Register, Charlene. "The Construction of an Image and the Deconstruction of a Star—Josephine Baker Racialized, Sexualized, and Politicized in the African-American Press, the Mainstream Press, and the FBI Files." *Popular Music and Society* 24, no. 1 (Spring, 2000): 31–84.
Rhodes, Don, and John Parris Springer. eds. *Docufictions: Essays on the Intersection of Documentary and Fictional Filmmaking*. Jefferson, NC: McFarland & Co., 2006.
Riesman, David. *The Lonely Crowd: A Study of the Changing American Character*. New Haven: Yale University Press, 1971.
Robinson, Randall. *The Debt: What America Owes to Blacks*. New York: Dutton, 2000.
Roediger, David R. *The Wages of Whiteness: Race and the Making of the American Working Class*. London: Verso, 2000,
Rogin, Michael. *Blackface, White Noise: Jewish Immigrants in the Hollywood Melting Pot*. Berkeley: University of California Press, 1996.
Rose, Tricia. *Black Noise: Rap Music and Black Culture in Contemporary America*. Hanover: Wesleyan University Press, 1994.
Rosenwald, Peter J. "Breaking Away 80's Style." *Dance Magazine*, Apr. 1984.
Ross, Andrew. *No Respect: Intellectuals and Popular Culture*. New York: Routledge, 1989.
Sachs, Aaron Dickinson. *The Hip-Hopsploitation Film Cycle: Representing, Articulating, and Appropriating Hip-Hop Culture*. Ph.D. diss., University of Iowa, 2009.
Sancton, Thomas. "The Race Riots," *New Republic*, Jul. 5, 1943. Reprinted in *Reporting Civil Rights, Part One: American Journalism 1941–1963*, 37–48. New York: Library of America, 2003.
Saxon, Alexander. "Blackface Minstrelsy." In *Inside the Minstrel Mask: Readings in Nineteenth Century Blackface Minstrelsy*, edited by Annemarie Bean, James V. Hatch, and Brooks McNamara, 67–85. Hanover: Wesleyan University Press, 1996.
Scheiner, Georganne. *Signifying Female Adolescence: Film Representations and Fans, 1920–1950*. Westport, Conn: Praeger 2000.

Schrum, Kelly. *Some Wore Bobby Sox: The Emergence of Teenage Girls' Culture, 1920–1945.* New York: Palgrave Macmillan, 2004.
Scott, Joan. *Gender and the Politics of History.* New York: Columbia University Press, 1988.
Shary, Timothy. *Generation Multiplex: The Image of Youth in American Cinema, 1981–1996.* Ph.D. diss., University of Massachusetts, 1998.
———. *Generation Multiplex: The Image of Youth in Contemporary American Cinema.* Austin: University of Texas Press, 2002.
———. *Teen Movies: American Youth On Screen.* London: Wallflower, 2005.
Shearer, Lloyd. "Break-Dancing." *Parade Magazine,* Mar. 3, 1985.
Sherman, Sharon R. "Bombing, Breakin', and Getting' Down: The Folk and Popular Culture of Hip-Hop." *Western Folklore* 43 (Oct. 1984): 287–93.
Shohat, Ella, and Robert Stam. *Unthinking Eurocentrism: Multiculturalism and the Media.* London: Routledge, 1994.
Simms, Margaret C. "The Economic Well-Being of Minorities During the Reagan Years." Washington, D.C.: The Urban Institute, Project Report, Oct. 1984.
Sklar, Robert. *Movie-Made America: A Cultural History of the American Movies.* rev. ed. New York: Vintage Books, 1994.
Snead, James. *White Screens, Black Images: Hollywood From the Dark Side.* New York: Routledge, 1994.
Snyder, Robert W. *The Voice of the City: Vaudeville and Popular Culture in New York City.* New York: Oxford University Press, 1989.
Spear, Allan H. "The Making of the Black Ghetto." In *The Urbanization of America: An Historical Anthology,* edited by Allen M. Wakstein, 269–75. New York: Houghton Mifflin Company, 1970.
Speed, Lesley. "Moving On Up: Education in Black American Youth Films." *Journal of Popular Film and Television* 29, no. 2 (2001): 82–91.
Stallabrass, Julian. *Gargantua: Manufactured Mass Culture.* London: Verso, 1996.
Stam, Robert. *Reflexivity in Film and Literature From Don Quixote to Jean-Luc Godard.* New York: Columbia University Press, 1992.
Stearns, Marshall, and Jean Stearns. *Jazz Dance: The Story of American Vernacular Dance.* New York: Da Capo Press, 1994.
Stein, Ellin. "Wild Style." *American Film* 9, no. 2 (Nov. 1983): 48–50.
Steinberg, Cobbett. "Dancing Men." *Ballet Review* 7, no. 1 (1978–79): 57–65.
Stewart, Jacqueline N. *Migrating to the Movies: Cinema and Black Urban Modernity.* Berkeley: University of California Press, 2005.
Stewart, Susan. *Crimes of Writing: Problems in the Containment of Representation.* Oxford: Oxford University Press, 1991.
Sullivan, C. J. "There's Hope for the South Bronx." In Berman and Berger, 76–89.
Sullivan, J., and L. Calicott. *Break Dancing: Step-By-Step Instructions.* New York: Beekman House, 1984.

Tarr, Joel A. "Infrastructure and City-Building." In *City at the Point: Essays on the Social History of Pittsburgh*, edited by Samuel P. Hays, 213–63. Pittsburgh: University of Pittsburgh Press, 1989.

Taylor, Jr., Henry Louis, and Song-Ho Ha. "A Unity of Opposites: The Black College-Educated Elite, Black Workers, and the Community Development Process." In *Historical Roots of the Urban Crisis: African Americans in the Industrial City, 1900–1950*, edited by Henry Louis Taylor, Jr., and Walter Hill, 29–50. New York: Garland Publishing, 2000.

Telotte, J. P. "The New Hollywood Musical: From *Saturday Night Fever* to *Footloose*." In *Genre and Contemporary Hollywood*, edited by Steven Neale, 48–61. London: BFI, 2002.

Terenzio, Maurice, Scott MacGillivray, and Ted Okuda. *The Soundies Distributing Corporation of America: A History and Filmography of Their "Jukebox" Musical Films of the 1940s*. Jefferson, NC: McFarland & Co., 1991.

Tinkcom, Matthew. *Working Like a Homosexual: Camp, Capital, Cinema*. Durham: Duke University Press, 2002.

Toop, David. *Rap Attack 2: African Rap to Global Hip Hop*. London: Serpent's Tail, 1991.

Traube, Elizabeth. *Dreaming Identities: Class, Gender, and Generation in 1980s Hollywood Movies*. Boulder: Westview Press, 1992.

Tyler, Bruce. "Zoot-Suit Culture and the Black Press." *Journal of American Culture* 17, no. 2. (Jun. 1994): 21–33.

Valis Hill, Constance. *Tap Dancing America: A Cultural History*. Oxford: Oxford University Press, 2010.

Variety. "Break Dancing Goes from Harlem Streets to the Croisette in Pics." May 9, 1984, 287.

Wallace, Michelle. *Black Macho and the Myth of the Superwoman*. London: Verso, 1990.

Watkins, S. Craig. *Representing: Hip Hop Culture and the Production of Black Cinema*. Chicago: University of Chicago Press, 1998.

Watt, Tessa. *Cheap Print and Popular Piety, 1550–1640*. Cambridge: Cambridge University Press, 1993.

Welsh, Jim. "Beat Street." *Films in Review* 35 (Aug./Sept. 1984): 435.

Williams, Melvin D. *The Human Dilemma: A Decade Later in Belmar* (A Revision of *On the Street Where I Lived*). Fort Worth: Harcourt Brace Jovanovich College Publishers, 1992.

Winokur, Mark. "Marginal Marginalia: the African-American Voice in the Nouvelle Gangster Film." *Velvet Light Trap* 35 (Spring 1995): 19–32.

Wright, Amy Nathan. "A Philosophy of Funk: The Politics and Pleasure of a Parliafunkadelicment Thang!" In *The Funk Era and Beyond: New Perspectives on Black Popular Culture*, edited by Tony Bolden, 33–50. New York: Palgrave, 2008.

Wood, Robin. *Hollywood from Vietnam to Reagan*. New York: Columbia University Press, 1986.

Youskevitch, Igor. "Masculinity in Dance." *Ballet Review* (Fall 1981): 90–1.

Index

Abstract Expressionism, 90, 120
Adventures of Huckleberry Finn, The (novel), 252n86
African American press, 17–18, 20–21, 27, 30–31, 115, 128, 154, 161–62, 171, 186, 210, 217n36, 218n56, 219n73–74, 232n48, 251n78
Ahearn, Charlie, 33, 35, 40–41, 51, 59–60, 83, 89, 92–93, 95, 98, 101–2, 104, 108–9, 111, 113, 115, 117, 119, 122–23, 145, 209, 237n93, 237n97; and aesthetic strategies within *Wild Style*, 236n90; and graffiti as *avant-garde* art practice, 91, 120–21; and musical film, 233n51; and utopian desires within musical film, 76
Airplane, 147
All That Jazz, 34–35, 72
Altman, Rick, 48, 50–51, 53, 92–93, 96–97, 102, 107, 121, 144, 230–31n29, 236–37n92
American Bandstand, 165
American in Paris, An, 35
American Mutoscope and Biograph Company, 12–14
Anagnos, Bill, 41
Anchors Aweigh, 78
Anderson, Eddie "Rochester," 97
Anderson, Laurie, 100
Animal House, 45
Arenal, Julie, 201–2

Armstrong, Louis, 17
Astaire, Fred, 35, 78–79, 116, 187, 235n76
Astor, Patti, 90, 234n66
Atwell, Rick, 196
Avalon, Frankie, 125

Babes in Arms, 125
Backstage musical, 51, 66, 92, 95, 98, 177
Baker, Josephine, 17–18, 20, 186
Bakhtin, Mikhail, 225n62, 231n32
Ballet, and gender, 198–201
Bambaataa, Afrika, 109
Banes, Sally, 109, 248n33, 250n61
Barkleys of Broadway, The, 78
Baryshnikov, Mikhail, 199
Basil, Toni, 175, 248n45
Basquiat, 230n19
Baudrillard, Jean, 143
Beals, Jennifer, 177, 178, 181, 184, 185, 190, 191, 253n97
Beastie Boys, 5, 114
Beat Street, 4, 33, 39, 40–41, 47–48, 95, 101, 115, 121, 166, 204, 221n5, 235n67, 250n63, 257n4; and "authentic" hip hop practitioners, 114; and breakdance manuals, 167; and choreography, 202; and commercial cooptation of hip hop, 142; and dilapidated housing, 105, 108; and family, 158–59; and location shooting, 114; and marketing, 209;

270   Index

musical genre, 49–51; postclassical musical, 75–77, 81; and urban topography, 54, 57, 59, 65, 71, 82–84; and women in hip hop film, 171
Beiderbecke, Bix, 187
Belafonte, Harry, 41–42, 221n4, 221n4–5
Bennett, Andy, 100
Benny Goodman Story, The, 187
Berkeley, Busby, 49, 157, 234n63, 237n96
Berman, Marshall, 56, 223n34
Berry, Chuck, 25
Berry, Fred "Rerun," 172
Better Off Dead, 153, 156
Bill Haley and the Comets, 155
Billson, Janet-Mancini, 169–70, 173
Birth of a Nation, 149, 188, 216n30, 251n79
Biz Markie, 3
Black Arts Movement, 176
Black Panther Party, 29, 176, 249n52
Black Swan Records, 19, 141
Blackboard Jungle, 155
Blackface, and minstrelsy, 9–10, 13, 15, 17, 149, 187–88, 199, 205, 215n19, 252n84
Blaxploitation cinema, 4, 22, 29–30, 161
Bledsoe, Jules, 20
Blond Venus, 186
Blondie, 158
Blow, Kurtis, 42, 51, 102, 114, 154
Bodnar, John, 180–81
Body Rock, 4, 33, 39, 42, 44, 46, 67–69, 84, 106, 179
Bogle, Donald, 23, 252n90
Bonnie Hayes and the Wild Combo, 157
Born Losers, The, 126
Boyz in the Hood, 70, 234n61
Branigan, Laura, 178
Breakdancing: and gender, 166–69, 171, 174; and montage, 77; and opinion of medical community, 164–65; and popular media, 165–66, 167
Breakfast Club, The, 127, 139–40

Breakin', 4, 33, 37, 39, 42–44, 50–51, 65, 67–68, 81–82, 114, 121, 158–59, 167, 205–7, 221n8, 222n11, 256n1; and African American press, 162–63; and "authentic" hip hop practitioners, 115; and children, 154; and exploitation cinema, 47–48; and marketing, 209; and postclassical "music man," 79; and women in hip hop film, 171, 177
Breakin' Through, 4, 33, 37, 39, 42, 44–45, 50–51, 69, 82, 84, 106
Breakin' 2, Electric Boogaloo, 4, 33, 37, 39, 50–51, 65–68, 75, 81, 101, 114–15, 121, 154, 158, 163, 167, 171, 205–7; and commercial cooptation of hip hop, 141–42; and exploitation cinema, 42–44; and family, 159; and postclassical "music man," 78–79
Bronner, Ethan, 110
Brown, James, 175, 248n45
Buddy Holly Story, The, 72
Burt, Ramsey, 199, 254n117–18
Busy Bee, 41, 116, 234n66

Cabin in the Sky, 22, 97, 107
Campbell, Don, 175
Canby, Vincent, 83, 134, 179, 240n33
Cannon Films, 42–43, 47, 65, 82, 161, 221n8, 256n1
Can't Buy Me Love, 130
Car Wash, 42
Cara, Irene, 184
Carmen: A Hip Hopera, 210
Carolina Blues, 23
Carousel, 230n29
Carter, Jimmy, 54–55, 57, 106
Chambers, Michael, 43, 115, 154, 162–63, 205
Chardiet, Jon, 41
Charisse, Cyd, 235n76
Chevalier, Maurice, 73, 121

Chicken Thief, The (1902), 13
Chicken Thief, The (1903), 13
Chicken Thief, The (1904), 13–14
Chong, Rae Dawn, 41, 114, 171, 235
Chong, Tommy, 114
Chopping Mall, 239n22
City Heat, 44
Classical musical genre conventions, 53–54, 65, 71, 72–73, 75–76, 92
Clean Block Campaign, 87–88, 105, 229n9
Cleaver, Eldridge, 249n52
Clinton, George, 29–30, 219n76
Clover, Carol, 182, 195, 254n116
Cold Crush Brothers, 108, 112, 141
Conceptual Art, 118
Congress of Industrial Organizations, 21
Cool as Ice, 70, 226n69
Cool pose, and gender, 170–71
Cooley High, 42
Cooper, Martha, 167, 213n2
Corman, Roger, 126
Covington, Paul L., 151
Crazy Legs (Richard Colon), 191–92, 205, 246n12, 255n136
Crenshaw, Kimberlé, 176
Cubism, 120
Cusack, John, 156

Da Hip Hop Witch, 210
Dames, 49, 78, 229n14
Dandridge, Dorothy, 22
Dauphin, Gary, 4
Davis, Guy, 41, 114
Davis, Ossie, 114
Dawn of the Dead, 239n22
Dawn of the Dead (2004 remake), 239n22
De Certeau, Michel, 82, 84
De Kooning, Willem, 91
Del Barco, Mandalit, 110
Delivery Boys, 4, 33, 39, 42, 45–46, 69, 84, 106, 211, 222n17, 250n63; and sublimation of violence through performance, 110
Denisoff, Serge, 179, 249n56
Devil's Angels, 126
Dickey, Lucinda, 43, 163, 205
Dietrich, Marlene, 186
Dirty Dancing, 34–35, 71, 73, 80–81, 127, 226n76
Disco Fever club, 51, 59
Doherty, Thomas, 43, 125, 205–6, 221n7
Don't Knock the Rock, 25–26, 125
Double Trouble (Rodney Stone and Kevin Smith), 98–101, 156
Doug E. Fresh, 235n67
Douglass, Frederick I., 161, 162
Down Argentine Way, 23
Downey, Robert, Jr., 136
Du Bois, W. E. B., 16
Durbin, Deanna, 125, 237n96
Dyer, Richard, 73, 77, 226n78, 253n98
Dynamic Rockers, The, 172

Ebert, Roger, 192, 249n55, 253n97
Ebony Film Corporation, 15
Edison Company, 12–13
Ellington, Duke, 22
Elliot, Missy, 3
Epstein, Marcelo, 44
Ero (Dominique Philbert), 87

Fab Five Freddy (Fred Brathwaite), 90, 234n66
Fairy tale musical, 48, 50, 52–53, 73, 80, 81, 184, 192
Falcon Crest, 44
Fantastic Five, 108, 112
Farrell, James, 132
Fast Forward, 6, 68–69
Fast Times at Ridgemont High, 36, 130, 132, 137–38
Fat Boys, The, 51, 75, 102, 114, 154–56
Fauvism, 120

272 Index

Female Break Force, The, 172
Feuer, Jane, 71–72, 80, 97, 230n25
Finish of Bridget McKeen, The, 12
Firstenberg, Sam, 43
Fisher, Jean, 122
Flashdance, 5, 33–34, 37–38, 47, 52, 71–73, 76–77, 127, 166–67, 177–78, 204–7, 210, 226n75, 249n55, 250n61, 253n100; and breakdance, 193–96; and doubles, 189–93; and the individual, 184–85; and music video, 179, 249n56; and Pittsburgh's steel industry, 180–81; and race, 181–84, 194–96
Flip Rock, 235n67
Folk musical, 22, 39, 48, 52, 65, 80–81, 86, 96–98, 100–108, 121, 230n29, 232n50, 250n63
Footloose, 34–35, 73, 127, 210, 226n76
Foreman, Murray, 4
Fort Apache, the Bronx, 83
Fortier, Carolyn, 86, 228n2
Foster, Catherine, 179
Freed, Alan, 6, 26, 29, 126, 219n71
Friday the 13th, 153, 160
Friedberg, Anne, 143–44
Funicello, Annette, 125
Funkadelic, 29
Furious Rockers, The, 174
Futurism, 120

Gabbard, Krin, 187–88, 193, 252n82
Garland, Judy, 97, 125
Garvey, Marcus, 16, 246n8
George, Nelson, 5, 180, 249n53
Giannone, Mary, 204
Gilbert, Eugene, 238n7
Gish, Lillian, 252n90
Glenn Miller Story, The, 187
Godard, Jean Luc, 235n73
Gold Diggers of 1933, 49, 229n14, 234n63, 237n96

Graffiti, 31, 90; and African American press, 86–89; and challenging the constraints of urban life, 93–94; and high art world, 95; as positive force, 87, 89, 91, 93–94; and relation of word to image, 118–19; and relation to advertising, 119; as social problem, 86–87, 88; and stemming violence, 109–11
Graffiti Rock, 165
Grand Bobalition, or "Great Annibersary Fussible," 7
Grand Celebrashun ob de Bobalition ob African Slabery!!!, 7–8
Grand Wizzard Theodore, 3
Grandmaster Caz, 3, 59, 158
Grandmaster Flash, 59, 158
Granger, Lester, 27–28
Great Fear of the Period That Uncle Sam May Be Swallowed by Foreigners: The Problem Solved, The, 10–11
Green Pastures, The, 22, 227n91
Griffith, D. W., 188
Grubb, Kevin, 114
Guerrero, Ed, 207, 216n30

Hairspray, 72
Hall, Adelaide, 20
Hall, Anthony Michael, 135
Hall, G. Stanley, 124
Hallelujah!, 107, 227n91
Handler, Ken, 46
Harlem, 16, 31, 42, 58–59, 102, 108, 151, 251n77
Harlem Renaissance, 17, 58
Harrington, Richard, 145
Hay, James, 71–72
Hazzard-Donald, Katrina, 171–72, 175
Hearts in Dixie, 22, 39, 107, 227n91
Hellinger, Mark, 19–20
Heyward, Julia, 100
High, Becky, 116

Higher Learning, 96
Hill District, The (Pittsburgh), 31, 42, 55, 60–62, 71, 84
Hinton, James, 93–94, 229n15
Hoare, Roseanne, 168, 173, 198
Holman, Michael, 165, 168, 169, 175, 255n136
hooks, bell, 249n52
House Party, 96
House Party 2, 96
How Bridget Served the Salad Undressed, 12
Hughes, John, 36, 126–27, 132, 134–35, 140, 238n10
Hughes, Langston, 16
Hughes Brothers, The, 4
Hurston, Zora Neale, 16

Ice Cube, 234n61
Ice-T, 114
Irish appropriation, of African American performance traditions, 6, 187
Irish immigrants, and African Americans, 10–12, 24, 60; representation of, 14

Jackson, Jesse, 55
Jackson, Michael, 162, 175, 196
Jacob, John E., 33
Jacobson, Harlan, 83
Jahan, Marine, 190–91, 195
Jay-Z, 4
Jazz Singer, The, 39, 95, 96, 187–88
Jeremy, Susan, 167–68
Jett, Joan, 181
Joffrey Ballet, 196, 256n137
Johnson, Linton Kwesi, 100
Johnson, Sunny, II, 178
Jordan, Chris, 189, 191–92, 195, 226n75
Jordan, Vernon E., Jr., 54–55

Keeler, Ruby, 78

Kehr, Dave, 71, 73, 76–77
Kelly, Gene, 35, 78, 81, 182, 198
Kempley, Rita, 145
Kendall, Richard, 203
Kid Fresh, 196
King Kong, 186
Kline, Franz, 91
Kohl, Herbert, 93–94, 229n15
Kool and the Gang, 102
Kool Herc, 141
Kool Moe Dee, 235n67
Krush Groove, 4–5, 33, 36, 39–40, 42, 75, 101, 106, 121, 127, 152, 171, 228n102; and "authentic" hip hop practitioners, 114; and commercial cooptation of hip hop, 141–42; and contemporary newspaper reviews/articles, 161–63; and location shooting in New York City, 59; and musical genre, 51; and teen film genre, 154–56; and urban topography, 81–84; and violence during film screenings, 146–49, 210, 244n88
Kudrow, Lisa, 211

Lady Pink (Sandra Fabara), 90, 234n66, 255n135
Lady Rock (Clarissa Lopez), 172–73
Lady Rockers, 172–73, 174
Lagersfeld, Paul F., 131, 240n28
Lake, Robert W., 128
Lamas, Lorenzo, 44, 69
Last Summer, 126
Lathan, Stan, 41, 209, 235n67
Lawrence, Jacob, 16
LeBrock, Kelly, 135
Lee, Spike, 4, 72
Legend of Billie Jean, The, 157
Les Carabiniers, 235n73
Lescaze, Lee, 56
Lil John, 3

Little Colonel, The, 78, 193
Little Richard, 25–26
Littlest Rebel, The, 78, 193
LL Cool J, 3, 5, 114, 147, 214n8
Lockers, The, 115, 172
Los Angeles, 31, 70, 83, 148, 159, 237n97
Losin' It, 45
Lott, Eric, 9, 187–88, 215n19, 252n84
Love Me Tonight, 50, 73, 92, 121
Lubin, 13–14
Lymon, Frankie, 25–28, 219n71

MacDonald, Jeanette, 73
Mailer, Norman, 94
Majors, Richard, 169–70, 173
Mall culture and history of malls, 127–28, 129, 135–40, 143–44
Marable, Manning, 107
Marcano, Josh, 46
Marci X, 211
Marx, Karl, 144, 221n1, 242n47
Massood, Paula, 4, 58, 224n51
Matheus, John Frederick, 20
Maximum Base Rent system, 57
McBroom, Durga, 182
McCarthy, Andrew, 133
McCulley, Johnson, 229n11
McKay, Claude, 16, 58
McKeever-Kaye, Kimberly, 175, 248n42
McLuhan, Marshall, 131
Meatballs II, 45
Meet Me in St Louis, 97, 230n29
Melle Mel, 235n67
Menace II Society, 234n61
Merton, Robert K., 131, 240n28
Microphone, 211
Millar, Jeff, 83
Mills, Florence, 20
Missing in Action, 161–62
Mitchell-Smith, Ilan, 135
Moby Dick (novel), 252n86
Moses, Robert, 56, 224n38

Moyers, Bill, 107
Mr. Freeze, 180
MTV (Music Television), 179, 180, 183, 249n56
Mulvey, Laura, 240n34
Murphy, Eddie, 162
Murphy, Francis L., 87

NAACP, 30, 151, 218n56
Nadell, Bonnie, 167
Nashville, 72
New Black Realism, 4, 33, 58–59, 70, 153, 163, 170, 224n51, 234n61
New Deal, 60, 133
New Edition, 114
New music man, 78–80, 84–86
New York City Breakers, 21, 165–66, 235n67, 255n136
Nichols, Kelly, 46
Nigger in the Woodpile, A, 13–14
Night of the Comet, 157
Nightmare on Elm Street, A, 147–48, 153, 159–60
Nijinsky, Vaslav, 199
Nureyev, Rudolf, 199
Nyman, Bruce, 150

O'Conner, Donald, 182–83, 254n116
O'Conner, Thomas, 134
Oklahoma!, 230n29
100 Men and a Girl, 125
Only the Strong, 111
Orchestra Wives, 23
Outsiders, The, 157

Palmer, Betsy, 160
Palmer, Robert, 100
Parliament, 29–30
Pennies From Heaven, 34–35, 72, 80
Peters, Ida, 59, 162–63
Peyton Place, 235n8
Phase2, 31

Index 275

Philip, Richard, 199–200
Pinkster, 9
Pirate, The, 23, 53
Plasketes, George, 179, 249n56
Platters, The, 25
Pollock, Jackson, 91
Port of Missing Girls, 124
Postclassical musical, 34–35, 39, 53, 71, 73, 76–77, 79, 227n80, 227n80–81
Postmodernism, 53–54, 72, 223n25
Potts, Annie, 134
Pough, Gwendolyn, 176, 247n26, 249n53
Powell, Dick, 78
Presley, Elvis, 186, 251n77
Pretty in Pink, 127, 139, 240n33; and style as class difference, 132–35
Prince, 160
Prince Ken Swift, 235n67
Pryor, Richard, 162
Psychedelic Furs, 133
Pump Up the Volume, 139
Purple Rain, 72

Quinones, Adolfo, 43, 115, 163, 175, 205, 221n8
Quinones, Lee, 89–90, 228n1, 234n66

Racial migration and suburbanization, 15–16, 60, 128–29, 130–32, 149, 151, 180–81
Randolph, A. Philip, 21–23
Rappin', 4, 33, 39–40, 42–43, 65–66, 71, 75, 79, 81–82, 84, 95, 101, 105, 121, 158, 204, 225n62, 250n63; and grassroots activism, 62–64; and musical genre, 50–51, 59; and urban decline, 61–62
Rapping, Elayne, 129–30, 153, 239n18
Reagan, Ronald, and his administration, 32–33, 41, 55–57, 67, 106–7, 153, 220n78–79, 221n4, 223n35, 225n67, 232n45–47

Rebecca of Sunnybrook Farm, 193
Rebel Without a Cause, 124
Red Alert, DJ, 157–58
Revolt (Joey Ahlbum), 116
Rhythm Technicians, 196
Ribeiro, Alfonso, 196
Riesman, David, 131–32, 239n23
Ringwald, Molly, 133, 162
Risky Business, 130
Ritchie, Lionel, 225n61
Rize, 210
Road to Ruin, The, 124
Robbins, Jerome, 108
Robeson, Paul, 17
Robinson, Bill, 17, 19–20, 22, 30, 78, 193, 218n61
Rock, Rock, Rock!, 25, 125–26; and interracial desire, 26–28
Rock Around the Clock, 25, 125–26
Rock Steady Crew, 21, 110, 166, 179–80, 183, 186, 192, 194, 234n66, 235n67, 246n12, 255n136
Rocky, 207
Rocky Horror Picture Show, The, 145
Rodrigues, Beatrice, 196
Rogers, Ginger, 187
Rogin, Michael, 188, 215n19
Roller Boogie, 147
Rooftops, 111
Rooney, Mickey, 125
Roosevelt, Franklin D., 21
Rosenwald, Peter, 179
Roxy night club, 69, 101, 114, 142, 174
Roy, Malinda, 196
Royal Wedding, 78–79
Run-D.M.C., 5, 42, 51, 102, 114, 141, 147, 154, 165
Rusler, Robert, 136

Saigon Electric, 211
San Francisco Ballet, 196, 200–201
Sanchez, James, 151–52

Sandler, Ken, 204
Saturday Night Fever, 34
Save the Last Dance, 210
School Daze, 72
Schultz, Michael, 42, 146, 210
Scratch, 210
Shake, Rattle, & Rock, 125
Shakur, Tupac, 3
Shary, Timothy, 124, 129–30, 234n62, 241n36
Shawn, Ted, 199, 254n117–18
Shelia E., 42, 51, 171
Sherman, Sharon, 96
Sherman Oaks Galleria, 137, 138, 140, 144
Shohat, Ella, 182, 186
Silberg, Joel, 42–43
Silver, Tony, 93
Simmons, Russell, 42, 114
Simon, Roger, 180–81
Sinclair, Abiola, 171, 221n5
Singin' in the Rain, 49, 182–83, 195, 264n116
Singleton, John, 4, 70
Siskel, Gene, 47–48
Sixteen Candles, 126, 153, 156
Sklar, Robert, 44
Slasher films, 127, 159–60
Slavery, 9, 14, 15, 17, 94, 144, 169, 215n18, 242n48
Smith-Madden, Valerie, 163
Snead, James, 78
Some Kind of Wonderful, 132, 140
Soundies, 22–24
South Bronx, 31, 35, 40–42, 49, 51, 59–60, 65, 71, 82, 86, 89, 95, 97–98, 103–6, 112–14, 122–23, 141, 151–52, 172, 213n2, 221n5; and heroin, 237n97; and urban decline, 54–58, 83, 223n26, 223n34–35
Speed, Lesley, 96
Spice-1, 234n61

Spying the Spy, 15
Stallabrass, Julian, 119–20, 236n86
Stam, Robert, 115, 182, 186, 235n72
Star Spangled Rhythm, 23
Stein, Chris, 158
Stein, Ellin, 113, 123
Steinberg, Cobbett, 198–99
Stewart, Susan, 104
Street Dance 3D, 210
Strike up the Band, 125
Style Wars, 93
Summer, Donna, 253n95
Superfly, 29
Sweat Equity Program, 57, 59, 64
Swing Time, 39, 187

Taki 183 (Demetrius), 94
Talmi, Akiva, 196, 200–201, 204
Tap Dance Kid, The, 196
Tate, Jimmy, 196
Taylor, Robert, 41, 166
Teatro Puerto Rico, 151–52
Teenage Crime Wave, 124
Teenage Gang Debs, 124
Telotte, J. P., 71, 73, 75, 227n80, 227n81
Temple, Shirley, 78, 193
Terminator, The, 44
Three Smart Girls, 125
Tims, Candace, 172
Tinkcom, Matthew, 52–53, 222n23
Toop, David, 5, 109, 233n55
Top Hat, 35, 39, 50, 92
Trip, The, 126
Two Knights of Vaudeville, 15
Two or Three Things I Know About Her, 235n73

Uncle Tom's Cabin (1927 film), 193
Underwood, Blair, 42, 114, 161, 163, 171
UTFO, 245n96

Valenza, Tasia, 42

Index   277

Valley Girl, 36, 132; and mall culture, 137–40; and children in teen film, 156–57
Van Peebles, Mario, 42, 62
Vanilla Ice, 69–70, 226n69
Vaudeville, 11–12, 15, 20, 24, 95, 216n29
Vereen, Ben, 45
Vlaminck, Maurice, 91

Walker, George, 12
Wallace, Michelle, 249n52
Walton, Lester, 17
Washington, Booker T., 20
Watermelon Contest (1887), 13
Watermelon Contest (1900), 13
Watermelon Eating Contest (1903), 13
Watermelon Feast, A, 13
Watermelon Patch, The, 13–14
Waters, Ethel, 19–20, 97
Watkins, Craig, 82
Wayans, Damon, 211
Weber, Michael, 180–81
Weekend, 235n73
Weird Science, 127, 130, 132, 241n36; and mall culture, 135–36
Welsh, Jim, 83
West Side Story, 108
Whitney, Mary, 199–200
Who Said Chicken? (1900), 13–14
Who Said Chicken? (1901), 13–14
Who Said Watermelon, 13
Whodini, 102
Wild Angels, The, 126
Wild Ones, The, 124
Wild Style, 4, 32–35, 39–40, 47, 49, 51–52, 54, 57, 60, 65, 71, 79, 81–86, 88, 95–97, 107–8, 110–11, 121–23, 141–42, 145–46, 156, 158–59, 167, 204, 211, 213n2, 228n1, 233n51, 250n63; and animation, 115–18; and documentary aspects, 112–14; and film musical audience, 97–102; and graffiti, 89–94, 103–4, 109, 118–20; and location shooting in New York City, 59; and marketing, 209; and styles of Modern Art, 91, 93, 120, 229n12, 236n90; and postclassical musical, 75–76; and representations of "home," 103–6; and women in hip hop film, 170–71
Williams, Bert, 12, 20
Williams, Melvin, 104–5, 231n42
Wilson, Lester, 202
Wise, Robert, 108
Wiz, The, 72

Yellowman, 100
Yolanda and the Thief, 53
You Got Served, 210
Young Man with a Horn, 187
Youskevitch, Igor, 198–99

Zappa, Moon Unit, 137
Zephyr (Andrew Witten), 31, 116–17, 234n66, 235n79
Zito, David, 81–82, 228n95
Zulu Nation, 109, 233n55

www.ingramcontent.com/pod-product-compliance
Lightning Source LLC
Chambersburg PA
CBHW030612230426
43661CB00053B/1947